KU-258-975

TEACH YOURSELF BOOKS

PRINCIPLES AND PRACTICE IN MODERN ARCHAEOLOGY

David Browne was educated at Warwick School and St John's College, Cambridge. He graduated in archaeology in 1971 and subsequently was engaged in research on Roman Britain at Cambridge. He has worked as Field Research Officer in the Department of Urban Archaeology, Guildhall Museum, Corporation of London. In this capacity he was concerned with excavations in the City. His fields of interest include classical history and archaeology, and the archaeology of the Americas.

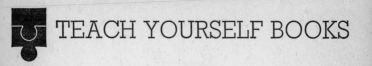
TEACH YOURSELF BOOKS

PRINCIPLES
AND PRACTICE
IN MODERN
ARCHAEOLOGY

David M. Browne

TEACH YOURSELF BOOKS
HODDER & STOUGHTON

ST PAUL'S HOUSE   WARWICK LANE   LONDON EC4P 4AH

First printed 1975

Copyright © 1975
David Browne

All rights reserved. No part of this publication may be
reproduced or transmitted in any form or by any means,
electronic or mechanical, including photocopy, recording,
or any information storage and retrieval system, without
permission in writing from the publisher.

ISBN 0 340 19816 8

Printed and bound in Great Britain for
Hodder & Stoughton, Teach Yourself Books, by
Richard Clay (The Chaucer Press) Ltd
Bungay, Suffolk

To Graham Webster

Contents

Preface   ix

1 **Archaeological Concepts**   1

Bibliography. Additional reading

2 **Finding an Archaeological Site**   30

Ground survey. Air photography. Magnetic prospecting. Resistivity survey. Electro-magnetic survey. Chemical prospecting. Bibliography. Additional reading. Ordnance Survey. Institute of Geological Sciences. The Soil Survey of England and Wales

3 **Excavation**   57

Trenching. Gridding. Open stripping. Digging procedure. Recording. Photography. Digging equipment. Personnel. Excavation of features—burial mounds, graves, ditches and banks, pits, timber buildings, stone walls, robber trenches. Bibliography. Additional reading

4 Conservation   110

Consolidation. Raising. Moulds and casts. Equipment. Organic material—bone, ivory, leather, textiles and basketry, wood. Metals—iron, bronze, silver, gold, lead, tin and pewter. Stone. Shale. Amber. Building materials—plaster, mosaics. Glass. Pottery. Notes

5 Analysis of Organic Remains   128

Animal remains: Human bone; Non-human bone. Birds. Fish. Molluscs. Microscopy and X-rays. Relative dating. Animal remains: Skin, etc.; Fibres. Radiocarbon dating. Vegetable remains: Pollen. Plant remains: Palaeoethnobotany. Coprolites. Wood. Dendrochronology. Bibliography. Additional reading

6 Analysis of Inorganic Remains   184

Stone: Chronological methods; Source analysis. Metals. Pottery. Glass. Bibliography. Additional reading

Appendix: Museums with Collections of Archaeological Importance   229

General Bibliography   242

Index   255

Preface

Archaeology is rapidly developing into a mature science in its own right. I have attempted in this book to introduce people unfamiliar with archaeology to a wide range of methods and ideas that are current in the study today. The pace of progress is such that we can confidently predict that much of what is being said and done at present will be drastically revised in the near future. Advances are being made on two fronts. First, archaeologists are thoroughly overhauling their theoretical outlook on the subject and, second, they are at work with more incisive analytical tools than ever before, particularly in the field of computers. I hope that this present survey will give some impression of these movements.

I must express my gratitude to various individuals who have aided in the production of this book. Many burdens were borne by my wife, Carrie. The typescript was expertly prepared by Jan Chapman. The illustrations are the work of Vanessa Mead. The photograph which appears last in the section of half-tones and which shows an inhumation burial after excavation is reproduced by kind permission of R. Jones and the Nene Valley Research Committee. The remainder of the photographs, which are of excavations at Chalton, Hants., under the auspices of the University of Southampton, appear by courtesy of D. Leigh, P. Addyman and T. Champion. The photographs themselves are by Trevor Hurst. Nicholas Chapman has given me valuable advice as editor.

Among specialists whom I have drawn on heavily for information, I would like to acknowledge the following: Philip Barker, FSA, Martin Biddle, FSA, A. J. Clark, Professor G. W. Dimbleby, Miss E. A. Dowman, D. W. King (Soil Survey), Professor A. C. Renfrew, A. H. Simpson (Institute of Geological Sciences), Paul Watts (Ordnance Survey), Dr M. Aitken, Dr Graham Webster and Sir Mortimer Wheeler. I would like particularly to acknowledge the co-operation of Messrs Thames & Hudson for their kindness in allowing me to refer to their excellent compendium *Science in Archaeology*.

To all the above persons and others that have helped me incidentally, I give my thanks. I, of course, bear full responsibility for the form of the book.

David M. Browne
Cambridge
31 May 1974

1 Archaeological Concepts

Archaeologists who have attempted to define their subject have usually done so in terms of what they wish to achieve through it. The result of this concentration on purpose has been a division of archaeologists into two main groups, those who see archaeology as a historical subject and those who see it as an anthropological one. Both groups tend to regard archaeology as a bunch of techniques used for reconstructing the past rather than a subject in its own right. British and European archaeologists usually belong to the historicising school. American archaeologists tend to be anthropologists. This stems from the fact that the majority of archaeology in the Americas is Indian archaeology and the standard way in which the Indians have been studied has been ethnographically and anthropologically rather than historically, and archaeology seemed to carry those studies logically back into the pre-Conquest period.

This book is founded on an alternative view to those expressed above and hopefully reflects a growing emphasis in modern archaeology. It starts from the observation that there is a certain body of data that is traditionally the concern of archaeologists and that this material can be recovered and studied only by archaeological means. Of course, to a certain degree, archaeological material can be used in an illustrative or corroborative fashion in other subjects, but its partiality and the inability to date most of it closely are serious restrictions. Once it is accepted that archaeological data does constitute a well-defined set within the general field of knowledge, then it follows that archaeology can be considered a subject in its own right of comparable status to both history and anthropology. It is the task of this chapter to define that separate body of knowledge and to show that archaeology is concerned with developing description and explanation of archaeological data in terms of itself. This does not exclude the possibility of calling in anthropological, or historical, or any other form of explanation as required, but it emphatically denies the right of any one of these to act as a controlling model.

Archaeological data is the material culture of the past. The archaeologist's job is to study objects made or modified by man. They may be massive composite artefacts, such as a medieval castle, or the simplest of tools, such as the battered pebbles utilised by the earliest hominids. They are only of antiquarian interest in themselves, however. The archaeologist is much more concerned with the phenomenon that artefacts are associated with other artefacts in regular patternings. The highest level of archaeological work is the explanation of these patternings.

There are many examples of the way in which artefacts occur in patterns. First, a commonly encountered recurrent association is the grave group. It has been observed that many people place various offerings in the grave with the dead, and leave them accompanied with weapons, pots, clothing and the like. It is also noted that regularities in the type of goods occur according to religion, sex, status or wealth.

On settlement sites certain areas are often marked off from others by the concentration there of particular artefacts denoting particular activities, and such activity areas may be a regular and distinctive feature of a particular culture. The kiva of the Pueblo Indians of south-west USA immediately springs to mind. The kiva was a largely subterranean structure used for religious purposes by the men's societies in the various villages.

At the broadest level, regional or other distribution patterns of artefacts can denote trade, gift exchange, culture diffusion, invasion or some other mechanism of movement. It is well known that settlements form distinct morphological and hierarchical patterns in a developed landscape.

When the archaeologist comes on to a site he finds artefacts arranged in a certain fashion. They are said to be in varying degrees of association. During the period of their use by living people artefacts are involved in various activities, often in conjunction with other artefacts. The physical positions assumed by artefacts in relation to other artefacts at various phases of the activities are termed articulations. An artefact's life ends when it is deposited. It may be deposited along with artefacts that it was in articulation with in life. It is said to be associated with these. Its degree of association depends on the degree to which the physical association reflects the physical articulation. Direct association is present when the association can be identified as being one deliberately intended in the living state. Paradoxically, a grave group is of this kind. Much of the last period of Pompeii closely approaches this, with the fittings of the houses still in the positions they occupied in AD 79. Direct association is held to closely resemble articulation. The recognition of articulation from association is an important interpretive step. Indirect association is fortuitous and the result of post-depositional factors, such as pit-digging or animal-burrowing.

Of course, perfect direct association is virtually impossible to discover outside cemeteries. All deposition involves some degree of dislocation in terms of reflecting the original articulation, and post-depositional factors can make this very severe. Thus the archaeologist's primary task is to reconstruct from a very partial position an approximation to the original direct association and then the articulation. The articulation cannot be realistically assessed without reference to the association in conjunction with the functional nature of the artefact, as what is being reconstructed is an activity. This is to say, for example, that it would hardly be possible to identify scraping of hides at a hunting site without first having at least a rough idea that the tools being found were of a suitable type for that function.

Archaeologists recognise a series of entities in a hierarchical progression which seems to correspond to real groupings of objects or their constituent parts.

The fundamental entity is the artefact. An artefact is any man-made or man-modified object. Childe (1956, 11) separated artefacts into relics, things such as pots, metal weapons and stone tools, and monuments, which include tombs, city walls, castles and the like. Deetz (1967, 48–9) distinguishes two basic procedures in artefact creation, the additive and the subtractive. Pottery is an example of an artefact created through the additive procedure, as the final product results from the controlled building up of a vessel from an original substance that bears little primary resemblance to the completed item. A flint implement is a subtractive artefact, as the fabricating procedure consists of removing pieces of the primary material to produce an object. The flintiness of the implement is still apparent, the essential difference lying in the transformed shape.

The specific form of an artefact is defined by two groups of actions. The first group is those acts involved in the making of the object and the second those acts for which the finished article is intended to be used. An artefact must therefore be considered the material manifestation of a sequence of human behaviour.

The artefact is the lowest level entity that can exist independently in a material culture system, but it is not the elemental archaeological entity. This is the attribute. An artefact is composed of a set of attributes. An attribute is the physical manifestation of a single human action or single sequence of actions which, in conjunction with others, was directed to the production of an artefact. The variety in the component attributes of an artefact is clearly limited by the precision of the maker's mental image of what he intends to make. Obvious examples of attributes are decorative motifs, forms of working edges and shape.

In recognising an attribute as the basis for an analysis, it is essential that the unit defined is an independent variable and has not arisen as the function of another variable. This is clear if an attribute is considered as the fossil of an action which has been directly applied to the material (Clarke, 1968).

Attributes exist in different states. The minimum number of states is two, presence and absence. A further state common in archaeology with incomplete objects is apparent absence, when an attribute cannot be said to have been either present or absent because the relevant part is missing. Other states can be considered as either quantitative or qualitative. In the first group fall the discrete measurements that can occur for an attribute such as length. The second set comprises the material manifestations of variation on a single action, for example the varied effects of soft-hammer as opposed to hard-hammer percussion (Clarke, 1968, 139–141).

The first stage in any archaeological analysis concerned with entities will be to define the attributes of an artefact. Theoretically, these could be infinite, but only a limited set are of any archaeological relevance. The importance of a particular attribute is dependent on the subject of the analysis. Thus the firing colour of a pot will be of interest in a study of pottery manufacture but of no relevance to a study of the development of forms.

Having defined his field of study and the relevant features for this, the archaeologist must consider his general approach to entity-building. This has traditionally been monothetic. This means that when constructing types, assemblages and cultures archaeologists draw up lists of attributes for each artefact. Artefacts are only considered as belonging to the same entity if they possess identical lists of attributes for the particular level under consideration. If an object has more or less than the stated attributes it is classified in another group. In this fashion a series of discrete units is constructed. A hierarchy of such units can be built in a dendritic pattern based on decreasing exclusiveness. Analysis proceeds by simple sub-division (Clarke, 1968, 35–38).

Mutual exclusivity is a major attribute of the entity type in this classificatory system. If, for example, the CBA Research Report 6 on Romano-British pottery is consulted it will be seen there that type status is restricted to virtually identical artefacts. It will be noticed that on this basis type becomes a very elementary entity, types are vastly multiplied and the organising power of the concept in relation to the data is very limited. In actual working many archaeologists have not oper-ated a strictly monothetic system because of this latter diffi-culty. What they have done is artificially limit the number of attributes considered as key, and then proceeded to classify monothetically. The restriction of attributes has led effectively to quasi-polythetic consideration. It should be stressed that the concept remains firmly monothetic.

Polythetism is an approach based on the observed vari-ability exhibited by single populations. It recognises that it is only necessary to possess a significant proportion of a set of key attributes to claim membership of a group. No particular attribute gains the artefact entry, but equally the lack of no single one means exclusion. A variety of combinations within certain parameters is found. The concept recognises that it is rare for populations to be discrete units. Populations are con-sidered distinct when the number of shared attributes falls below a certain proportion of the total content of each.

The idea of recurrent sets must be emphasised in conjunc-tion with polythetism, for it is the basis of the hierarchical scheme of entities discussed here. A repeated set of attributes or artefacts is termed a complex by Clarke (1968). Without the idea of recurrent sets all objects must be considered unique and non-comparable. In reality it is clear that two things are said to be alike because a certain set of the total attributes that they possess, and that are considered relevant, are closely similar if not identical. The level of affinity of any two entities depends on how restricted a set of attributes is being con-sidered. Thus at type level a pot and a sword would be said to be unalike because the analysis is considering only certain functional attributes, whilst at culture level they might be considered identical as products of a single people.

There is no problem in accepting the concepts of artefact and attribute outlined above. When it comes to the recognition of types, however, we enter the most controversial sphere of fundamental archaeological concepts. It is not intended to deal with the nihilistic view that denies the existence of types, but it is necessary to indicate the problems that the recognition of the entity involves. It seems self-evident that there are readily distinguishable functional types of artefacts such as pots and axes. They are distinguished by their possession of different recurrent sets of specific attributes which are directly relevant to the function of the object. It is proposed to refer to functional types as classes of object. The concept of types is restricted to subdivisions within artefact classes.

The most common way in which type is envisaged is by considering the manufacture of an object. A manufacturer sets out to make a number of examples of an object according to a standard pattern fixed in his mind. All the products which conform to that standard pattern are said to be of the same type. This simple definition is more difficult to apply to archaeological material. The reason lies in the inevitable variation that creeps in between two products as a result of the limits of accuracy of reproduction that exists in the manufacturing process and the non-essential variation in matters such as decoration that is allowed, according to the predilections of the worker and his market. The more mechanised or refined a process of manufacture, the more likely that variation within types will be limited. Therefore a greater degree of variation is to be allowed for in the production, for example, of a stone axe by percussion than for a wheel-made pot. The archaeologist's problem is to know where to draw the line between variation that was deliberate and related to producing new types and variation that was tolerated within a type. It is at the procedures used to define these thresholds that criticism can validly be levelled. All depends on the correct assessment of relevant attributes, and attribute states. It will be noted that the definition of type within class adopted here demands a generally high level of similarity between individual artefacts and corresponds, for example, to Clarke's subtype entity rather than his type. To avoid terminological confusion every attempt should be made to restrict the use of the word type to this first, grouped, archaeological entity.

If a general hierarchy for archaeological entities is being developed, then it is legitimate to question whether it is valid to equate in level types across classes. In other words, can a pot type be considered to be of the same order as a sword type? This will be considered reasonable if reference is made back to the operating model of the creation of a type. Irrespective of class, the objects are the result of a repetitive process operating according to a standard idea of output.

It is worth emphasising the common process link that is the basis of artefact, type and class production. Each entity is regarded as the result of a deliberate action by an individual towards a specified end.

However, within most manufacturing processes are the materials for change. A variation that might arise through chance in the process of production might be found to be advantageous and be incorporated in a revised version of the original type. New ideas that do not arise directly from manufacture can also be added and type change can occur. In both ways many, possibly all, of the key attributes of the original type are retained alongside the new ones and a high level of linkage may exist between two types. Many such linkages are observed in archaeology and have given rise to the practice of typological ordering, that is postulating developmental sequences on the basis of the degree of attribute linkage between types. The underlying concept is evolutionary and, whilst subject to considerable criticism, has proved of much value in providing a rough ordering of artefacts, many of which have been shown to have stratigraphical and chronological validity. A set of artefacts that show a high level of affinity arising through the modification of successive types by the incorporation of new, beneficial variety is called a type series. The type group is a contemporary set of artefacts that share a high level of affinity based on the modification of a single type. As it is often the case that an original form is retained alongside the modified, it is quite possible for one type to be linked to another in both a horizontal (type group) and a vertical fashion (type series). This is the main problem with typology. It places too much emphasis on variation arising through time and, in a chest-of-drawers fashion, tends to arrange artefacts in an excessively vertical order. The problem is overcome by considering artefacts as assemblages in associated contexts. Deposits which contain artefacts that are likely to have been directly articulated are extremely important for showing those types that co-existed and indicating the degree of overlap in time between them. When the fault of considering artefacts in a unilinear fashion is carried through to cultures, mistakes in temporal placement have occurred, as for example in the case of the French Upper Palaeolithic for which coeval cultures, occupying geographically distinct areas, were at one time arranged in chronological sequence.

The type complex is an important concept as it recognises recurrent associations of particular artefact types. Repeated associations of types can arise from a number of sources, such as manufacture at the same centre and utilisation as part of the same activity. An example is the repeated occurrence of specific types of vessel such as glass jar, ceramic jar and dish and metal patera in Romano-British cremation burials.

When artefacts are found together in direct association, the set that they form is termed an assemblage. When a series of assemblages sharing a high proportion of similar artefact types is found within a defined region, it is said to constitute an archaeological culture.

V. Gordon Childe was responsible for the development and application of the concept of archaeological cultures, and it remains the most important synthesising concept in archaeology. This is because most people have been prepared to accept Childe's assumption that a culture can be equated with a people and that changes observable in cultures can be ascribed to historical-type events such as emigration and invasion. Application of such ideas to European prehistory allows a readily comprehensible picture of development to be constructed.

It is important to the process of reconstructing the past to understand what 'culture' implies. Culture is peculiarly human. It is the extra-somatic, non-instinctive behaviour of human social groups. Its specific form varies with the particular group. It is universal to all. Culture can be subdivided into a number of subcultural spheres, the chief of which are social, economic and religious. Forming a distinct sphere but found cross-integrated with the other spheres is material culture. Each subcultural unit has its own specific form of material representation which is interrelated with that of the other spheres.

An archaeological assemblage comprises part of the material element of the culture of a particular social group. No one assemblage or single type of assemblage represents the whole culture. Carelessness in this aspect has led to mistakes in the past. For example, the so-called Bronze Age Wessex Culture of Britain was constructed from the funerary assemblages representing a small privileged class of Bronze Age society. An archaeological culture is constituted only when assemblages representing all the material aspects of the culture of a particular social group are integrated.

A culture occurs within a definite geographical region but is not necessarily restricted in time.

Most books about the prehistory of a particular region are written as culture histories. The archaeologist first defines the characteristics of the assemblages that constitute the culture. This done, he uses specific aspects of these assemblages to serve as the basis for the reconstruction of the various activities undertaken by the people represented by the culture.

Cultures cannot exist independently of the natural environment. There is a constant interaction between material culture and the surroundings in which it is utilised. The most direct way in which this is apparent is in the economic subsystem of a culture. The configuration of the artefact assemblages concerned in subsistence activities is dependent on the nature of the activity and the availability of raw materials for their manufacture.

This is not to say that there is a strict deterministic relationship between natural habitat and cultural form. There is very considerable scope for variation within similar environments.

One of the fundamental distinctions in prehistory between groups of cultures is that between those dependent on various systems of hunting and gathering and those based on agriculture of some form. The two modes of subsistence give rise to entirely distinct manifestations in material culture.

Hunting, fishing and gathering cultures will be represented by assemblages containing a variety of combinations of artefacts such as bows, atl-atls, projectile points of stone, bone and antler harpoon heads, traps, knives, scrapers and hooks. The specific form of the combination, together with a faunal analysis of the site, will inform about the precise nature of the activity. Many hunting cultures share very similar subsistence patterns and it is often the non-utilitarian-inspired variability in the form of the artefacts rather than quantitative differences in the composition of assemblages that allows distinction between cultures.

The range of variation between modes of hunting and gathering and level of cultural development can be very great. The highest level of development is represented by the sedentary coastal villages of the Canadian north-west coast Indians, whose elaborate culture was based on exploiting the annual salmon run. These Amer-Indians had a great variety of material culture and had developed an intricate and highly symbolic art style expressed principally in wood-carving. The lowest level of development is represented by the very meagre tool kits of the Bushmen of the Kalahari, the Aborigines of the Australian Central Desert and the Paiute of the Great Basin, USA. A minimal tool kit does not, however, imply a similar level of economic or social organisation. The subsistence strategy of these peoples is very complex, involving the successive exploitation of different ecological niches at different seasons in order to maintain survival in very hostile environments. An equally complex social system helps further to regulate the distribution of subsistence activities and the intake of the products. Archaeology is unable to inform much on this aspect of culture. Locational analysis and study of faunas does help to indicate whether a mixed economic strategy involving seasonal movement was in operation.

There is a similar considerable variety in the nature of agricultural practice and the associated material culture. One can contrast the irrigation-based civilisations of Egypt, Mesopotamia and India with the shifting maize and manioc cultivators of the South American tropical forest. It is clear that the correlation hunting/gathering = low level of material cultural development, agriculture = higher level does not hold fully. It is possible to rank the north-west coast Indians with agricultural peasant villages of the Middle Ages in terms of their variety of material culture. The fundamental difference between the two settlement entities is the ability of the agricultural village to withstand a greater range of adverse conditions and partake in a broader socio-cultural organisation which can further guarantee its survival and expansion. Agricultural communities are capable of a much more developed form of social co-operation leading to civilisation than are the generally small-scale, mobile communities of hunters.

Any culture history of an area will be concerned to identify the point in time at which this crucial transformation in subsistence type occurred. It should be borne in mind that for over 99% of man's time on earth his economy has been based entirely on hunting, fishing and gathering. The mechanisms of the domestication of plants and animals is the subject of much current research (e.g. Ucko and Dimbleby (eds), 1969). The British Academy is sponsoring a research programme on the origins of agriculture directed by E. Higgs. Some of the techniques of floral and faunal analysis in use are described in Chapter 5.

Because of the difficulties of chronology and the paucity of material, it is also inevitable that the majority of attention in culture history is given to the cultures of the last 10 000 years or so. Here it is possible to analyse in detail subsistence patterns, settlement patterns, clothing, technology, transport, trade, social life, art and religion.

The archaeologist is particularly concerned to explain the processes of culture change. He will see the content of assemblages changing as new configurations occur in the same area, replacing older ones such that new cultures must be said to have formed.

David Clarke (1968) has recently discussed cultural process and suggested a tentative classification, which is discussed here. He links observed patterning of artefacts with the various social and demographic reasons that might give rise to them.

Diffusion has been a favourite explanation for culture change. Clarke recognises three forms. Repatterning in assemblages can occur as a response to an external stimulus without involving borrowing or reproduction of a particular trait. This is termed stimulus diffusion. It could be argued that the development of the Indus Valley civilisation was an example of stimulus diffusion, the impetus towards city-based organisation coming from intercourse with the Sumerian area. Very few Mesopotamian traits can be identified in the Indus area, but the chronological relationship of the two civilisations, their proximity and the convergent similarity of their natural environments render the idea of stimulus from one area to another a likely explanation.

Artefacts from one cultural area were often distributed beyond their region of origin by trade or some other exchange mechanism. This is termed secondary diffusion. These artefacts were incorporated by the other group and copies made if they proved useful additions to its cultural equipment. Adjustments to the compositions of assemblages thus occur. Some of these can be quite drastic, such as the introduction of metal tools which had a catalytic effect on the development of the mode of production and subsistence in parts of prehistoric

Europe. Within a culture new elements can be generated at particular points through invention and then be distributed through trade, intermarriage or gift exchange to the whole culture areas. This process is called primary diffusion.

Intrusion/substitution, acculturation and assimilation, which can occur at the technocomplex, culture group, culture and subculture level, are the three other major processes involved in changing the configuration of an assemblage. Invasion by another people can lead to a complete replacement of one culture by another. An example of this would be the apparent obliteration of the pre-Greek-speaking cultures of much of the mainland of Greece by the invasions of Greek speakers. To obtain almost total cultural substitution it is not necessary to replace completely one population with another, only for what remains of the pre-existing group of people to accept the incoming culture and abandon its own.

Acculturation is said to be occurring when two cultures become increasingly similar as a result of interaction between their respective groups of people by intermarriage, trade or sharing of certain resources. The full development of this process is cultural fusion. The reverse process, the break-up of a culture into two or more, can be called cultural fission. This can occur as communities become isolated from one another by physical barriers. The development of many small cultures in the valleys of coastal Peru at various stages in the pre-Columbian era is an example.

Assimilation of one culture by another can occur after the military conquest of a region. There are a number of examples from the Roman Western Empire where Celtic culture was assimilated to the imported classical. Elements of the assimilated culture are still in evidence but no longer in a dominant position.

An artefact type can become obsolete and be replaced by a new invention. There is a constant loss from the artefact population of a culture through time and this is the major source of change within the system.

One other entity may be mentioned because of its importance for Palaeolithic studies. This is the technocomplex, a term coined to describe a set of assemblages comprising similar classes of artefacts although varying considerably in the specific types present (Clarke, 1968). This represents the tool kits of many groups of people following roughly similar subsistence patterns in like environments and who were probably part of a large, related language and racial group although culturally distinct. This term probably describes accurately the situation of the Lower and Middle Palaeolithic Acheulean or hand-axe cultures of Africa, Europe and Asia.

We must turn from this necessarily brief review of the basic concepts concerning objects in archaeology to a consideration of the ideas of time that the archaeologist employs and how he establishes chronological relationships between artefacts, assemblages and cultures. Typology has been mentioned above and physical methods are dealt with in a later chapter.

The earth is at least 4500 million years old. Life emerged over 1000 million years ago. The mammals first appeared some 200 million years ago. Man as a creature possessed of culture, capable of manufacturing tools belongs to the last 2 to 5 million years of the earth's history. This is a very small fraction of geological time. The earth's history is divided into five eras, which are, earliest to latest, the Azoic, Proterozoic, Palaeozoic, Mesozoic and Caenozoic. These are further subdivided into periods. The Mesozoic (the Age of the Reptiles) is of interest, for it is in its first period, the Triassic, that mammals are found in the fossil record. The Caenozoic is more relevant, for through its successive periods, the Palaeocene, Eocene, Oligocene, Miocene, Pliocene and Pleistocene, can be traced the emergence of the genus *Homo*. The Caenozoic is split into the Tertiary and the Quaternary. Man belongs largely to the two periods of the Quaternary: the Pleistocene (the period of the Ice Ages) and the Holocene (the post-glacial period).

The establishment of the antiquity of man was one of the major achievements of nineteenth-century science. Three important steps were necessary (Daniel, 1967, 57). First, stone tools, fashioned by men, had to be recognised as such. The significant events for this recognition had occurred before the beginning of the nineteenth century with the opening up, first, of the Americas and, more recently, of the Pacific area where peoples could be observed using as tools and weapons objects that had previously been described as thunderbolts or fairy stones. The second step was the acceptance of the true antiquity of geological time. The prevailing view until the early nineteenth century was that of diluvialism. This explained the derivation of the earth's strata in terms of a series of catastrophic floods such as are recorded in the Bible. This explanation made it easy to maintain the traditional chronology of the earth held to by the Church. This put the creation, according to the calculations of Archbishop Ussher, at 4004 BC. Charles Lyell (1797–1875) introduced a new principle into geological thinking, that of uniformitarianism. He pursued this in his *Principles of Geology* (1830–3). The principle states that the processes of the past were the same as those in operation at the present. It is not possible to invoke as explanations of geological strata processes of deposition that cannot be observed today. The obvious consequence of the application of this principle is the recognition that the earth must be many million years old, for it would not be possible for the proposed processes to be effective in less time.

The third step for the establishment of the antiquity of man was the recognition of the true association of human products with geologically old deposits. John Frere had arrived at such a conclusion at the site of Hoxne, Suffolk, as early as 1797; but it was Boucher de Perthes, working in the Somme Valley at now famous sites like Abbeville and Saint-Acheul from the 1830s, who was responsible for demonstrating the association of hand-axes with Pleistocene gravel deposits containing extinct fauna. Boucher de Perthes' work was greeted with much hostility in France and it was, in fact, two British scientists, Sir John Prestwich (1812–96) and Sir John Evans (1823–1908), who visited de Perthes' sites and, convinced of the veracity of his findings, brought them to the full attention of the scientific world in papers to the Royal Society and the Society of Antiquaries in the memorable year 1859.

Besides putting man into his true context in the general history of life, a process accelerated from the time of the publication of *The Origin of Species*, nineteenth-century antiquaries were concerned to give order to the many products of man that were encountered and which could not be assigned to the Classical or Biblical world. A Dane, Christian Jurgensen Thomsen (1788–1865), has the credit for the invention of the Three-Age System which is still with us as a general organising force. Thomsen was faced in 1816 with the problem of giving a coherent arrangement to the newly created National Museum in Copenhagen. With the orderliness of a warehouse clerk, he divided the collection according to the material from which it was made, namely Stone, Bronze and Iron. He held that this was the general chronological trend in technological development. He published his scheme in his guide-book to the museum in 1836 (English version in Lord Ellesmere, *A Guide to Northern Antiquities*, London, 1848). Thomsen's successor at the museum, Jens Jacob Asmussen Worsaae (1821–85), carried forward and extended the scope of Thomsen's work. He was able to demonstrate the validity of the sequence by applying the basic principles of modern excavation. He also sought to integrate monuments such as barrows into the chronological scheme and engaged himself on comparative studies within and beyond Denmark.

It was recognised early that the Three-Age System could not accommodate adequately the finds by Boucher de Perthes and others. John Lubbock (later Lord Avebury; 1834–1913), who is famous as a politician for such benefits as the Bank Holidays Act 1871 and the Ancient Monuments Act 1882, was also responsible for coining the terms Palaeolithic and Neolithic. In his *Prehistoric Times* (1865) he subdivided the Stone Age into a period characterised by chipped tools associated with the Drift and its extinct fauna (Palaeolithic) and a period of polished stone tools (Neolithic). Lubbock clearly recognised that the age system did not necessarily apply universally at the same time and that there was a considerable overlap between ages. In 1866 Hodder M. Westropp introduced the further division of the Stone Age, the Mesolithic, the period of small chipped flint implements.

The twentieth century began with European archaeology firmly based on a Five-Age System. During the later nineteenth century a number of scholars, using the typological method and the principle of cross-dating, had developed elaborate subdivisions of the main periods. Oscar Montelius was chief among these. He subdivided the Neolithic into four periods and the Bronze Age into five. Other systems were devised by de Mortillet, Dechelette and McCurdy (Daniel, 1967, 261–3).

During the nineteenth century an alternative to the technological model was developed. This is known as the ethnographical stage model. Scholars, using the observations of ethnographers, divided the peoples of the world according to their level of economic and social development. It was thought that man had progressed through these various stages to achieve civilisation in some parts of the world. An early example of the model was published by Sven Nilsson (1787–1883) in 1838 (*The Primitive Inhabitants of Scandinavia*, London, 1868). He divided mankind into savages, herders, agriculturalists and civilised peoples. The classic example of the model is that put forward by the American Lewis H. Morgan in 1877 based on studies of Indians, particularly the Iroquois. The development of mankind was divided into three stages, Savagery, Barbarism and Civilisation. The first two stages were subdivided into Lower, Middle and Upper Statuses.

Vere Gordon Childe, the greatest synthesiser of prehistory to date, combined the Five-Age System, the ethnographical stage model and the culture concept in his two works *Man Makes Himself* (1936) and *What Happened in History* (1942). These works can be argued to represent the highest development of all these model systems. Childe isolated what he considered to be the two most significant events in human history, the Neolithic Revolution and the Urban Revolution. As he envisaged the events, the first transformed man into a food producer with the development of agriculture and the second brought forth the rise of civilisations.

This brief sketch has not been intended as a history of archaeology. The reader should consult the works of Glyn Daniel to pursue this subject further. What it has attempted to show is the development of the basic systems used by archaeologists to arrange their artefacts in a time dimension. It will be noted immediately that the systems described are all systems for the relative chronological placing of objects not of absolute dating. This was recognised by the initiators. Thomsen, for example, clearly saw that in parts of the world the Age of Stone was still in existence. Also, it was recognised that whilst the systems had a wide application it was not universal. This was particularly true of the Americas, where no stages equivalent to the Bronze and Iron Ages can be identified. It was necessary to develop an entirely separate stage model for the Mexican, Mayan and Peruvian areas. The general model employed was that of the Developmental Stages. Cultures were arranged in relative order according to their level of development. Level of development was measured by the number, range and complexity of the artefacts composing the assemblages. Thus a standard model for Peru was composed of the following periods: Pre-agricultural, Early Agricultural, Formative, Cultist, Experimental, Florescent, Expansionist, Urbanist and Imperialist. The Pre-agricultural and Early Agricultural were grouped in the Incipient Era; the Formative, Cultist and Experimental in the Developmental; the Florescent in the Florescent; and the Expansionist, Urbanist and Imperialist in the Climatic (Mason, 1957, 16–17). In Mexico a similar scheme of eras, the Pre-classic, Classic and Post-classic, was used. Each stage in the developmental sequence was marked either by cultural change, such as the emergence of the Mochica in Florescent North Coast Peru, or by the introduction of some significant feature, such as maize. As with the European stage system, the model has fallen into disrepute and is now little used, except at the most general organising level, because it contains so little information concerning culture history and is such a crude representation of culture change as to have ceased to have any analytical value.

Whilst archaeologists are generally abandoning, or at least tacitly ignoring, the more embracing stage schemes of the past, they nevertheless continue to operate two important stage concepts in organising assemblages, those of period and phase. Just as the Bronze Age can vary in length depending on the region in which it is found, so the period and phase are not time units of constant length. This makes them difficult to use consistently. On the site of a Roman villa, the term period will be applied to successive major structural changes that are detected. On a Middle Eastern tell, one period might be distinguished from another by a complete change in culture. In the first case a period might last twenty years, whilst in the latter it could be several hundred.

The nature of archaeological evidence and the requirement for a concept that links entities in time as well as in space makes it inevitable that a hierarchy of terminology will exist. Two major types of period/phase can be recognised. The first is the cultural period/phase and the second the site period/phase. The first is defined from both stratigraphic and typological-taxonomic studies, whilst the second is defined purely on stratigraphical grounds.

Two assemblages can be said to belong to the same cultural phase if they show a closely similar quantitative and qualitative content of types such as is only likely to have arisen through the close contemporaneity of the two groups producing the assemblages. Such contemporaneity is best firmly established by cross-dating links, and absolute dates derived from techniques such as radiocarbon (C14) dating wherever possible. A cultural period is a summation of a set of phases and represents a distinct stage in the development of a culture. Such a development of a culture has been modelled by Clarke (1968, 257 *et seq.*). He suggests that cultures go through a four-stage development, termed pre-formative, formative, coherent and post-coherent. Clarke terms these 'phases', but as they are not the minimal time entities that his general definition of phase proposes, the term 'period' is more appropriate. The pre-formative stage is characterised by considerable variability in the assemblages of a culture. This variability decreases in the formative stage and the distinctive features of the culture begin to appear as closely correlated sets of attributes. The coherent period sees the culture at its most developed; its features are being increasingly elaborated and there is much experimentation with new types. In the post-coherent stage the variety of types and their degree of sophistication is much reduced. Clarke's important work *Analytical Archaeology* should be consulted for further detailed discussion of the basis, and the implications, of this stage model.

Periods and phases can be more easily defined on a site. A new period can be said to be initiated when structural or stratigraphic evidence suggests that a significant change in the use, access to or occupants of a building or activity area has occurred. A stratigraphic or constructional phase is initiated by a minor addition or alteration to a site conducted as a single activity. The period or phase is the unit of time represented by the number of years between the initiation of one period or phase and another. Thus it is variable in length. It will be appreciated that in telescoping site period/phases into cultural ones it is possible, even though unlikely, that several site periods might be subsumed under a single cultural phase.

The concept of stratification is fundamental to the demonstration of all schemes of sequence in archaeology. It is the primary means of demonstrating the positions of assemblages relative to each other. Without the clearest understanding of stratification all attempts at accurately establishing degrees of association of artefacts will be frustrated. The principle is taken from geology. Deposits or strata of rock can be observed superimposed one on another. The stratum at the bottom of a series will have been laid down earliest and those above it successively through time from bottom to top. Palaeolithic implements are found incorporated in geological strata, but archaeological stratigraphy is not usually of the same order of magnitude in thickness or extent.

Stratification occurs on sites of human occupation through two main agencies, natural deposition and human activity. It is of great importance to be able to identify which agency is involved. For example, a layer of wind-blown sand on a midden might indicate a period when the mound was deserted. Clearly, if the sand had been deposited by humans, the history of the site would require an entirely different interpretation. It is of crucial importance to approach the interpretation of any deposit found on a site through the question, 'How was it formed?'

There are a great variety of sources for layers built up by human activity. Among the chief found are: construction layers, deposits of material associated with building; demolition layers, material spread over a site from the destruction of a structure and rubbish deposits. Whilst major activity might be represented by extensive horizons of deposit which can truly be called strata, most archaeological stratification is not in the form of true strata but is composed of small layers of material usually limited in depth to a few centimetres and in extent to particular features such as pits or the rooms of a building. If two rooms of a building have undergone separate alterations, then the layer sequence in each will differ from that of its neighbour. An individual archaeological layer can be as small as the silting deposit that forms in the top of a stake hole after the timber has been removed. Thus a complex, deep site such as a tell, some of which are several hundred metres of accumulated deposit, and in Britain a Roman town, will consist of a vertical accumulation composed of horizon strata representing the beginnings and ends of significant periods and thousands of minor layers formed as the result of single actions such as the sealing of a cess pit. If the site is dismantled layer by layer, the depositional history can be recovered in reverse down to the earliest occupation of the ground.

An understanding of the processes of deposition of each layer is essential in order to be able to assess the degree of association of objects found within them. If, for example, a

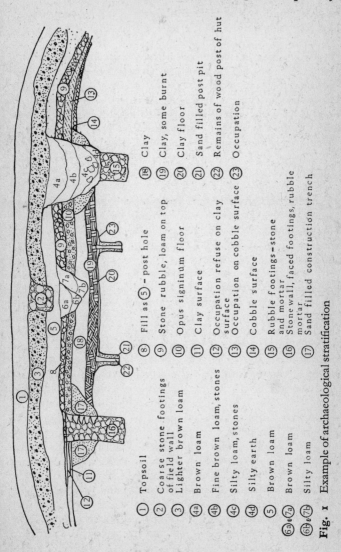

① Topsoil
② Coarse stone footings of field wall
③ Lighter brown loam
④a Brown loam
④b Fine brown loam, stones
④c Silty loam, stones
④d Silty earth
⑤ Brown loam
⑥a⑦a Brown loam
⑥b⑦b Silty loam
⑧ Fill as ⑤ — post hole
⑨ Stone rubble, loam on top
⑩ Opus signinum floor
⑪ Clay surface
⑫ Occupation refuse on clay surface
⑬ Occupation on cobble surface
⑭ Cobble surface
⑮ Rubble footings — stone and mortar
⑯ Stone wall, faced footings, rubble mortar
⑰ Sand filled construction trench
⑱ Clay
⑲ Clay, some burnt
⑳ Clay floor
㉑ Sand filled post pit
㉒ Remains of wood post of hut
㉓ Occupation

Fig. 1 Example of archaeological stratification

rampart is thrown up using earth from the surrounding ground halfway through the history of a long-occupied town, it is very likely that few of the objects found together in the mound will be contemporary with each other and none contemporary with the construction of the defence. The longer a site has been occupied and the more intensively it has been dug into, the greater the degree of displacement of objects that can occur. Roman pottery is commonly found in fills of medieval rubbish pits in British towns that have been continuously occupied. In a deeply layered site the general trend in the age of the objects will be to get progressively younger towards the top, but redeposition will mean that many layers will contain much material residual from earlier levels. It is important to recognise this situation and to separate it from cases of late type survival. The complexity of archaeological stratigraphy cannot be too fully stressed. Each site is distinct and linked only by the twin concepts of stratigraphic order and uniformitarian explanation of that order.

The contemporaneity of two assemblages or cultures can be established by cross-dating. Cross-dating exists when types x of assemblage A are found associated with types y of assemblage B in assemblage B's region and when types y of assemblage B are found with types x of assemblage A in assemblage A's region. By creating a chain of cross-dating across a landmass it is possible to link cultures chronologically. In the days before radiocarbon dating this was how the chronology of prehistoric Europe was established. The cultures of the Balkans were tied into the chronology of Egypt through finds of south-east European material in Egypt and finds of Egyptian exports in Greece and the Aegean area. South-east Europe was in turn linked to Central Europe and so on. Much of the Egyptian material could be assigned a date in calendar years and, making due allowance for survival, it was possible to give a date to cultures with which it was found associated. The result was a short chronology for European prehistory that has not stood the test of the recent C14 recalibration. This, however, proves not to be through any fault in the principle but through a carelessness in the recognition of cross-linked traits (Renfrew, C., 1973).

When physical methods are not employed, an assemblage is dated either from the association of the layer within which it is found with a datable event or by the presence of objects within the assemblage to which a date can be assigned. In Britain a classic example of a deposit to which a date can be assigned is the Boudiccan fire layers found at Verulamium (St Albans), Colchester and London which belong to the great native rebellion of AD 60. Most of the material found in these layers can be said to have been in use at the time of or shortly before the destruction. The same is true for all the objects found in the latest pre-disaster positions at Pompeii. Closely datable deposits such as these are unfortunately rare.

The most obvious example of a directly datable object is something such as a Roman coin, which can be assigned to a year of minting, or at least to one of a small number of years, because it usually gives such details as the number of consulships or the number of times tribunician power has been renewed by the Emperor, the dates of which are known from literary and epigraphic sources. The example of the Roman coin is a convenient one for demonstrating the important principle of *terminus post quem* dates. Just because a coin can be dated in its minting to, say, AD 76, this does not mean that this is the date of the deposit in which it is found, or the date of its associated artefacts. The coin may have been in circulation several years before being lost and buried. Its present position in the ground could even be due to redeposition. All that it is strictly proper to say is that the coin gives the date after which the deposit must have been formed; how long after is a matter for the archaeologist to decide in each case. One of the signs looked for in the case of a coin is the amount of wear that it has suffered. If the coin is in mint condition it is likely that deposition took place soon after issue. However, it should be noted that certain coins were hoarded for a long time and turn up in much later deposits. The same principle applies to other artefacts directly datable or not. A layer is dated by the latest object found within it, irrespective of what percentage may be of earlier type. It is clearly extremely important when excavating to ensure that no mixture of the finds between layers occurs. A date is usually arrived at on the basis of groups of artefacts considered to be contemporary with each other and an estimate is made of their likely joint lifespan before being discarded.

Occasionally it is possible to come upon an object, or layer, that can give a *terminus ante quem* for an assemblage. An obvious case is the Boudiccan sack deposit. All layers below it must be pre-AD 60. If a coin hoard, the deposition date of which can be closely assessed, is found dug into a floor or the filled-in top of a ditch, this gives the date before which a layer must have formed. Potentially, all objects found in stratigraphic positions which are demonstrably later than others are capable of giving a *terminus ante quem*. This capacity is restricted by the inability to date most objects closely.

This chapter has been concerned to outline the basic concepts of entities and time with which the archaeologist operates. It is now necessary to move to a study of how the archaeologist obtains his evidence.

Bibliography

Childe, V. G., *Man Makes Himself*. London: C. A. Watts, 1936.

Childe, V. G., *What Happened in History*. London: Penguin Books, 1942.

Childe, V. G., *A Short Introduction to Archaeology*. London: Muller, 1956.

Clarke, D. L., *Analytical Archaeology*. London: Methuen, 1968.

CBA (G. Webster (ed.)), *Romano-British Coarse Pottery: a student's guide*, Research Report 6. 2nd ed. Cncl. Brit. Archaeol., 1969.

Daniel, G., *The Origins and Growth of Archaeology*. London: Penguin Books, 1967.

Deetz, J., *Invitation to Archaeology*. New York: American Museum of Natural History, 1967.

BRITISH MUSEUM,

Ellesmere, Lord, *A Guide to Northern Antiquities*. London: Bain, 1848.

Lubbock, J., *Prehistoric Times*. 6th ed. London: Williams & Norgate, 1900.

Lyell, C., *Principles of Geology*. London: Murray, 1830–3.

Mason, J. A., *The Ancient Civilisations of Peru*. Harmondsworth Press, 1957.

Nilsson, S., *The Primitive Inhabitants of Scandinavia*. London: Longmans, Green & Co., 1868.

Renfrew, C., *Before Civilisation*. London: Jonathan Cape, 1973.

Ucko, P. J., and Dimbleby, G. W. (eds), *The domestication and exploitation of plants and animals*. London: Duckworth, 1969.

Additional reading

Binford, L. R., *An Archaeological Perspective*. New York: Seminar Press, 1972.

Binford, S. R., and Binford, L. R. (eds) *New Perspectives in Archaeology*. Chicago: Chicago University Press, 1968.

Bray, W., and Trump, D., *A Dictionary of Archaeology*. London: Penguin Books, 1970.

Ceram, C. W., *Archaeology*. New York: Odyssey Press, 1965.

Ceram, C. W., *The World of Archaeology*. London: Thames & Hudson, 1966.

Chang, K. C., *Rethinking Archaeology*. New York: Random House, 1967.

Chang, K. C. (ed.), *Settlement Archaeology*. Palo Alto, California: National Press Books, 1968.

Childe, V. G., *Piecing Together the Past*. London: Routledge & Kegan Paul, 1956.

Clark, J. G. D., *Archaeology and Society*. 3rd ed., London: Methuen, 1957.

Clark, J. G. D., *World Prehistory*. 2nd ed. Cambridge: Cambridge University Press, 1969.

Clark, J. G. D., and Piggott, S., *Prehistoric Societies*. London: Hutchinson, 1965.

Clarke, D. L. (ed.), *Models in Archaeology*. London: Methuen, 1972.

Daniel, G., *The Three Ages*. Cambridge: Cambridge University Press, 1943.

Daniel, G., *A Hundred Years of Archaeology*. London: Duckworth, 1950.

Daniel, G., *The Idea of Prehistory*. London: Penguin Books, 1962.

De Laet, S. J., *Archaeology and its Problems*. London: Dent, 1957.

Dymond, D. P., *Archaeology and History*. London: Thames & Hudson, 1974.

Forde, C. D., *Habitat, Economy and Society*. London: Methuen, 1964.

Grinsell, L., Rahtz, P., and Warhurst, A., *The Preparation of Archaeological Reports*. London: John Baker, 1966.

Hawkes, J., *The World of the Past*. New York and London: Alfred A. Knopf and Thames & Hudson, 1963.

Heizer, R. F., *Man's Discovery of his Past*. Palo Alto, California: Peek Publications, 1969b.

Hole, F., and Heizer, R. F., *An Introduction to Prehistoric Archaeology*. 3rd ed., New York: Holt, Rinehart & Winston, 1973.

Leone, M. P. (ed.), *Contemporary Archaeology*. Carbondale and Edwardsville: Southern Illinois University Press, 1972.

Piggott, S., *Approach to Archaeology*. London: A. & C. Black, 1959.

Renfrew, C. (ed.), *The Explanation of Cultural Change: models in prehistory*. London: Duckworth, 1973b.

Rouse, I., *Introduction to Prehistory: a systematic approach*. New York: McGraw-Hill, 1972.

Strong, D. E. (ed.), *Archaeological Theory and Practice*. London and New York: Seminar Press, 1973.

Trigger, B. G., *Beyond History: The Methods of Prehistory*. New York: Holt, Rinehart & Winston, 1968.

Ucko, P. J., Tringham, R., and Dimbleby, G. W., *Man, Settlement and Urbanism*. London: Duckworth, 1972.

Watson, P. J., Leblanc, S. A., and Redman, C. L., *Explanation in Archaeology*. New York and London: Columbia University Press, 1971.

Willey, G. R., and Phillips, P., *Method and Theory in American Archaeology*. Chicago: Chicago University Press, 1958.

2 Finding an Archaeological Site

The remains of past human activity are scattered in vast quantities over much of the world's land surface. Sometimes they are immense and perfectly obvious structures, such as the Pyramids, Hadrian's Wall and Stonehenge. There is no archaeological skill required in locating such monuments. There may, however, be considerable physical discomfort involved in the search. The cities and temples of the Classic Period Maya are hidden in the jungles of Guatemala and Honduras and, even with all the aids of modern transport, survey and excavation of the sites is a difficult and expensive task. Problems of access of this sort are rarely encountered in Britain except in mountainous regions.

Most ancient sites are not as readily discernible. They fall into two categories. The first comprises those remains which are partially visible above ground. The second group can no longer be seen by the naked eye at ground level. This latter class includes the majority of archaeological relics. To detect the presence of both types of remains archaeologists use a few easily understood techniques.

Before considering these procedures, it is necessary to understand how ancient sites come to be in the state in which archaeologists find them. Detailed consideration is given to a number of common features in Chapter 3 and here attention is drawn to the principles only. A structure can go out of commission in three main ways. In the first, it can be abandoned by its users and left derelict. Deprived of maintenance, it is at the mercy of the elements and rapidly deteriorates. The first parts to suffer are the perishable items such as the timber members. Thus in, for example, a brick or masonry building with wood fittings it will be roofing, doors, windows and flooring that will break up first. The primary deterioration period in this instance is usually short. After this, the more solid parts of the structure will stand for a considerable time, showing only minor collapse. Vegetation will have begun to colonise various bits of the site from the early days of its dereliction and this will contribute to its decay and to the partial covering of some of the lower parts of the structure, along with earth brought by the action of wind and water. Below-ground chemical and bacterial agents are potent in decay processes. If no serious disturbance was to occur henceforth, then the likely outcome would be the slow break-up of the upper parts of the building combined with the slow burial of the lower elements, producing a mound which itself would be subject to denudation that further diminishes its prominence. It should be emphasised that this example serves only to indicate some general processes and simplifies what is a complex system of interacting agencies. A major catalyst in the sequence outlined above is human interference in the form of the robbing of building materials from abandoned sites for reuse in contemporary structures. Many Roman towns, such as Wroxeter and Verulamium (St Albans), have served as the quarries for medieval domestic and, more particularly, religious edifices. In this manner buildings are rapidly reduced to foundation level.

Robbing is an example of demolition—the second way in which a structure can end its life. The third way is destruction, either by accident, for example in a fire, or deliberately by enemy action. As far as the subsequent history of the site is concerned, there is little distinction between the two means. Structures treated in these ways are unlikely to show above ground as they immediately become subject to geomorphological processes, particularly buried through soil development.

It is rare nowadays that the archaeologist has the time, money or, probably, inclination to descend into the country-side with the object of making a discovery for the sake of making a discovery. It is much more likely that he will have a particular problem in mind before undertaking any fieldwork. Not all problems will be purely academic. Whilst a researcher may be searching for further examples, say, of a particular type of Roman fort, he may also be conducting more generalised enquiries into the archaeological content of an area in advance of a motorway or large-scale urban development. Whatever the objective, the techniques are held in common and are usually used in combination. Ideally, fieldwork is not an end in itself. Often it is the next best solution when time is short, but normally it should be regarded as the basis for further analytical work and hence its value is directly proportional to its degree of organisation in terms of the specific purpose for which it was conducted.

It may be asked why there should be so much concern with fieldwork. An important reason is the archaeologist's reliance in analysis on the distribution map. The value of the conclu-sions that he draws from such maps is related to both how he uses them and how accurate a representation the map is of the spatial distribution of the class of sites about which he is argu-ing. Recent work in Britain has emphasised how partial and biased a sample many of our maps are. It has been suggested that the demonstrated density of Romano-British homesteads in Cornwall reflects not the original distribution but the distri-bution of archaeological survey parties (Thomas, in Fowler, 1972). The incompleteness of distribution maps is common-place knowledge to archaeologists. This has not prevented many unintelligent statements from being made. It is a funda-mental procedure in all science to consider the nature of sampling error in the evidence, and archaeology is not exempt from this. One means of roughly quantifying the problem for a given survey area is to collect figures of the number of sites in different classes known at various intervals in the past. This will allow broad trends in the accumulation of knowledge to be gauged and intelligent guesses about the future productivity of the region to be made.

Fieldwork entails two main operations, recognition and recording. Recording usually comprises a mixture of verbal description, measurement and photography. Measurements are obtained through standard surveying methods which are described in most archaeological textbooks, some of which are listed in the bibliography at the end of this chapter. Photographic procedures are the same as those employed in excavation and are described in the next chapter.

Prior knowledge is undoubtedly required to recognise the nature of an archaeological site. It is impossible to generalise usefully about the infinite variety of sites of different periods that will be met with or the artefacts yielded by them. The reader should consult the bibliography. He will find the book *Field Archaeology*, published by the Ordnance Survey, very valuable in this respect. Even better is to get to know an experienced archaeologist who is prepared to give guidance on reading and on which sites and museums to visit. Many local societies organise field trips.

Familiarity with the geography of the area to be searched is the second most important requirement. The researcher should provide himself with the available maps. Britain is fortunate in having the excellent map cover provided by the Ordnance Survey. The smallest scale of Ordnance map useful to the archaeologist in the field is the 1 inch to the mile (1:63 360). This can serve as the map on which integration of a regional study takes place. It is a convenient scale at which sites can be seen both in their local and in a regional setting and compared with each other. If the main purpose of the survey is to collect surface artefacts, then either the $2\frac{1}{2}$-inch or 6-inch to the mile maps are appropriate for plotting densities. The 6-inch map can often serve for planning, but for this operation the most appropriate scale is the 25-inch for rural areas and the 50-inch for some urban centres. Often, it is desirable to draw a separate plan at even larger scales whilst in the field and relate this to the Ordnance map later. When plans are required it is customary to draw them on the spot rather than log a series of measurements, which is the normal surveying practice. This is because an archaeological drawing tends to be peculiar to the individual responsible for it, emphasising those things which he considers significant in the object being surveyed. Archaeologists differ in their assessments of significance and it is quite possible for two entirely different drawings of the same site to be made by different people, neither 'wrong' but constructed according to separate terms of reference. Resurveying of monuments is usually rewarding.

Two of the many advantages of the Ordnance maps should be specially noted. By showing bench marks, contours and spot heights they provide a ready-made system for relating sites into the general topography of a region. Secondly, through the National Grid Reference they provide an infinitely expandable numerical method of registering location.

Geological information is most readily obtained by reference to the maps and accompanying memoirs of the Institute of Geological Sciences (previously the Geological Survey of Great Britain). These are printed in a standard colour code on an Ordnance Survey 1 inch to the mile base map. Two types are published, one showing the solid geology only, the other showing the superficial deposits of gravel and alluvium or drift. These latter maps are the more important to the archaeologist as the well-drained, light soils of the drifts were primary areas of ancient settlement. In the absence of a full coverage of the country by the Soil Survey, the geology maps are the best guides to the general character of a region's soils. Unfortunately, some of the maps are out of print or otherwise not easily obtainable and some memoirs are out of date. The aid of a local geologist should be enlisted when possible. It should always be borne in mind that the boundaries of deposits shown on the maps are approximations. Should it be of importance at a site to establish the detailed edge, then this can be rapidly achieved by use of an auger. Also, the Geological

Survey does not record shallow deposits of drift. These can be of local significance in soil formation and should be looked for in the field.

The Soil Survey of England and Wales provides for a few areas detailed maps and memoirs on the local soils. These can be of great value in understanding the soil cover of a particular site, but care should be exercised if it is intended to use the map as a guide to ancient conditions. Soil types have been subject to transformations due to the impact of agriculture and, particularly, changes in drainage patterns.

Present-day vegetation very rarely resembles ancient conditions, but some knowledge of prevailing species is useful in helping to assess the amount of environmental change that has occurred in an area. Local naturalists' clubs are the best source of information. Unusual patterns of growth in some species may indicate the location of buried features.

When planning a survey it is a routine practice to make oneself familiar with any previous archaeological work done in the locality. A gazetteer is compiled using information derived from excavation or survey reports in journals, museum records and local helpers. This work will show up areas of ignorance and suggest fruitful lines of research. A national gazetteer is maintained by the Ordnance Survey. A list of major collections of air photographs is included at the end of this chapter.

Documentary evidence can sometimes come to the aid of the archaeologist. Place names and field names can indicate sites no longer visible and also provide a clue to past environment. The Domesday Book for Cambridgeshire records the name of a village called Werateuuorde (Wratworth) (Domesday Book, XIII, XIV, XXIV, XXIX, XXX). This settlement lay partly in the parishes of Orwell and Wimpole. After the sixteenth century both the site of the village and the name were lost, and without the documents we would be ignorant of its existence. The presence of a structure, in this case a Roman villa, is suggested by the field name Sunken Church Field at Hadstock, Essex (VCH Essex iii, 135-6). Place names can be used to show the former extent of woodland. The occurrence of the words 'leah', '(ge)haeg', 'ryding', 'stocking' and 'holt' on a number of occasions in the parishes of south-east Cambridgeshire betray the widespread nature of the oak forest on the boulder clay in former times (Reaney, 1943).

Names also inform about the purpose of structures. At Stapleford in Wiltshire excavation of an enclosure called South Kite failed to reveal its purpose. A nineteenth-century tithe map of the parish records its name as 'The Coneygar', thus showing it to be a medieval rabbit warren. The other uses of documents in reconstructing the history of sites are considered later (Taylor in Fowler (ed.), 1972).

Further examples of useful documentary work in field archaeology are the tracing of Roman roads from place names such as 'straet' and from the courses of parish boundaries on maps made prior to the reforms of the late nineteenth century. The sites of many prehistoric barrows are marked on the old Ordnance maps but not on the present ones. Documents have been used to trace deer parks in Dorset and maps to find old wind-pumping mills in the Fens (Fowler (ed.), 1972). These few hints should be enough to show that most surveys will benefit from an informed visit to the local archivist's office, usually situated close to the centre of local government.

Ground survey

Because it is very time-consuming this fundamental procedure in fieldwork is becoming less common on a large scale, although motorway building has produced some notable examples, such as that of Peter Fowler along the M5 line and the work of the M40 Research Group (Rowley and Davies, 1973). The very great value of widespread groundwork can be judged from the labours of Hallam and Bromwich in the Fenland. Here, painstaking collection and survey, combined with an almost uniquely revealing air photograph record of the complete Roman landscape, has allowed broad conclusions concerning the chronology and economic basis of Roman Fenland settlement to be made and has provided a basis for a campaign of extensive excavation when finance is available (Philips (ed.), 1970).

Ground survey can only be accomplished satisfactorily on foot. Usually more than one person is necessary if surveying with instruments is involved. Bromwich's work shows that the lone worker is not excluded. The team will be looking for one or more of the following three things: unusual patterns of soil colour or texture, or unusual patterns of vegetation growth; unusual rises or dips in the ground; scatters of artefacts.

It is important to walk and record within standard area units. The maximum size for such a unit should be no greater than the smallest expected site size. The use of a standard unit allows for easy statistical manipulation of the results, proper assessment of finds densities and rapid comparability. It is not adequate to use existing divisions of the landscape as collecting units. Having worked out the size of the unit to be used, usually a square, parties work progressively across the survey area demarcating the collecting zones with lines of ranging poles.

A standard record sheet or card should be filled out for each survey unit. This can take a variety of forms, but it should have sections which record the following sorts of data:

1 Location. This should always be in the form of the National Grid.
2 Name of site. This is not essential but, if used, should be as local a term as possible, such as a field name or the title of a nearby farm.
3 Record number. This is often omitted when the grid reference is used instead.
4 Site environment. Geology, soil type, topography, drainage, vegetation, present use.
5 Observed features. This section is descriptive of the remains found. It will usually be accompanied by drawings and photographs.
6 Collection notes. Here it is normal to give the date of the record, the name of the recorder and notes on any samples taken.

Where samples are taken, every care should be exercised that the receptacles are clearly and indelibly marked with a code that is systematically related to the record sheets. The whole survey can be rendered useless if the finds bags are mislocated. Normally all artefacts visible on the surface are collected regardless of age. There has yet to be a study that investigates whether systematic relationships exist between surface and subsurface finds, and at present this author stands by the assumption that, for extensive sites, surface collections are likely to be representative of the range of artefacts present but not necessarily of the relative proportions. This assumption requires as total a collection as possible. Total collection helps also to guard against the 'false' site. The practice of manuring fields with farmyard refuse is ancient. In more recent times refuse derived from fairly long distances has been spread on fields from tractor-drawn carts. It is always possible that this could contain quite ancient artefacts disturbed by digging at the source. These will only be present in small numbers relative to the more modern bric-à-brac. Ignoring the recent material, however, might give undue emphasis to the finding of ancient material. Of course, recognition of the source of such a manure spread would lead to the true site of the derived objects.

The fieldworker usually has to cross other people's land. He must always gain permission to do so to avoid the possibility of prosecution and to defend the good name of archaeology. Always observe the Country Code. Finds made in the survey belong to the owner of the land on which they were found and cannot be removed without his permission. Polite explanation to an owner of the objectives of the work usually results in full co-operation.

Air photography

Air photography is the largest single source of new discoveries in archaeology. Its use as an archaeological survey tool was pioneered by Major G. W. G. Allen and O. G. S. Crawford between the wars, and its most productive recent exponent has been Professor J. K. S. St Joseph of the Cambridge University Committee for Aerial Photography. Whole ancient landscapes have been revealed in such places as the Fenland and along the gravel terraces of most of the rivers of midland and southern Britain. The standard view that the Midlands was too heavily wooded to have supported any sizeable prehistoric population has been overturned by finds in the Avon, Severn, Trent and other valleys. The effect this has on our view of prehistoric Britain is only just beginning to be examined (e.g. Webster and Hobley, 1965, 1–22).

Sites can be revealed from the air by a series of indications. Upstanding earthworks can be studied to best advantage in low, raking sunlight when rises cast dark shadows which contrast sharply with the highlights of the slopes facing the sun. Depressions are in deep shade except for a part of the lip. The whole chiaroscuro effect can be very revealing. Observation of sites under snow has produced spectacular results. Professor St Joseph has recently published a fine photograph of the Hadrian's Wall fort of Housesteads under a light snow cover taken in bright winter sunlight. The details of the fort and its vicus are remarkably clear (JRS, LXIII, pl. XV). Differential melting of snow or hoar frost sometimes shows up features such as ditches when in cooler depressions the snow lingers longer than elsewhere on the site. At the early Roman fortress of Longthorpe near Peterborough, Professor St Joseph noted in 1964 that the line of buried ditches could be detected because snow over them was melting before that over the rest of the field (JRS, LV, 1965, 74).

Soil marks are seen in land bare of crop or vegetation. Any removal of earth from the ground involves at least a minor change in the mechanical composition of that earth relative to that from which it was derived. Hence it cannot be replaced in the ground without usually giving visual indication of disturbance. Disturbance, i.e. ditches, pits, banks and the like, will show as differences in texture and colour according to derivation and composition. Soil marks are usually noted after ploughing or earth scraping. They can be seen on the ground but, if extensive, are best appreciated from the air.

When ancient sites are covered by planted crops, differences observed in the growth patterns of the crops can indicate their existence. The theory is very simple, the reality very complex. Results are closely dependent on a variety of interacting factors, so that repeated survey of a region over a number of years and seasons is required before a full picture can emerge. Influencing factors inducing variability of results are soil types, crop growth (cereals are usually more susceptible than root crops, grass is least revealing), microclimate, drainage, elevation, degree of slope, weather conditions and seasonal conditions. Exceptionally dry conditions at the critical late period of growth in cereal crops often yields the very best results.

If a ditch, pit or hollow of some other kind has been dug and subsequently filled with earth of richer organic content than the surrounding ground, then the following effects are observable in a suitable crop such as wheat. Growth of the crop over the features will be slower but richer. Whilst the rest of the crop will be ripening to a light, yellowish colour, the crop over the buried remains will retain a greenish hue indicating the line of the features. In the late season, however, the more thoroughly matured feature-based crop will take on a darker yellow colour and often grow to a greater height than the surrounding crop. If the grain over the features is markedly higher than the rest, it will cast a shadow in raking light.

When a crop grows over a buried feature such as a wall or metalled road, the inverse effect is in operation. The crop ripens relatively quickly but progresses little further. It can be seen yellowing whilst the rest of the field is green. Later in the season the rest of the crop will overtake the crop over the foundations, and if marked stunting of growth has occurred shadows will be cast in the hollows created.

Interpretation of air photographs is fraught with difficulties. Much prior knowledge of what has proved to be archaeological and what has not is required. The results of recent agricultural and construction activity constantly show up and can mislead the unwary. In south-west Cambridgeshire, RAF photographs showed a line that was first thought to be that of a Roman road. What was observed in reality was the oil pipeline to the RAF station at Bassingbourn. Geological features are also common. One regularly met is the polygonal patterning of a bedrock surface caused by the cracking of the ground and the filling of the fissures with a sludge during periglacial conditions. There is much to be said for consulting the landowner of a field suspected of containing archaeological remains before interpreting a photograph. He can give an account of recent utilisation, such as the location of field drains, old ponds, manure stacks and Second World War emplacements. The bibliography includes works with collections of interpreted air photos.

There are two main types of air photograph, the low-level oblique and the high-level vertical. The oblique photo is in more general use in archaeology as it usually reveals greater detail about individual sites or aspects of them. It is common practice to fly over a site at between 60 and 150 metres (200 and 500 feet) or 300 and 450 metres (1000 and 1500 feet), approaching it from a number of angles to accommodate variations of relief and light. A drawback of the oblique shot is the visual distortion created by the relatively low angle of photographing which makes it difficult to draw a highly accurate plan on to an Ordnance Survey base.

The vertical photograph, taken normally at about 3000 metres (10 000 feet), is more suitable for mapping. It has rarely, however, provided sufficient detail for archaeological purposes as the available photographs have not been taken with archaeology in mind. The photos have been made in unsensitive crop conditions. Expense limits the archaeologist's ability to commission a run at suitable times. Most modern cartography is achieved through the use of vertical air photos and considerable advances have been made in the precision of the photogrammetric technique. The procedure involves the planning of a flight path between two known points in conjunction with a set of ground control points at a constant altitude. A fixed camera with a lense of standard focal length takes a series of photographs, of which adjacent shots overlap in their coverage of a land area by 60%. Such a pair of photos can be viewed stereoscopically, giving a three-dimensional view of the land surface. Photogrammetric machines are capable of creating detailed contour maps of great accuracy by plotting from these 3-D pictures.

Magnetic prospecting

(Source: Aitken, 1969. I would like to thank Dr Aitken for his permission to use his material.)

Magnetic prospecting and resistivity surveying are techniques for locating features over a restricted area and are usually used as adjuncts to excavation.

The first method can be used to find fired material such as kilns, furnaces, ovens and hearths, pits and ditches, structures and ironwork.

Most rock or soil contains the iron oxides magnetite and haematite. A single haematite particle constitutes a magnetic domain. In material not subjected to heat, the domains are randomly orientated and mutual attraction–repulsion renders the total magnetism weak. Heating weakens the magnetisation of single domains, some of which tend to line up on the axis of the force lines of the earth's magnetic field. As the material cools, the domains stay fixed on this acquired alignment, whilst the magnetisation of individual domains returns to that prior to heating. The material exhibits increased magnetism as the cancelling-out effect between domains has been replaced by an additive one. Above 675°C there is no increase in the permanent magnetism acquired on cooling. The property is termed thermo-remanent magnetism. Calculable fractions of the potential thermo-remanent magnetism of a given material are attained on heating to a lower temperature.

The process is more complicated for magnetite. The amount of magnetisation acquired is greater, but the acquired domain alignment is less stable. The specific thermo-remanent magnetisation gained by fired clay varies with the degree to which conversion from magnetite to haematite occurs during heating.

Thermo-remanent magnetism is not the property that is responsible for the magnetic anomalies registered by ditches and pits. Most rock and soil is susceptible to a certain degree of induced magnetism in the absence of heat. The fills of pits and ditches often have greater susceptibility to induced magnetism than the surrounding deposits. This is detected as a magnetic discontinuity. The greater susceptibility is associated with either the higher organic content or the presence of burnt material in the feature.

Where a feature possessing either thermo-remanent magnetism or a high susceptibility to magnetisation is present, there is a localised distortion of the earth's magnetic field. This is measured as a deviation from the normal magnetic intensity of an area. The measurement unit is a gamma. Britain's normal intensity is 47 000 gamma.

Dr M. Aitken of the Research Laboratory for Archaeology and the History of Art, Oxford, who has pioneeered much of the work in this subject, gives four rules for use in interpreting the distortion created by an isolated archaeological feature, (Aitken, 1969, 687). First, the anomaly maximum occurs to the south of the feature but is not displaced by more than one-third of the depth of the centre of the feature. Secondly, the distance between the two points where the anomaly is at half its maximum value is not less than the depth of the feature. Thirdly, a reverse anomaly can be found as far north as the feature is deep. The reverse anomaly is only greater than 10% of the maximum anomaly if modern iron is present. Lastly, at distances beyond three times the depth of the feature, the observed anomaly is very small.

In the case of continuous archaeological remains like ditches, the anomaly varies according to orientation, for example that for a north–south ditch is much more marked than that for an east–west one.

The proton magnetometer has a bottle of water or alcohol with an electric coil wrapped around it as its detector. Before measurement, a current of 1 amp is passed through the coil for 3 seconds, creating a magnetic field along the axis. Most of the protons of the nuclei of the hydrogen atoms present in the water or alcohol align to this. When the current is switched off, the protons gyrate around the direction of the lines of force of the earth's magnetic field. The gyration frequency is directly proportional to the intensity of the earth's magnetic field. The gyrations of the protons are detectable by the alternating voltage they produce in the coil and this is passed through a flexible cable to an amplifier in a meter. The meter is sensitive to fractions of 1 gamma. The current passed through the coil is automatically timed in the instrument, and when it is shut off frequency measurement is conducted and registered on the indicating meters, where the lower the number shown, the greater the magnetic intensity.

The proton gradiometer depends on the same principle. A bottle is set at both ends of a vertically held staff some 1·5 to 3·0 metres long. If there is no anomaly there are the same proton frequencies from each bottle, and if these are linked in series to an amplifier a signal of 3 to 4 seconds is given. With an anomaly, slightly different frequencies are set up between the two bottles, with the result that the length of the combined signals is shorter. The stronger the anomaly, the shorter the signal. The instrument shows the time the signal takes to reach zero.

A simplified and cheaper version of the gradiometer is the 'bleeper'. This comprises only the bottles, an amplifier and a loudspeaker. The signal length is estimated by the operator. It is called a bleeper because of the bleeps given off as the signals move in and out of phase at different amplitudes.

Best results with a gradiometer are obtained by keeping the upper bottle at a height above the ground greater than the size of the anticipated remains and the lower bottle about 30 cm above the ground. The gradiometer picks up quite small anomalies and is not notably affected by widespread disturbance. It is not hindered by magnetic storms or d.c.-driven vehicles.

The differential fluxate magnetometer operates on a different principle. The detectors are two strips of mu-metal set vertically above each other. A meter registers different magnetic intensities. The instrument gives continuous readings and is not as severely affected by strong external magnetic gradients, such as occur near iron, as the proton magnetometer, but it is heavy and requires considerable labour in setting up.

Surveying is carried out by setting out a square grid of wooden pegs over an area. A plastic-covered net is stretched out between the four corner pegs of each square, creating a shorter-spaced grid. The bottle is moved regularly to corner points on this grid and readings are taken. If required, shorter-spaced readings can be taken to investigate strong anomalies.

A number of factors can make a site unsuitable for magnetic prospecting. Excessive vegetation and trees may severely hinder the cable. Interference can come from a.c. electric cables, transmitting stations, iron litter, pipes and wire fences. Igneous rocks have considerable thermo-remanent magnetism and it is impossible to survey on Tertiary basalts. D.c. lines only affect the proton magnetometer.

Magnetic prospecting has achieved its greatest successes in detecting isolated features of fired clay, particularly kilns. To justify its use it must be shown to be much quicker and less consumptive of effort than digging, for which it is never a substitute.

Resistivity survey
(Source: A. Clark, 1969.)

Professor R. J. C. Atkinson was the first archaeologist to make use of resistivity survey in archaeology. He utilised it for the rapid and accurate detection on the ground of ditches and pits associated with henges at Dorchester, Oxfordshire (Atkinson, 1953, 32).

Resistivity survey is superior to magnetic survey in its

ability to detect linear remains and buildings. Water in soil contains salts derived from the soil matrix and humic acids of organic origin. It is the presence of this water that allows the soil to conduct electricity. If two electrodes are placed apart on a deposit and a current is set up between them, then the ratio of the voltage applied to the strength of the current is called the resistance. Moist ground usually has less resistance because of the good conductivity of water. The strength of the salts and acids present also affects the resistance. The surveyor is looking for subterranean features that have a resistivity which contrasts with that of the general soil pattern. His best results are likely to come from the free-draining loam soils developed on gravel or chalk. Here pits and ditches will have an easily detected contrasting resistivity with the subsoil. On clays this is not as easy, but stone structures can still be found. The results on sandy and stony soils are poor as they tend to suffer from dryness, which makes it difficult to conduct electricity. Subsoils that are not uniform in their consistency demand special care. Drift deposits vary considerably from different grades of gravel through sands to silts and clay aggregates, and these changes can occur over a small area. Each of the different deposits is likely to have a different resistance. On chalk and limestone, solution hollows filled with clay occur. Without an appreciation of these possibilities it would be easy to identify features incorrectly. I. Scollar has developed techniques for isolating man-made remains from geological effects (Scollar, 1959).

It has been found that in recently ploughed fields results can be unreliable because of the relative dryness of the upper soil, and in this case the operator should be sure that the probes make contact with unloosened soil.

As a rule, high resistivity is registered by brick and masonry buildings, and low by pits and ditches. A robber trench will react as a ditch, whilst a stone-filled ditch will act as a wall.

There are a number of instruments available. Atkinson worked with a Megger Earth Tester, a rather heavy instrument depending on hand generation of electricity but equipped with a dial which registers values directly. The Megger is less reliable in dry environments. The Tellohm and the Gossen Geohm are similar instruments, from which readings are taken by setting a dial on zero. Such instruments are termed null-balance types.

The Martin-Clark Meter is of this type. It is hand-held, requires only very short leads and is equipped with an efficient changeover switch, a feature which cuts out the time-wasting involved in the other instruments in resetting the probes. Four probes, the required minimum in surveying, are in operation and a fifth spare probe acts as the first of the four in the switchover for the next reading.

The distance apart that the operator places the probes is important as it governs the amount and reliability of the information that he is likely to gain. Features are usually detected to a depth approximately equal to the distance between the probes. Guides to the scale of buried remains are provided by air photos or on site by use of an auger. It has been found that spacing of a metre is adequate for most purposes.

Two basic methods of survey can be employed. The first is the single straight line traverse and the second the area survey, which is conducted by setting up a square grid of parallel straight line traverses. The probes are moved along a plastic or linen tape measure. The single traverse is used for determining the line of a long ditch or wall, whilst the area survey aims to recover plans. In the latter a scale plan is produced on which are drawn contour lines connecting equal resistance values and giving, roughly, the limits of the features.

A number of scientists are working on refinements of the above procedures. A. Clark has developed an easily portable table-like arrangement in which the probes are set in a square, which seems to give better results than the standard linear setting (Clark, A., 1969, 706). I. Scollar has developed techniques that make it possible to eliminate non-archaeological anomalies (Scollar, 1959, 284).

Two configurations of probes are available for the Martin-Clark meter. The first is the old Wenner arrangement, one of the disadvantages of which is the double-peak effect obtained on some readings (Clark, A., 1969, 704). The second is the double-dipole configuration whereby one current and one potential electrode are interchanged in position, giving an arrangement of current, current, potential, potential. The double-dipole arrangement allows straight switching without alteration of the external connections. There is better definition of small features and the double-peak effect of the Wenner configuration is eliminated.

There is another configuration that can be used in the field known as the twin electrode arrangement. The pairs of electrodes are separated entirely from each other by at least thirty times the electrode spacing. One pair is fixed at the periphery of the site, whilst the other can be moved about at will. With this configuration there is much freedom of movement, the orientation of the probes is irrelevant and the double-peak effect of the Wenner configuration is eliminated. The method has proved very successful on uniform subsoils but is not yet fully tested on variegated soils.

I would like to thank Mr A. Clark for his permission to use material in his article and for extra details of the method. The form of this summary remains my responsibility.

Electromagnetic survey

Experiments to date have indicated that, for archaeologists, electromagnetic instruments are of most use in their primary role of metal detection rather than as detectors of underground soil features.

The soil conductivity meter (SCM) detects the variation in the electrical conductivity and the magnetic susceptibility of a soil. However, it is only capable of picking up the anomalies created by features of no more than two-thirds of a meter in depth. Operating at a low frequency at South Cadbury where the topsoil was thin, it was used with some success to detect magnetic features (Tite and Mullins, 1970).

Foster and Hackens (1969) have demonstrated how a pulsed

induction meter (PIM) can aid in the search for small metal objects. They used a Decco Mk. 4 Pulse Induction Metal Detector to pinpoint coins and other small objects on and in the floor surfaces of the rooms of Greek (Hellenistic) houses at Delos.

The instrument consists of a coil and a meter. The coil (in fact, an assemblage of coils of different sizes) is moved to points on a nylon grid by one operator whilst another person records the readings from the meter. The smaller the coil, the smaller the objects detected. Lead, silver, iron and bronze objects were found in this manner and pottery also showed up. As it was discovered that the strength of the signal varied with the different types of material, it was possible to predict with a high degree of accuracy the metal that a particular reading represented.

Metal detectors are available commercially at low prices. This has given rise to the deplorable practice of treasure-hunting on archaeological sites. One of the main purposes of this book is to emphasise that archaeology is a rigorous, scientific discipline dealing with a particular range of evidence and that one of the primary features of that evidence is the way in which it lies in the ground. If those relationships are disturbed by uncontrolled digging, irreparable damage is done. People who use these detectors to locate artefacts and then dig down to extract them are ignorantly looting the past. Further, they are usually breaking the law in that they are entering someone's land without his permission and taking away his property. Remember that anything that is not treasure-trove belongs solely to the owner of the land on which it is found, not to the finder.

Chemical prospecting

Phosphate analysis is the main form of chemical prospecting that is at present used in archaeology. When organic materials decay they leave behind phosphatic residues which mark their presence. If it is wished to test whether a deposit might have incorporated residues of animal or human occupation, for example the remains of cattle excretion in a kraal, samples are taken and subjected to a simple test for the phosphate content. This test is described by Goodyear (1971, 209–10). An enhanced phosphate presence is taken to indicate some activity, but it is impossible to say whether it was animal or human. Another use is to indicate the position of a body in a burial (a problem at Sutton Hoo) where the skeleton has completely decayed.

Other forms of chemical survey that might come into more common use are the various spraying techniques using chemical solutions that can be employed to emphasise the presence of a particular element over an area (Biek, 1969, 121).

Bibliography

Aitken, M., *Magnetic Location*, in Brothwell and Higgs (eds), Science in Archaeology. 2nd ed. London: Thames & Hudson, 1969, 681–94.

Atkinson, R. J. C., *Field Archaeology*. 2nd ed. London: Methuen, 1953.

Biek, L., *Soil Silhouettes*, in Brothwell and Higgs (eds), 1969, 118–23.

Clark, A., *Resistivity Surveying*, in Brothwell and Higgs (eds), 1969, 695–707.

Foster, E., and Hackens, T., *Decco Metal Detector Survey on Delos. Archaeometry* 11, 1969, 165–72.

Fowler, E. (ed.), *Field Survey in British Archaeology*. London: Council for British Archaeology, 1972.

Goodyear, F. H., *Archaeological Site Science*. London: Heinemann Educational, 1971.

Ordnance Survey, *Field Archaeology in Great Britain*. New revised edition, Southampton: HMSO, 1974.

Phillips, C. W. (ed.), *The Fenland in Roman Times*. London: Royal Geographical Society, 1970.

Reaney, P. H., *The Place-names of Cambridgeshire and the Isle of Ely*. Cambridge: Cambridge University Press, 1943.

Rowley, T., and Davies, M., *Archaeology and the M40 Motorway*. Oxford: Oxford University Press, 1973.

Scollar, I., in *Bonner Jahrbücher*, 159, 1959, 284.

Tite, M. S., and Mullins, C., *Electromagnetic prospecting on archaeological sites using a soil conductivity meter*. Archaeometry 12, 1970, 97–104.

Webster, G., Hobley, B., Baker, A., and Pickering, J., *Aerial reconnaissance over the Warwickshire Avon*. Archaeological Journal 121 (for 1964), 1965, 1–22.

Additional reading

Aitken, M., *Physics and Archaeology*. New York: Interscience Publications, 1st ed. 1961, 2nd ed. 1974.

Beresford, M., *The Lost Villages of England*. London: Lutterworth Press, 1963.

Bradford, J., *Ancient Landscapes, Studies in Field Archaeology*. London: Bell, 1957.

Crawford, O. G. S., *Archaeology in the Field*. London: Dent, 1953.

Ditter, A., and Wendorf, F. (eds), *Procedural Manual for Archaeological Field Research Projects*. Santa Fe: Museum of New Mexico Press, 1963.

Fowler, P. (ed.), *Archaeology and the Landscape*. London: John Baker, 1972.

St Joseph, J. K. S. (ed.), *The Uses of Air Photography*. London: John Baker, 1966.

Trorey, L., *Handbook of Aerial Mapping and Photogrammetry*. Cambridge: Cambridge University Press, 1950.

Wainwright, F., *Archaeology, Place-names and History*. London: Routledge & Kegan Paul, 1962.

Ordnance survey

This note is intended to give a brief review of the services provided by the Ordnance Survey. It is based on information kindly supplied by Paul Watts of the Sales Promotion Department. The address of the Ordnance Survey is Romsey Road, Maybush, Southampton, SO9 4DH.

A new edition of the book *Field Archaeology in Great Britain* is now available. This is of vital importance for anyone wishing to learn of the great variety of types of monument that can be met in the field.

Maps available

Ordnance Survey maps not specifically for archaeological purposes are published at a variety of scales. All contain information that the field archaeologist requires and most mark the sites of antiquities.

ONE-INCH MAPS	These are being replaced by the new 1:50 000 maps. The new maps for a line south of Lancaster to Bridlington were published in 1974. Those north of the line are due in 1976. The 1:50 000 maps incorporate all the information of the one-inch series in metric form and in a less crowded fashion.
QUARTER-INCH (1:250 000)	This scale is primarily intended for the motorist, but it is of use to the archaeologist for making regional comparisons. A famous example of the use of the quarter-inch is Cyril Fox, *Archaeology of the Cambridge Region*, Cambridge, 1923.

A number of tourist and special maps for various areas are available. One of the special values of these is the coloured accentuation of relief. They serve students of the cultures of highland Britain.

1:25 000 MAPS	Two series are available. The first series: most of Britain, except the Highlands and the Islands, in 2027 sheets. 160 sheets of the updated second series have been prepared.

1:1250 MAPS	Available for all towns and urban areas containing more than 20 000 people.
1:2500 MAPS	Available for most of Great Britain, excluding mountainous and moorland regions. The earlier series or County Series is based on pre-1939 surveys. This is being replaced by the post-1945 National Grid Series. The most recent publications of this series are in fully metric form.
1:10 000 and 1:10 560 MAPS	Most of the country, except for parts of Scotland, is now covered by National Grid based sheets. The 1:10 560 maps are being replaced by the 1:10 000 series. Contours are given in metric, and in the latest issues new contours of 5- and 10-metre intervals are used.

The Ordnance Survey publishes some specifically archaeological maps. These are as follows:

Southern Britain in the Iron Age   1:625 000
Roman Britain   1:1 000 000
Britain in the Dark Ages   1:1 000 000
Britain before the Norman Conquest   1:625 000

Each of the above maps records the positions of a broad range of types of antiquity of the relevant period. They are of necessity composite, including finds differing in age by sometimes up to several centuries. Two thematic maps are also published. These are *Ancient Britain* 1:625 000, which shows about 1000 sites classified by ages, and *Monastic Britain* 1:625 000, which shows the location of medieval religious houses.

The important monuments of Hadrian's Wall and the Antonine Wall are excellently served by detailed maps at 2 inches to the mile and 1:25 000 respectively.

The Ordnance Survey publish geological maps on behalf of the Institute of Geological Sciences.

The Ordnance Survey does not publish maps of Ireland.

Maps of Northern Ireland are issued by the Chief Survey
Officer, Ministry of Finance, Ordnance Survey, Ladas Drive,
Belfast, BT6 9FJ. Maps of Eire are issued by the Assistant
Director of Survey, Ordnance Survey, Phoenix Park, Dublin.

Other services rendered by the Survey include the supply of
survey control data such as triangulation point and bench
mark values; information concerning surveys before they are
published; transparent copies of maps that can be used for the
production of copies, enlargement and reduction of standard
scale maps; various mounting services; and the supply of information through microfilm facilities.

Ordnance maps are subject to Crown copyright. They can-
not be reproduced without the permission of the Director-
General. Enquiries should be addressed to the Copyright
Section. A charge is made for rights of reproduction.

Institute of Geological Sciences

This brief summary of the services available from the Institute
is based on information kindly supplied by A. H. Simpson,
Head of the Editorial and Publication Section. The Institute's
address is Exhibition Road, London, SW7 2DE.

Maps
Most of the Institute's maps are published by the Ordnance
Survey.

> 1 inch to 25 miles. Map of the British Islands. 5th edition,
> 1969.
> 1 inch to 10 miles. Maps of Great Britain.
> ¼ inch to 1 mile. Maps of England and Wales. These are
> being replaced with 1 : 250 000 scale maps.
> 1 inch to 1 mile and, gradually replacing these, 1 : 50 000
> maps of England and Wales.
> 2½ inches to 1 mile. Maps of England and Wales.

One-inch maps are also available for Scotland and Northern
Ireland.

Other publications

The Institute issues a wide range of technical publications which can be of value to an archaeologist. The full details of these can be obtained on application. The main series are the following:

> One-inch Sheet Memoirs (New Series). These accompany the maps.
> British Regional Geology Handbooks.
> Bulletins of the Geological Survey of Great Britain.
> Reports of the Institute of Geological Sciences.
> Mineral Monographs.
> Geophysical Papers.
> Geomagnetic Bulletins.
> Seismological Bulletins.
> Water Supply Papers.

The Soil Survey of England and Wales

The aims of the Soil Survey are to describe, classify and map the soils of England and Wales. The results are presented in the following series of publications.

Maps

Large scale. A selection of soil maps at a scale of 1:25 000 (about 2½ inches to 1 mile) for each county is being produced, in some cases accompanied by interpretative maps of land use capability and drainage. Maps are already available for districts in Cheshire, Cumbria, Derbyshire, Devon, Dyfed, Essex, Gloucestershire, Herefordshire, Kent, Norfolk, Nottinghamshire, Warwickshire, Worcestershire and Yorkshire.

The following soil maps on Ordnance Survey 1 inch to 1 mile 3rd edition sheets are available:

Blackpool (66), Leeds (70), Southport (74), Preston (75), Formby (83), Beaumaris (94), Rhyl (95), Bangor (106), Denbigh (107), Derby (125), Wem (138), Melton Mowbray (142), Ely (173), Aberystwyth (163), Church Stretton (166), Llanilar (178), Ludlow (181), Cambridge (188), Aylesbury

(238), Abingdon (253), Bridgend (261/2), Cardiff (263), Reading (268), Weston-super-Mare (279), Wells (280), Glastonbury (296), and composite sheets of Anglesey, Pwllheli, Exeter/Newton Abbott and Malmesbury/Bath.

Smaller scales. Soil maps at a scale of 1:250 000 are available for Lancashire, Shropshire and Hertfordshire, and at 1:625 000 for the West Midlands. A series of county maps at 1:250 000 are to be produced.

Other publications

Soil Survey Records accompany the 1:25 000 soil maps. They contain detailed accounts of the soils, and chapters on the physical environment, soil classification, agriculture, land use capability and drainage.

Memoirs similarly describe the 1 inch to 1 mile maps.

Special Surveys and Bulletins describe non-standard surveys, including Romney Marsh, Sussex Coastal Plain, West Midlands, Lancashire, Exmoor Forest, Breckland Forest and the Castleford district area of Yorkshire.

Technical Monographs describe work in the laboratory or field undertaken in support of the mapping programme, for example: Land Use Capability, Soil Classification, Micromorphology, Field Handbook and Laboratory Methods. An Annual Report is produced which gives information on the present mapping programme.

A full list of publications may be obtained from the Soil Survey of England and Wales, Rothamsted Experimental Station, Harpenden, Herts, AL5 2JQ. There is always much unpublished information at regional and local offices, freely available to the public. A list of addresses is given in the Annual Report.

There is a similar organisation for Scotland with its headquarters at the Macaulay Institute for Soil Research, Department of Soil Survey, Craigiebuckler, Aberdeen, AB9 2QT.

3 Excavation

Excavation is the main source of new information to the archaeologist. The range and reliability of that information is directly dependent on the standard of this work. All excavation involves destruction, total excavation involves total destruction. Because of this no one should put a spade into the ground before he has very carefully considered the reasons for, and the methods of, so doing.

Excavation planning starts not in the field but in the study. Nowadays, save in salvage work, a dig is planned with definite academic objectives in mind. It is problem-orientated. This is not to say, as there is an unfortunate tendency in some archaeological circles, that recovery will be limited to answering only the original questions. All digs contain a majority of unexpected features which can only be dealt with as they arise in the light of principles developed in other excavations. An excavator will attempt to recover the maximum information from his site and will be constantly asking new questions of it as he proceeds. It would be naïve to think that it is possible to approach a site with a completely open mind. A particular decision to dig immediately defines to a certain extent the framework of thinking about the site, and it requires constant personal discipline in questioning his own judgement for the director to obtain the maximum from his work.

Assuming that an excavator has stated his problem and chosen his site, then there are three standard ways in which he can open up the ground exclusive of the special arrangements made for barrows.

1 Trenching

The use of the trench or cutting is long-established practice. It is now admitted to be of limited usefulness. Its advantages are that it is labour-saving, easy to control and gives a rapid vertical view of a site. The serious archaeological objection is that it fails to allow an extensive view of the site, often giving only fragmentary and obscure glimpses of the plans of structures. Multiple trenching does not offset this disadvantage and there can come a stage with this response when open stripping is more economical of labour.

Cuttings are limited in modern practice to the excavation of linear earthworks where a vertical understanding is of greater importance than a horizontal one. But even in this case it has been found profitable to make such cuttings as broad as possible to counter the possibility of missing lateral variability in a ditch or bank. The need to strip extensively stretches of bank in order to pick up structures such as wooden towers is worth stressing.

2 Gridding

Gridding is the form of area excavation usually associated with the name of Sir R. E. Mortimer Wheeler. It was developed by him primarily as a method of close control over complex stratigraphies on settlement sites. The method is now unfashionable for technical reasons outlined below, but its importance historically in the general improvement of the standard of field archaeology cannot be overstated. Wheeler states the following reasons why he adopted the system. First, by digging in a grid of squares or 'boxes' it is possible to control the digging and recording through subdivision. The grid can be easily extended in all directions without dislocating the survey data. A large number of vertical sections is present throughout the excavation. The interconnecting system of baulks makes the removal of spoil simple (Wheeler, 1954, 82).

In the standard procedure the grid was composed of squares with 10-, 20- or 30-foot sides with intervening baulks of 2- or 3-foot width. The actual excavation units were laid out in association with a grid of pegs from which measurements were recorded.

It was normal practice for the supervisor to excavate, within the square, a smaller hole in one corner to a level lower than the general level in the box in order to gain a preview of changes in the stratification. Wheeler held emphatically that stratigraphical digging could only be controlled from the side. He stated as a universal principle: 'vertical digging first, horizontal digging afterwards' (Wheeler, 1954, 85).

3 Open stripping

This approach is rapidly replacing gridding as the main form of area excavation. Of course, broad clearance of sites is nothing new, as reference to pre-First World War Society of Antiquaries Research Excavations will show. What is modern is the application to the work of strict stratigraphic principles every bit as stringent as those of the grid system. The use of the system arose because of the unsuitability of the grids to extensive sites with little vertical stratigraphy and in which total comprehension of the plan was essential, particularly where timber buildings were concerned, as at Cheddar (excavated by Philip Rahtz). It was originally argued that the method could not be easily applied to deeply stratified sites such as Roman towns. This has been demonstrated to be untrue, at places such as Wroxeter, as long as the severe problems of earth removal and large-scale man management have been mastered. The return in archaeological information has been immense. (For Wroxeter see Barker, 1971, 1972.)

Grids create certain problems which the digging of larger

areas overcomes. First, because of baulks and the differential rate of working in different squares, it is rarely possible to see the total plan of a site at a single time on the ground. Instead it is necessary at least in part to build plans up on paper from the records for individual boxes. This inevitably seems to lead to a lack of uniformity, frequently to minor but irritating misalignments and some confusion in the understanding of a plan. This can be accentuated if, as often happens, the baulks obscure elements. It has been known for complete lengths of wall to be hidden under trench divisions.

This does not happen with open area digging which is specifically controlled in terms of revealing unitary plans. This does not mean the neglect of superimposition and stratification, nor the demise of the section. With the grid the position of most sections is predetermined and fixed for the duration of the excavation before the full content of the site can possibly be assessed. With stripping, a choice can always be made in the position of any section whenever it is required. Normally sections do not stand throughout an excavation and a continuous record is made by carefully readjusting the position of a datum along a determined section line. The maintenance of one control standing section is, however, desirable.

The two main problems are labour control and recording control. It is standard to have subdivisions of large areas under several site supervisors. Such subdivision usually conforms to subunits of the survey grid established for the site which is described below. By a system of area notebooks and a concordance book—the responsibility of the senior supervisor—the stratigraphic record is fully maintained. It is worth emphasising that the large-scale operations described here depend on a high degree of organisation with a skilled staff, each with clearly defined responsibilities within a flexible, hierarchical direction structure. These large digs demand considerable delegation to trusted assistants, but they should never degenerate into committee-run operations. The director's position as co-ordinator remains essential. This is not the task for even the willing amateur.

Spoil removal generates special problems. Unless a mecha-nised conveyor belt can be provided, long wheelbarrow runs are usually unavoidable. The use of motorised dumpers is increasing.

Open stripping is applicable to all sites. Restrictions that do arise are usually from non-archaeological sources. In urban rescue work the excavator is often restricted to the land threatened by redevelopment and this means that large trenches rather than true strips are opened up. Time and avail-able labour are other factors, although the present writer holds that only rescue excavations are valid when there is an in-sufficiency of these; and research digging should never be initiated until resources adequate to do true justice to the site, within the limits of contemporary knowledge, are available.

Digging procedure

All modern earth-removing procedures during excavation conform to the principles of stratigraphy which have been outlined elsewhere in this book. There are two basic rules: one is positive, the other negative. The archaeologist generally comes on the deposits which compose the site in the reverse order to which they were laid down. He must remove these deposits as strictly as is practicable in that reverse order until at the end of the dig he can 'invert' his findings and set about writing a description of the sequence in its proper order.

Strata are never regular level units. Floors, levelled demoli-tion dumps or construction make-up layers are likely to be the closest approach to this. Sites, therefore, should never be treated as if they were composed of horizontal layers. This might seem self-evident in the light of the principles already stated, but a widespread practice, fortunately very restricted in Britain, was to dig in arbitrary levels. Wheeler in a classic pas-sage with accompanying diagram admirably demonstrated the 'utter absurdity' of the method (Wheeler, 1954, 70). The pro-cedure was to dig down in predefined horizontal units or spits. In the elaborate version of the practice the precise location of every object on the site might be measured. But all this hard work is totally meaningless archaeologically. Wheeler's diagram (Wheeler, 1954, Fig. 11) shows how objects separated by several thousand years can occur at the same level. Whole culture sequences were originally created in the Americas on the basis of recovery by this technique coupled with ceramic seriations of the material so derived. One report by an eminent American professor using the method on a midden even admits that in section the strata visibly sloped several feet downwards within the cutting! Lest the reader consider that the above remarks are anachronistic, it should be noted that the author met the method in use in Germany on a Roman colonia in 1970.

The standard method of digging is called contour excavation. To describe how this might proceed let us take the example of excavating the deposits shown in Wheeler's diagram (Fig. 2). The topsoil, layer 1, would be removed with pick and shovel in an orderly fashion working down and conforming to the slope. At spaced intervals over the area of work, digging would be slightly more advanced vertically in control pits designed to give a preview of the underlying layer or layers. As soon as a vertical change in deposit is encountered, the emphasis changes to removing the remainder of the upper layer extensively and carefully to expose the underlying and, in this case, first two archaeological deposits, layer 2 and the tree pit. The use of control pits avoids overdigging, especially when heavier tools are being employed, and it is possible to examine carefully the surface of a fresh layer for signs of, for example, erosion. It should be noted that recording procedures described below come into operation as soon as a new layer appears and it is bad practice to record after the removal of a layer.

Removal of layer 1 reveals layer 2 covering most of the excavation area but also a discoloration of roundish shape. There are two possibilities concerning the relationship of the discoloration to 2. The first is extremely unlikely, being that the discoloration represents the truncated top of a heap of material over and against which 2 has accumulated. The second is the common explanation, being that the material is the top of the filling of a hole cut through layer 2. It is important that

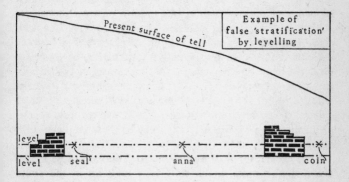

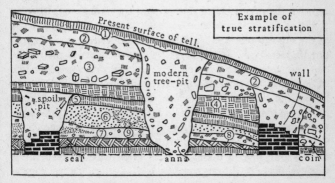

Fig. 2 Diagrams illustrating the stratification of a city-mound (*bottom*) and the fallacy of recording by mechanical levels (*top*)
(*After Wheeler, 1954*)

the excavator makes his mind up correctly as it determines his next move. Having correctly decided on the second explanation, because the discoloured soil was deposited later than layer 2 he will commence removing it and continue to do so until it is entirely gone. By carefully following the contour of the division between the deposit and the other deposits, what will emerge will be the precise shape of the pit which the material filled. By the same procedure, the subsequent sequence of removal would be: 2, spoil pit over monastery wall, 3, 4, spoil pit over Harappan wall, 5, 6, 7, 8, 9. The principle is simple as stated above, but the practice is often very difficult. Sometimes discolorations can hardly be detected. Changes from one deposit to another are often gradual. In extensive sites it is common for features of entirely different dates to be cut from the same horizon and it is impossible to decide their relative sequence. Each feature has special problems to be looked for, and some of these are dealt with below.

Two exceptions to the rules outlined above can be made. When disturbances which start very high up in the strata sequence are large and very deep it is often impracticable to remove them entirely in one go and they are taken down in stages as the general area is lowered. Massive holes from early in the dig can obstruct spoil removal, normal strip trowelling is hampered and, as the sides tend to weather prematurely, exposed deposits in the sides disintegrate with attendant loss of evidence. It is not normal to remove masonry walls, particularly if the site is to be preserved for public viewing. Adjustments are made in the digging order which do not at the same time upset the proper recovery of associational evidence.

If a deposit has formed gradually and relatively uniformly over a long period it can be very thick with no discernible distinctions in it, although there may be vertically a typological or cultural sequence in the artefacts. If this seems to be the case, then this is the only justification for resorting to artificial spit recovery. The important point is that the arbitrary levels are created within what appears to be a uniform stratum and each spit is carefully removed with an eye to any possible change, whereupon the method is immediately abandoned. The mechanical ease of the technique should not blind us to its very limited archaeological value.

Recording

There are standard general practices in British excavations for recording, although the details vary. What is described here are those methods used by the author or described by reputable excavators.

Essential in all excavations are fixed points from which to take horizontal and vertical measurements. To deal with levelling, a solid fixed point close to the periphery of the site is used as the reference datum. In Britain it is usually possible to obtain the height above sea-level of this datum by levelling it in to a nearby Ordnance Survey bench mark. The methods of levelling with a simple level are fully described in Fryer (1961) or Coles (1972). The level is set so that the telescope can rotate in a horizontal plane. A graduated staff is held on the reference datum and a reading taken. The staff is then moved to the point to be levelled in, which during an excavation usually lies at a lower level than the reference point. The difference between the two readings is the distance below site datum of the feature being measured. It is normal to level the surface of a site before excavation and to produce a contour plan. This is achieved by taking a grid of measurements from which a contour drawing is produced by interpolating lines showing chosen vertical intervals. During excavation all archaeological surfaces are levelled, allowing a study in changing site topography to be undertaken in conjunction with the plan. All datum points used in section drawing are levelled, thus rapidly tying in many layers to the Ordnance datum (OD).

To make horizontal measurements it is necessary to establish fixed points from which tape measures can be conveniently strung. These normally take the form of either wooden pegs with nails placed in the top or metal rods. It is essential that these are set firmly so as not to move in use. Some form of a grid of pegs is normally used and the method employed by Martin Biddle is described below as an example. Two main alternative ways of fixing a point by horizontal measurement can be used. The first is by triangulation, that is by taking

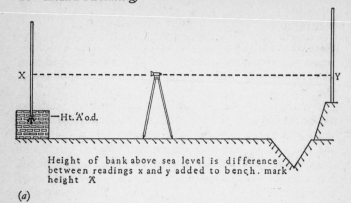

—Ht. 'A' o.d.

Height of bank above sea level is difference
between readings x and y added to bench. mark
height 'A'

(*a*)

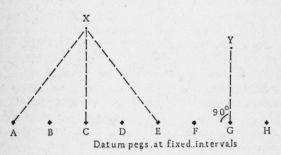

Datum pegs at fixed intervals

Position of X fixed at the intersect of arcs drawn from
A and E. Arc drawn from C as check. Y fixed by
measuring out at right angles from G

(*b*)

Fig. 3 (*a*) Simple levelling. (*b*) Fixing horizontal positions

measurements to the spot from two fixed points a known
distance apart. In drawing this out the two points are placed
at the correct distance apart according to the scale of the plan
on a straight line. The distance from one point to the spot is
drawn with a compass, and similarly for the other. The
point of intersection of the compass arcs marks the spot. In
practice it is advisable to take measurements from three points

to counteract error, and the angle of the intersection between two tie lines should always be kept as close to 90 degrees as possible.

Measurement by offsets is popular for its speed. Lines are taken to a spot such that they form a right angle to the fixed line from which they originate. The length of the offset line and its position along the fixed line are noted. The method is less accurate the longer the offset line because of the difficulty of estimating a right angle over any great distance. Direct measurement to obtain the right angle in every instance would render the method more cumbersome than triangulation.

All modern work is according to the metric system. At Winchester, Biddle used a co-ordinate system for planning and recording precisely the position of all important finds. The system is based on a theoretical point of origin 0/0 well beyond the excavation to the south-west. Biddle recommends that the point of origin is set beyond the dig such that the values on the axes in the excavation differ to avoid confusion. The divisions of the axis of the co-ordinate grid are marked around the excavation by lines of pegs at set intervals apart. Within the excavation long nails or steel rods are driven in on a regular grid on the axes. Each peg of this internal grid has a unique co-ordinate number expressed as eastings/northings in the manner of the National Grid. Any single object's exact location can be expressed in terms of these axes. Spot levels taken in conjunction with the co-ordinates all have unique numbers. If the grid spacings are 2 metres no lengthy measurements are involved; for example, no offset will be longer than half the length of the side of the internal grid square. Within the squares ready-made drawing grids are used. These are made of a light metal frame in the form of an open square internally subdivided by taut nylon string into 10-cm squares. Use of the grid facilitates drawing, which is usually with minimum measurement guided by the 10-cm squares (Biddle and Kjolbye-Biddle, 1969).

Levels are usually logged in an orderly fashion in a note-book used for recording the details of site surveying. The note will give the level, the number of the layer and the horizontal location at which the reading was taken. The survey notebook should also include a description of the peg system being utilised and the information that allows this to be related to the National Grid. All major measurements, such as overall dimensions of structures, should be logged and reliance should not be placed solely on the plans for these. As in all archaeology, the detail with which this is done depends on available time and labour.

All drawings (mainly sections and plans) should be given a reference number and an index according to location, period and subject kept in the survey notebook. Drawings require a title, orientation, a key to any conventions used, a scale, a date and a signature.

Choice of the scale of the drawing is dictated by the size of the area being drawn and the paper available. 1:10 is normal for sections and plans, although 1:20, 1:50 and 1:100 can serve some planning purposes.

Planning method has been outlined above. The most important rule is always decide precisely what is to be drawn before drawing it. This always saves time in the long run. This is not to suggest that once a scheme has been derived it should be followed slavishly. Often the physical act of drawing, and the many minor mental decisions made, stimulate new thought about a subject. It should be borne in mind that the drawings of a site constitute one of the sole bits of surviving evidence after an excavation and they should therefore always be carefully considered.

Common equipment for planning is: metric retractable measuring tapes (steel or plastic-coated linen), 30-m ones usually suffice, and small (3-m) hand tapes; plumb-bob; spirit level; drawing-boards (sturdy but easily portable); drawing implements (in the field these tend to be pencil, ruler, beam compass and rubber). Drawings are executed on a transparent plastic film laid over graph paper, which provides guide lines. Biddle recommends Ilford Azoflex. Some archaeological units use ready-prepared standard transparent sheets. The advant-

ages of this material over normal paper are that it can withstand water, does not shrink, can be used in combination with
other sheets in an overlay system and copies can be readily
made from them.

The drawing of a section requires the same amount of
thought as does the planning. It is good practice not only to
think about the section as it is emerging during digging but
also to have a long summarising think before putting pencil to
paper. Sections should have been chosen both to give a representative vertical view of the site stratigraphy at one point and
to make certain points about the site sequence. A single drawing on this basis is worth hundreds of words.

To draw a section a carefully levelled horizontal line is
strung across the middle of the section face. It is from this
string datum that all measurements are made. Above or below
the datum is strung, parallel to it, a tape. The zero point on the
tape will lie vertically in line with one end of the datum. The
loop end of the tape can be hooked over a nail, whilst the
other end can be held to a nail by a clothes-peg. It is important
that both the string and the tape are kept taut throughout the
drawing operation. Using a measuring rod the layers are plotted by measuring up and down from the datum at known
points along the line. It should always be remembered to relate
the datum level to the site datum.

In drawing plans and sections it is normal to employ conventions to represent different deposits. No standard system
exists, but there are some commonly recognised symbols,
which are shown in Fig. 4. Precision is the requirement of a
successful technical drawing. For this reason more artistic
methods of giving impressions of the gradation of deposits
are not commonly used. Photos can serve this purpose. If the
excavator has decided that a line of distinction between a deposit can be seen, he must have the courage to show such,
giving in writing and with the help of photos and samples the
reasons for drawing the line. Often attempts to show grading
are in reality a mask for indecision. However, at the other
extreme, distinctions that are spurious should not be created

	Sand		Brickwork
	Gravel		Brick rubble
	Fine gravel		Stonework
	Gravel and sand		Stone rubble
	Brown earth		Tile
	Occupation soil		Plaster
	Water laid muddy deposits		Mortar
	Brick earth		Flint
	Clay and gravel		Concrete
	Clay		Wood
	Brown sandy loam		Ash
	Chalk		Charcoal
	Humus		Carbon
	Oyster shells		Peat
	Cess		Opus signinum
	Burnt daub		Clay (state burnt)

Fig. 4 Symbols for sections

in a false show of precision. The decisive factor in deciding on distinctions between deposits is an understanding of the process of deposition, which is the basic task of the excavation. In representing the deposits what is aimed for is the balance between clarity of line where the stratigraphy warrants it and the use of a combination of conventions that bring out the nature and variety of the section deposits.

Each stratigraphic unit is assigned a unique number immediately it is encountered. Number systems vary. One common method is to carry a dual series of numbers. One set refers to features such as pits, walls and post holes, and the layers within each feature are given a subsidiary sequence of numbers or letters. The other set refers to widespread deposits, such as demolition spreads, that cannot be described as features. This author has always considered this method unnecessarily numerate and prefers the other system which simply gives every single stratigraphic unit a number as it is come upon. This includes walls and other structural deposits. On an extensive site with many intrusions with deep fills, it is common for a number of the features to be in different stages of excavation. With the common-series number system, a new number can be readily assigned to a new layer and a record entered in the layer book without worrying about consistency of numbering. Entries in the book and a feature index relate layer to layer and layer to feature. A single-number system also assists finds' recording and marking. Any system that is stratigraphically based will do, provided that it yields all the required information in the simplest possible way.

Labels are ubiquitous to archaeological excavations. When a new layer is uncovered it is immediately assigned a code number and a label is placed in the deposit. The label will be of strong card or, increasingly, of waterproof plastic and on it will be registered the site, area and layer code in indelible ink. A common form of code might be CC 4 29, which could stand for Cambridge Castle site, area of excavation number 4 and layer number 29. There is little to be gained by including any more information on this label. Two of the same labels will also be placed in the trays provided for the reception of the common finds such as pottery from the layer. These trays and their attendant labels are changed for each layer. The same label is also attached to the container for the special finds usually called 'small finds'. These are things such as coins, metal objects and glassware, or almost anything that is thought worthy of having its position in the ground precisely measured. General finds tend to be recorded only in their stratigraphic units. Small finds are assigned an individual number and a separate register is kept for them. The number is recorded, on the label and the object itself, in a triangle. The register should contain an entry by number which records the stratigraphic context, the measured position and a brief description of the object itself. The register should also contain an index to the objects by material.

Many excavators prefer file cards to a register and some of the advanced workers are instituting punch-card systems similar to that utilised by the Ancient Monuments Laboratory and shown in Fig. 5. The evolving of record systems suitable to storage in computerised memory stores is just beginning in archaeology.

It is worth stressing that any find that leaves the site without a label and which therefore cannot be related to a particular deposit has lost a lot of its archaeological value. This is where site discipline is of paramount importance. All the skill expended in extracting delicate objects from the ground can be dissipated through carelessness in the record, which is still all too common on sites.

Along with the plans and sections, the site notebook is the most important evidence of the site after excavation. If there is one really serious failure among many otherwise excellent excavators it is the haphazard way in which they keep written records. Even when voluminous notes are kept it is often very difficult for an independent scholar to gain any good idea of the site from them. There is a tendency to carry much detail in the head, and to forget to make detailed records of obvious features simply because they are obvious. One test of a good

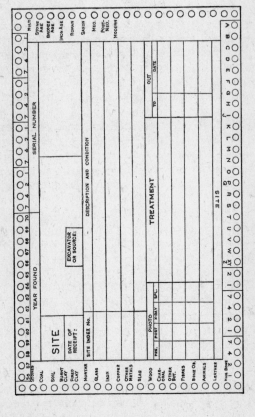

Fig. 5 Example of a punch-card record

(By courtesy of Mr L. Biek)

excavator is the clarity with which he can explain his site in writing.

Site books should firstly have numbered pages to allow for cross-reference. Much of the success of the record depends on the adequacy of the cross-referencing. Throughout the book the layer record must be related to the indexed plans, sections and other drawings. Wherever possible, written description should be accompanied with drawings to scale or at least sketches. With this in mind the most suitable form of record book is one with lined paper on the right-hand side and metric squared paper on the left.

A standardised system of entries should be used that gives rapid access to the sort of information that is usually required of a layer. A single page per layer is suitable. Each page is headed by the layer number. This should be followed by information on the location of the layer, that is its horizontal position in terms of the site co-ordinate pegs and its stratigraphical position in relation to other layers. After this the thickness, section contour and position of the surface of the layer in terms of OD is noted. The main description of the layer follows next. This is best split into two parts, the first part being purely descriptive, giving the fullest possible detail about composition, colour, texture, porosity, etc., and the second part giving an interpretation of the derivation and process of deposition of the deposit. Reference to supporting evidence such as drawings and photos should be included. The final entry lists the finds from the deposit. Small finds numbers are given here as well as a general description of artefacts. Critical dating pieces should be specially mentioned. If no finds were made in a particular layer, then this should be noted.

The entries in the site book should be as factual as possible, and where opinion is given it should be indicated as such. The site book is not a diary and should not be kept in that form. It is rarely of archaeological interest at what time a find was made. The book is a dry, unemotional record of an investigation. This is not to discourage the keeping of a site diary as well. This can keep records of progress and record the names of helpers. It may even harbour the wilder speculations we all make but should not at that stage commit to the permanent record. It has been found, incidentally, that some people have a psychological dislike of amending entries once made. This is unscientific. No record in the site book should be deleted, but it should be superseded as required with a note to that effect. This allows the director's train of thought to be followed through the excavation.

Photography

Photography has made substantial technical advances since the Second World War and the archaeologist is faced with a bewildering variety of equipment that will provide excellent results. It is not the intention of this section to provide a guide to available cameras. Reference should be made to the manuals mentioned in the bibliography. Instead, here are considered the requirements of archaeological photography in terms of results.

Two types of photograph are taken. The first is the photograph that is publishable. This requires careful preparation of the site before it is taken. Whenever time permits, all photos taken should be of this type. The second type is usually called a record shot, as it is taken to illustrate a particular point but at a time when the site is not in as clean a state as it might be. It is desirable to make a constant photographic record during the excavation and it is not always possible to keep the site in an ideally tidy condition, particularly in a rescue situation. Only a tiny fraction of the photos taken can be published because of the high printing costs, which increases the value of the record shots stored with the other site records and makes it imperative that they are of as high a quality as possible.

Just as with a drawing, an archaeological photograph is made to illustrate a particular point. Therefore it is important that the subject to be photographed is well prepared and the photograph well composed. Preparation of the subject usually means cleaning. Masonry, brickwork and floors of solid materials should be thoroughly brushed to remove particles of earth and, where necessary, the surfaces washed or scrubbed to remove clinging dirt. No detail should be allowed to be blurred. Earthen features such as section faces, pits and post holes may require precise scraping or cutting with a trowel or knife. If weather conditions such as excessive dryness lead to lack of distinction between layers, it is permissible to use aids such as sprinklers to water section faces. It is not good practice to use scoured lines for emphasis or even tape lines to show layer boundaries, as the dominant effect they tend to have in a photo can give a sometimes misleading impression of the clarity of a distinction. Such interpretive devices should be banished from site photography. It should also be stressed that it is not only the immediate subject of the picture that must be spotless but also the surroundings if these are to appear in the photo.

Once the site is cleaned, thought must be given to the composition of the shot. An artist's, as well as a scientist's, sense is needed here. The technical devices of scales and numbering have to be subordinated to the subject-matter in the picture. The provision of a scale is essential in the photograph. For fairly large-scale pictures, metric red and white ranging poles are required. One is set vertically and one horizontally. Small black and white scales (cm) are used for smaller subjects. It is important that the poles are kept parallel to the plane of the intended picture to avoid visual distortions of the scale. Some excavators like to photograph layers with legible labels placed in them and some also provide a ticket indicating the direction of north on the photo. A human scale is sometimes preferable to or can be used in combination with poles, particularly when photographing large-scale monuments or shooting from a distance.

It is a good idea for the director of an excavation to observe from the beginning of the dig the lighting conditions that prevail locally. These will markedly dictate the best time at which to take pictures. In very poor lighting, use can be made of flashlight equipment. What is required for all subjects is an even lighting which brings out to the maximum the texture of the feature under study and any contrasts between it and its surroundings.

It is not intended to discuss technical features of taking photographs. It should be noted, however, that all photos should be executed in black and white in the first instance as it is very unlikely that colour prints will be reproduced in publication. This is not to discourage the taking of coloured slides and prints as part of the record. For colour work, filters will often be required and some experimentation on site is advisable. A camera with the facility to attach a variety of lenses is an advantage. A wide-angle lens is often required on site.

Increasing use is being made in archaeology of photogrammetry, especially as an adjunct to and a check on planning. Using a camera attached to a quadropod, a series of overlapping vertical photographs is taken at a constant elevation over the surface of a site. These can be viewed stereoscopically and plans produced from them using a stereo-plotting machine.

Digging equipment

There are certain tools and other equipment which are commonly used on sites. Those mentioned here are a selection.

It is now a frequent practice to open up a site by mechanical means. This is labour-saving and, if conducted carefully, does no archaeological damage. On urban sites it is often necessary to remove a metre or more of relatively modern masonry, brick and concrete before deposits of archaeological interest are encountered. As these digs are usually pressed for time, pneumatic drills, concrete-breakers and mechanical excavators are employed. Machines often to be seen digging trenches are the JCB 3c and the HY-MAC. For extensive stripping a small bulldozer is suitable. Other plant that may be required includes small cranes for lifting buckets of earth from deep holes and pumps for removing water from waterlogged sites. Plant hire is an expensive business and should be well thought out beforehand to obtain the maximum benefit for the minimum outlay.

All sites require accommodation, security and safety. A wooden hut (or huts) is normally erected on a site if no other accommodation is available. These come as $3 \times 2 \cdot 5$ m or $6 \times 2 \cdot 5$ m lock-ups, prefabricated and usually requiring three men to put them up rapidly. They are unstable in high winds unless held down by ropes slung over their roofs. Alternative forms of accommodation can be caravans or, in towns, derelict property. Whatever type is chosen it is needed for tool storage, accommodation for the finds and shelter for the workers.

To give some measure of security against man and animal it is normal to erect a fence around the dig. The common form is 1 m or $1 \cdot 5$ m chestnut paling secured to stakes. Wire fencing and hoarding are alternatives.

If deep trenches are being dug, shoring should be erected by a company specialising in this sort of work. If labour is being employed, as is usually the case in Britain in permanent units, then shuttering is required by law below $1 \cdot 2$ m. There is no virtue in working in hazardous conditions and attention should always be paid to safety. On a large team it is worth having a safety officer with first-aid experience. Remarks concerning securing trenches apply equally to spoil heaps, which should be revetted to a reasonable angle of rest and checked regularly for movement if they are close to trench edges.

The pick and shovel are the most important of the heavier hand tools employed. The pointed end of the pick is used to loosen and lever the earth. Intelligent use of the pick is required so that clods are created with minimum damage to any contained artefacts and through feel, as well as by sight, changes in deposit are recognised. The pickman should work consistently towards himself so as not to trample on what he has previously loosened and should try to maintain a constant depth to his picking. This will make it easy for the man with the shovel to clear away cleanly into a wheelbarrow. Both the pickman and the shoveller should be collecting artefacts, and no unbroken clods should find their way into the barrows.

Pick and shovel removal is only justified in topsoil or on large sites that are being excavated under pressure of time. Sterile layers of construction material can also be treated this way. However careful the watch on the soil, there is an inevitable loss of finds by this method.

Wherever possible, less robust tools are used to loosen the ground. These are principally the pointing trowel (between 5 and 10 cm) or the small pick. The trowel is the characteristic tool of the archaeologist. It is used to cut a shallow depth of ground and to scrape clean the newly exposed surface. Its shape and size make it a convenient tool for exposing and isolating artefacts. It removes a limited amount of earth at any one time and it is possible to keep a close watch on finds. A small hand shovel can be used to transfer the discarded soil to a bucket and thence to a wheelbarrow. The hand pick or its relative the entrenching tool can be used to similar effect as the trowel and is particularly useful for hard deposits. A trowel can be used in combination to achieve clean surfaces.

The spade and the fork do not figure much in archaeology. The spade is a cutting implement and its broad blade can do a lot of damage to objects if it is driven blindly into a deposit. In the hands of a skilled person it can be used for trimming operations. A fork is only justified in an emergency when artefact recovery is the main aim. Otherwise it is unsuitable for stratigraphic digging because of the messy surfaces that it creates.

A turf-cutter is useful for cutting sections for drawing or photography. Knives of various blade widths can be used for trimming and for the finer work of isolating objects and lifting them.

Brushes and brooms, if used intelligently, can aid the clear appreciation of features, especially masonry. Clearly their use is inappropriate on damp deposits, where they will smear.

Finds are collected in trays. These come in various sizes in metal, wood and plastic. To save money, digs often use old pie or tobacco tins or the like. One tray is used per layer. A supply of strong paper and polythene bags is also essential and standard-size cardboard boxes can be used for storage. The various containers required in first aid and conservation are described later. For small objects, such as coins, little envelopes are traditionally used.

Among the miscellany of other tools that can come in useful may be mentioned shears, sickle, axe, hammer, sledge-hammer, mallet for wooden pegs, and the main carpenter's tools such as saws.

Nails (8 and 15 cm) and string that does not stretch unduly are needed for labelling, laying out grids and section drawing.

Nailbrushes and toothbrushes are used for washing pottery and other robust objects. Basins are needed for water.

Sieves are not as common as they might be on archaeological sites (particular those of the later periods). This is probably because Roman sites, for example, tend to produce large amounts of finds and this quantity blinds the excavator to the still larger amounts that are being unintentionally lost through normal digging methods. Fine sieving would be the ideal on all sites, but the operation is so time-consuming and the quantity of material to be treated so immense that it is just not feasible for most sites. However, it is essential to incorporate a sample sieving into a digging programme in order to assess the loss of 'invisible' information.

The other major class of equipment required on a dig is that belonging to the record side, which has already been dealt with. This is in summary: survey gear (level, staff, tapes, rulers, compass, plumb-bobs, spirit level), drawing equipment (drawing-board, masking-tape, graph paper, transparent plastic sheets, scale ruler, beam compass, range of pencils, indian ink—black, red and white—biros, rubbers, set-square), and other items such as notebooks, file cards, labels and miscellaneous stationery.

There are undoubtedly omissions from the above section but the main range should have been indicated. Workers will find that they have individual preferences for certain types of equipment, especially when it comes to the choice of art materials for the records, and also in the emphasis given to the use of different tools for digging. As long as it is remembered that what is required is the most precise, efficient and accurate way of completing the job in question, then the details are not important.

Personnel

How an excavation is staffed is clearly of importance in determining the success of a dig. There is again no uniformity in this matter as the sponsoring of excavations varies so much and also the scale. What will be mentioned here will be the sort of gradations the author has met and worked with in the field. Whilst the titles and precise combinations might vary, the roles are reasonably universal.

Digs are rarely committee-run affairs in the field and it is not altogether desirable that they should be so. Normally one man is the *director* with overall responsibility for the conduct and publication of the excavation. Increasingly directors are employed by committees which provide the finance and to whom the director is accountable. If he is fortunate, the director's committee will be composed at least in part of senior archaeologists on whom the director can draw for advice. It is a fool who is not prepared to listen to others during his work or to subject his efforts to close scrutiny. In anticipation of work on a site the director should contact experts in the sphere in which he is working and invite them to visit the site during the digging. The present author has advocated for some time that there be set up a panel of experts by period who should have powers of inspection of all excavations financed with public money. The present Inspectorate system is not adequate in this respect.

The director should be a competent excavator and have the academic ability to interpret his findings. This might seem self-evident to the beginner, but so many excavations are undertaken in this country by unqualified and incompetent people that it needs repeating. No one should dig without the express approval of an acknowledged expert. He should be able to give evidence of both digging and academic training. There is a welcome move afoot under the auspices of the CBA to form a professional association for archaeologists with proper requirements for professional qualifications aside from those supposedly granted by a university degree.

Supposing the requisite technical competence in the director, his job is an unenviable one. First, by digging he has committed himself to a period of work of approximately four times the length of the actual excavation. No one should dig a site unless the outlet and time required for publication are secured. Non-publication of work is the single most serious offence committed by professional and amateur archaeologists.

The director is responsible for the administration of the dig. This includes gaining permission to excavate, hiring labour, hiring plant and equipment and paying wages. On a large excavation some of these tasks would probably be delegated to a deputy director.

During the excavation it is the director who is responsible for the interpretation of the stratigraphy and the basic finds. No major deposit should be excavated without him first examining it and giving instructions as to its treatment. The removal of delicate objects will be done by him or under his direct supervision. No important drawing will be made and filed without him having checked it. The director will give the instructions concerning photography. In sum, the director should have maximum contact with the inch by inch removal of the site as far as is compatible with administration chores. It is just not good enough to pay periodic visits to an excavation, as is still the practice with some directors.

After the excavation it is the job of the director to see that there is a rapid publication of the results of the work. Most directors are specialists in a single period or type of objects. By and large, most archaeologists are knowledgeable about the artefact content of the site rather than the non-artefactual. It will usually be necessary to obtain specialist help in the analysis of the finds. The co-ordination of these contributions into the final report is the responsibility of the director. Indeed, a good director will have planned from before the commencement of digging an integrated programme of specialist help.

The site supervisor is the backbone of modern British archaeology. As paid labour in the sense of the old navvy or day-labourer is no longer common on archaeological sites, the site supervisor takes on the role of foreman in relation to the paid and unpaid voluntary workers that make up the labour force. He deals with the efficient usage of labour and its problems in the first instance. The whole dig can be jeopardised if the supervisor is either incompetent or unable to handle people.

Site supervisors need to be very experienced excavators who have worked on a variety of sites. They are very often university students intending a career in archaeology. They need to have an academic as well as a technical competence in the subject. Too many possess one or the other. Their duties are the control of a part of the excavation. This entails the making of the records and the instruction of the workers in the progress of the digging. They will make the minute by minute decisions about earth removal, only calling in the director when a major decision is required. Site discipline is in their hands. They are expected to dig along with the other workers and should be responsible for the advanced digging designed to obtain a preview of the next strata. They are responsible for seeing that trays and sections are labelled.

With modern pay scales based on the Department of the Environment rates it is possible for a supervisor to earn over £40 a week.

On large excavations assistant site supervisors are found. They are less experienced than the site supervisor and should receive some instruction from him. Otherwise they undertake those tasks of the supervisor that are delegated to them. A particularly common one is the drawing.

It is not uncommon, although this role is frequently incorporated into the supervisory posts, to have a full-time drawing team. This is satisfactory for routine drawing, but the individuals should be skilled draftsmen and even then not left to their own devices as so frequently happens. The director should involve himself directly in the drawing of crucial sections and plans.

People in the assistant supervisor/assistant grade can earn between £20 and £30 a week.

Another very important member of the assistant grade is the finds assistant. He or, as is very often the case, she is responsible for the cataloguing, storage and first aid of finds. The director is wise, having given his approval to the system to be used, not to interfere in the running of this side of things— which, more than most things on site, must be absolutely orderly. Cataloguing entails keeping the registers or file cards up to date. The director must at any one time be able to get at information on the finds from any part of the site. To make an intelligent catalogue the assistant needs considerable knowledge of what he is handling. He should be able to spot unusual and significant pieces and bring them to the director's attention. Little first aid should be carried out on site, and this only in emergencies. The finds assistant should act as the direct liaison between the dig and the conservation laboratory. It is an added advantage if the finds assistant can also act as a draftsman.

Various other specialist posts can be found on excavations, although it is more normal for the roles to be combined with one of those mentioned above. These include photographer and surveyor. Few digs are large enough to warrant a full-time surveyor; the same is true of photography, which by and large should be in the hands of the director. Draftsmen and illustrators are more properly regarded as part of the post-excavation programme.

The ordinary digger in Britain is usually either an unpaid volunteer working in his spare time, a paid volunteer (often students on vacation) working for a consistent but restricted length of time or a full-time paid worker earning from £3 to £5 a day (although rates are not uniform). The last category is increasing in number and often includes young graduates or school-leavers. The trend will probably continue as there is an expansion of full-time regional units.

The digger can vary from the totally inexperienced, needing training and careful watching, to the reasonably experienced who can soon be expected to take on the responsibilities of an assistant supervisor. The digger acts to the instructions of the supervisor. He does the actual earth-moving and the collection of artefacts and other remains. Clearly some tuition is required if this is to be done well, and the digger needs constant watching. Training in the use of tools is often required. The discipline of archaeology must be instilled in the worker and any idea of a treasure-hunt atmosphere quashed. Handling volunteer labour is a very delicate business requiring care. It should be remembered that volunteers may not be physically used to some of the jobs and should not be asked to do them without some demonstration. At all times their interest should be maintained by giving information about what is being found and its significance. On the other hand, archaeological excavation is a scientific operation and is not designed for the amusement of volunteers, who must be expected to conform to all the standard rules of practice and to work in a steady fashion in accordance with the instructions of a supervisor. Digging instructions are not the subject of debate for the uninitiated. The supervisor must cultivate a friendly but businesslike attitude to the work. An eye for personality will enable him to isolate the chatterer or malcontent.

There are a few unscrupulous people who go on excavations in the hope of making finds which they can pocket and sell. Some individuals masquerade as helpers in order to assess a site's potential for saleable items and then return after hours to engage in clandestine digging. Amateurs who use metal detectors to locate antiquities and then dig on the spot are another menace. All such people should be unceremoniously removed from sites and subjected to the maximum prosecution in law.

A final word with regard to personnel returns to the duties of the director. His overall task is to produce good archaeology in the shortest possible time for the minimum amount of money and with the maximum amount of enjoyment. The comfort of the workers should always be in his mind. There is no virtue in hardship and the merry navvy attitude met with has no place. A happy dig is usually a good one.

Excavation of features

In the first part of this chapter the general practice of excavation has been discussed. In the second part the archaeological problems presented by certain common features, and the methods necessary to deal with them, are described.

Burial mounds

Barrows were once thought to be fair sport for the casual digger and the history of their excavation abounds with horrifying stories of multiple barrow ripping within a single day. For a full discussion of the archaeological significance of the burial mounds of the Neolithic and Bronze Ages, the reader should turn to the works by Ashbee listed in the bibliography. The remarks made here can apply to the burial mounds of all periods.

A barrow, as does any burial, represents a single sequence of ritual actions. By studying the arrangements made for burial and traces of the activities, such as feasting and ceremony, associated with it the archaeologist gets about as close as he is ever likely to without the help of literature or inscriptions to the beliefs and practices of ancient religions. This means that not a scrap of data can be squandered and that the excavation must be designed to give as total a view as possible of the ritual events. This means total excavation in all except emergencies.

Two main methods of digging round barrows have been used. Both are preceded by a detailed contour survey of the mound before digging commences. The first method, used particularly by Sir Cyril Fox, is the strip method. This entails excavating the barrow by removing parallel strips successively. The strips are about 1·5 m wide and are totally removed before

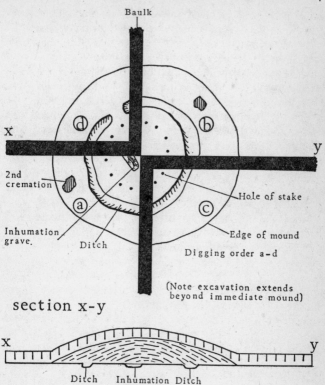

Baulk

x

y

2nd
cremation

(a)

Inhumation
grave.

Ditch

Hole of stake

(c)

Edge of mound

Digging order a–d

(Note excavation extends
beyond immediate mound)

section x–y

x

y

Ditch   Inhumation   Ditch
grave

Fig. 6 Barrow excavation

the next one is begun. The method provides many sections
across the mound but they are all on one axis. At no stage is a
good overall view of the barrow obtained, and this depends on
the accuracy of the plans.

The main method is the quadrant. The barrow is divided
into quarters by two lines of pegs. Opposite quadrants are
excavated alternately. Baulks about a metre wide are left

standing between the quadrants. By this method area excavation is combined with complete cross-sections on two axes.

Very large barrows can be handled by the grid method, although the multiplicity of baulks can obscure features.

In the quadrant method a quarter of the mound is first excavated down to the surface of the buried soil below the barrow. Then the corresponding section of the ditch is removed. This procedure is repeated until only the baulks are standing. These are then taken down and the pre-barrow soil dug away. The pre-mound earth is of great interest as the surface might show traces of plough furrows and the soil itself might harbour pollen, seed, insect and molluscan remains that will yield information about the microclimate environment at the period preceding construction.

When digging these structures there are many things to be on the lookout for, such as timber remains within the mound. Many barrows were erected over mortuary houses. Not all the timbers were set in the ground and traces can be preserved within the body of the mound. Barrows were commonly used after their construction as convenient burial-places. Such secondary burials must be distinguished from satellite burials, which are those burials other than the main one which were deposited in association with the building of the barrow. Pits and stake and post circles are other features likely to be met.

The other main class of barrow, the long barrow, requires a different excavation approach. Professor W. F. Grimes, working on Cotswold megalithic tombs, made preliminary cuttings across the mound to obtain knowledge of the depth and nature of the deposits. This done, the cuttings were extended as horizontal strips over the whole mound. A special problem was the structure of the cairn within the mound. To study this, stripping proceeded down to the surface of the cairn. The top surface was cleaned up and every stone drawn. Pitched groups of stones were indicated as these were the structural units comprising the cairn. The stone groupings were then removed in the constructionally reverse order (Grimes, 1960).

Wheeler points out the two basic requirements in the setting out of a long barrow dig. The first is a longitudinal section through the whole mound and the second is a series of sections across the ditch (Wheeler, 1954, 121). This can be combined quite easily with the benefits of open stripping shown by Grimes (Grimes, 1960). Ashbee's recent work will give the reader details of the sort of features to be met in the earthen long barrow—particularly the wooden mortuary houses that form the infrastructure of the monuments (Ashbee, 1970).

Graves

It is more frequent for the archaeologist to deal with the single burial in a flat grave. The first thing to ask is whether any form of marker gave for a time the location of the burial. T. Lethbridge more than once remarked on the almost total lack of overlap of graves in some Saxon cemeteries in the Cambridge region and reasonably ascribed it to the existence of markers such as small mounds (Lethbridge, 1926, 79).

Burials were either by inhumation or by cremation. In the latter case the body was usually ceremonially burnt close to the burial spot and the calcined bone and ashes collected and placed in a container which was buried in the ground. Containers can commonly be leather bags, pots or glass urns. The actual container can be accompanied by grave goods, such as other pots and ornaments. The excavator must first find the outline of the burial hole and then carefully empty its fill. The hole is normally sectioned, with one half of the fill being entirely removed before the other in order to study the post-burial depositional history of the hole. The objects within the hole are left *in situ*. The other half of the fill is then removed. This results in the isolation of the burial objects in the positions they have come to rest in relation to each other. It must be decided whether this represents the original arrangement. A detailed plan of the positions is made. If the container for the cremation was of organic material it may not have survived except for traces, such as the iron fittings of a box or soil representing the rotted wood of a casket.

Inhumations require equal attention. If possible, a specialist should inspect the exposed remains *in situ*, or failing this a very detailed series of photos should be taken. It is not usually worthwhile to section a grave such as this except in a running fashion as the work proceeds downwards. The grave fill is removed to expose the details of the skeleton and any accompanying goods and a careful plan is prepared. A sharp lookout is kept for nails or staining that might indicate a vanished wooden coffin.

Ditches and banks

Of the greatest importance in the study of the natural processes that affect an earthwork is the experimental earthwork on Overton Down, Wiltshire, constructed under the auspices of the British Association Committee on Archaeological Field Experiments in 1960. The general idea behind the project was and is to study the processes at work and their depositional results on the ditch and bank by cutting sections at intervals of two, four, eight, sixteen and thirty-two years. Certain materials were incorporated in the earthwork and the results of the actions of natural agencies on these is also being studied. P. A. Jewell, and P. A. Jewell and Professor G. W. Dimbleby have provided accounts of the specifications for the experiment and the report of the sections cut after two- and four-year intervals (Jewell, 1961; Jewell and Dimbleby, 1966).

The setting up of the experiment is based on the uniformitarian assumption that the processes observable as operating today were the only processes operating in the past. The site is on chalk downland and consists of a linear bank and ditch with the long axis on horizontal ground to avoid any complicating slope effects. The ditch was dug 90 ft (27 m) long, 10 ft (3 m) wide at the top and 8 ft (2·5 m) wide at the bottom. It was separated from the bank by a 4-ft (1·2-m) berm, the difference between the bank and the edge of the ditch.

As data from which to measure soil movement, six 9½-ft (3-m) long steel tubes were secured with concrete in the ground along the spine of the bank. When these had been set, 30-cm square turves cut from the surface of the ditch were laid

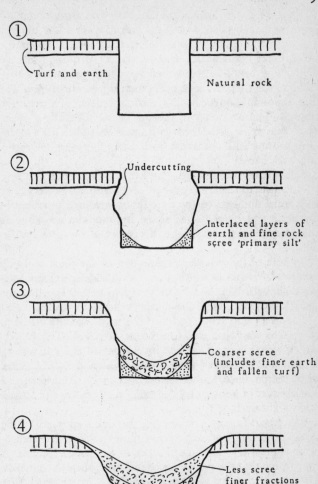

Fig. 7 Development of a ditch profile

as the core of the bank. The soil and flints from under the grass were then piled over the turves to form a low mound, $2\frac{1}{2}$ ft (75 cm) high by $8\frac{1}{2}$ ft (2·5 m) deep. The main body of the mound was constructed, in three stages, of chalk from the ditch. The break between each stage was marked by road chippings, a different rock being used for each interface. The final appearance of the bank in section was that of a truncated triangle. The constancy of this profile was carefully checked along the length of the bank with a metal template. As a means of measuring soil movement polythene tubes were set vertically in the bank.

Before construction began, broken flower pot was scattered over the site to represent pre-earthwork pottery. Pottery discs with serial numbers to 500 were set in measured positions in the berm and on the ditch sides. Lycopodium spores were scattered before the building of the bank to simulate the pollen rain.

As part of the experiment a section of the ditch was dug using primitive tools, antler picks, wicker baskets and shoulder-blade shovels. The picks were found to be efficient, but the shovels only came up to one-third of modern standards.

The other important aspect of the work was the burial of objects to see what transformations occurred. The objects buried were billets of oak and hazel (charred and uncharred), cooked and uncooked sheep bone, cremated human bone, wool, cotton, linen, leather tanned in five ways, fresh-fractured flint, pottery of known clay and firing temperature and human bone of known blood groups.

The report is only available for the first four years of the experiment, but it already reveals characteristics that archaeologists must take account of when digging such features. It is probable that the principles behind the processes on chalk soil extend to other soil types, and this is being tested in a parallel experiment on sandy soil at Wareham.

It is worth repeating in detail the observations reported by Jewell and Dimbleby. After seven and a half months, scree had accumulated in the basal angles of the ditch. In the bottom of the ditch, the lowest level of accumulation consisted of a thin band of earth derived from the topsoil. Over this was fine chalk rubble and crumbs of earth. Clean coarse rubble accounted for the upper 25 mm or so. The scree at the basal angle protected it from weathering, but the sides above the scree showed evidence of denudation such that slight undermining at the lip could be seen. Calcareous mud filled the slight pits in the floor of the ditch.

Six months later the continuation of slow weathering of the sides during the summer was noted. After twenty and a half months, more scree had accumulated and the sides of the ditch above the scree showed considerable collapse so that there was a marked overhanging of the turf at the lip of the ditch.

Heavy rain brought the first fall of undercut turf on to the centre of the ditch floor. This was recorded after twenty-five and a half months. At this time also the increasingly deep scree on both sides of the ditch had coalesced in the middle, giving a parabolic profile. Along the centre line lay rolled chalk and flint.

The section of the scree showed it to be made up of alternately coarse and fine bands, and this seems to correspond to winter and summer deposition respectively. By now there was a very concave profile to the slopes above the scree with the turf overhanging precariously.

With two years and eight months passed, the scree on the sides had accumulated to within 30 cm of the chalk surface. Because of snow falls many of the turves on the lip had fallen off and rolled down to fill the hollow of the coalesced screes. Some of the big pieces stayed part of the way up the slopes, and rubble piled up on these and spilled over them.

One of the most important general observations that could be made was that the rate and quantity of deposition fell off appreciably with time. In the second two years only a quarter of the material of the first two years was deposited. This is at least partly due to the fact that the growth of screes protects the source of scree, the ditch side, from denudation.

After four years it was noticed that in the move towards

slope equilibrium some degrading of the top of the scree had occurred. Very few other turves had fallen. Of those that had, those which had landed roots down were growing grass and those which had ended up grass down had broken up. The scree now had a lower angle of rest than before, 32 degrees rather than between 35 and 38 degrees. The top of the scree was finer grained and the thin soil layer at its base had undergone calcium carbonate impregnation. Worms seemed to have been less active in the ditch than they were in the bank.

The bank after seven and a half months showed little change except for some disintegration of its surface, which had become loose through freeze–thaw and wetting–drying action.

After twenty and a half months, the crest of the bank had sunk about 75 mm. At twenty-five and a half months, this shrinkage had continued and the layers making up the bank were exhibiting rounded profiles. This rounding was associated with a 25% to 27% shrinkage of the turf and chalk and soil core of the mound. The base of the bank had spread and grass was colonising the new deposits. Mole activity had disturbed the bank. Some downslope movement was noted which was seen to decrease with depth. Considerable consolidation of rubble layers within the bank had occurred.

At thirty-two months, the effects of frost shattering on the surface were noted. The heaving had left a spongy surface.

After four years, the trends of sinkage of the bank crest and rounding of the make-up layers were seen to be continuing. Downslope movement was proceeding at a reduced rate and very little extra spread of the base was occurring as grass growth was stabilising the tails. Grass growth at the front of the bank acted as a barrier to downward movement and humping of deposits was noticed there.

In the bank the rubble make-up was becoming cemented by redeposited calcium carbonate. This meant a certain amount of aggradation. Texture changes were also taking place as the rubble was reduced in size, this process advancing faster in the chalk than the flint and at the surface before the centre of the mound.

The recorded observations suggest that aspect does not play a significant role in the rate of weathering.

The bank remained virtually bare of vegetation after four years, the only significant colonisation occurring at the tails.

Earthworm activity was subdued in the first two years but was prolific after four and had led to considerable vertical displacement of the Lycopodium spores.

Molehills appeared along the edge of the bank during the first two years and in 1962 a run disturbed the buried surface for 1 metre from the bank edge. After thirty-two months, the moles had penetrated 2 metres into the bank and a run went into the turf core of the bank in search of earthworms.

One or two points arising from the above details might be further stressed. As the lower slope of the ditch is masked very quickly, it is here that the closest resemblance to the original profile is preserved.

With a berm of one or more metres the processes of weathering will probably not lead to large-scale slumping from bank into ditch; instead, an overall equilibrium of profile will be attained. Therefore, if large deposits of bank material are found in a ditch, it is likely that they have been dumped there.

Accumulations of soil at the tails of banks can occur by moles transferring it there. Worms help to diffuse soil widely in a bank. All this can lead to artefact displacement.

Particle size tends to vary with the seasons. Harsher winter conditions allow larger fragments to be detached, whilst finer detritus characterises summer conditions.

Slumping of ditch-lip deposits which might contain non-contemporary artefacts warns that the association of every item must be closely scrutinised.

A greater degree of comminution was noted at the ends of the bank than at the sides. This suggests that conical structures may develop finer textures before a long bank.

The experiment at Overton Down shows the sort of things that the archaeologist must be on the lookout for when digging ditches. They must be examined both horizontally and vertically. Philip Barker has recently re-emphasised the need for multiple cuts across a ditch. Working at Hen Domen, Montgomery, on a small timber castle of motte-and-bailey type, he dug seven sections across an 18-metre length of the motte ditch and they were all different (Barker, 1969).

The first two observations to make concern the size and shape of the ditch. It is necessary to assess the original shape of the feature. This will be done by examining the relatively undisturbed profile under the earliest deposits. From the deposits and an estimate of their rate of deposition the lifespan of the ditch can be guessed.

Dating a ditch requires the most careful attention to the degree of association of the artefacts contained in the fill. It is usually thought that the finds from the primary fills are most likely to be contemporary with the construction of the ditch. The primary deposit is often referred to as the 'rapid silt'. The assumption is a dangerous one, as the Overton Down data shows. Material from the topsoil can be much earlier than the cutting but can find its way to the ditch bottom in the first silt. It is not uncommon to find the effect known as interdigitation or reversed stratigraphy in a ditch deposit sequence. By this, older material becomes stratified above younger because the deposits are derived in succession from different sources.

In the sequence of deposits the excavator should always be asking himself, how did that deposit get there? In other words, he must think process. Time and time again it is possible to meet directors and supervisors who can produce excellent descriptions of their strata and yet have not the faintest idea of the processes whereby they formed, or worse still have vague stock expressions such as 'silting' or 'dump'. The archaeologist is rarely, amazing as it may seem, trained as a soil scientist and he must therefore be prepared to take relevant advice.

The sort of deposit that will be met includes dark lines of organic material representing vegetation growth during minimal erosion phases. Another one might be fine clay muds that formed during times when there was standing water in the ditch.

It should be remembered that many ditches underwent more than one life-cycle. When they became choked with material they were recut. Even where the recutting very closely follows the original line, some trace should be visible in section. If at all possible, recuts should be spotted in plan first and the excavation should proceed vertically in this knowledge in order to separate the artefacts precisely. Only when a ditch has been considerably enlarged on the same line is no trace found of a recut.

Ditches were often kept clean and much of the primary deposit would be removed in this fashion. Traces can usually still be found in the basal angles.

It was common practice in most periods to dump refuse into ditches, and this refuse can be identified in tip lines. If the life of a ditch and rampart is truncated by the slighting of the bank, then the bank deposit will be found filling much of the upper part of the ditch. Over this might occur the topsoil that filled the hollow after abandonment.

The first task in studying a bank is to decide how it was built. There was a great variety of methods of construction in antiquity. A common one was to use the sequence adopted at Overton Down, that is lay out a core and marker bank of material derived from the top of the ditch zone and then dump loads of subsoil from the ditch over the core. Examination of the tip lines shows the direction of the dumping. Small ditches were sometimes dug to mark the line of a bank.

Under many banks the pre-existing ground surface is preserved and this should be treated, as that found under barrows, as a source of environmental information.

Banks can undergo renewal during their life, as can ditches, and this is usually manifest in additions to the body of the mound. Care must be taken not to confuse the latter stage of construction dumping with later addition. Traces of a turf-line separating the phases should be sought.

A form of banking commonly met is the counterscarp, found on the opposite lip of the ditch and designed to expose an assailant more easily to fire.

Builders used a number of devices to give their banks a sheer face rather than a natural or glacis-type one.

Roman military engineers used turf which survives as dark organic bands. The Turf Wall of Hadrian's Wall at High House, west of the River Irthing, is 6 m wide built of coursed turves 45 × 30 × 15 cm. The height to rampart walk may have been about 4 m. A continuous strip of turf 75 m wide had been removed for the building.

Wood is a much more common revetting material. In very complex constructions, the rampart material can be boxed in between timber uprights joined to cross-beams that pass along the front and rear and through the body of the bank. Traces of these horizontal timbers can be found. Sometimes the bank is founded on a corduroy of logs. Timber uprights can be set on the ground or in the ground in a trench or series of pits. Examination of the timber settings can inform about the history of the structure. It may be possible to say whether the structure was dismantled or left to dilapidate.

Masonry revetments present their own problems. Graham Webster has provided an excellent summary, on which the following account is based, of the possibilities that can be found for the relationship of a wall to a rampart (Webster, 1963, 82–3).

In the first case a wall could be built freestanding and the rampart added to it. It is likely, although not necessary, that the wall was finished on both sides and traces of working, such as mortar mixing floors and waste stone splinters, might be found under the bank. In the second instance the wall and bank may have been built in phase with one another. Working traces might be found within the rampart at stages in its construction. The wall is unlikely to be finished on the blind side and no construction trench would be evident. If a wall was an addition to an existing bank, as is often the case in Romano-British town defences, the front of the bank is slighted to provide a construction trench in which the builder worked. The mason worked in the trench, backfilling partly as he went to raise his working platform. Chippings and mortar are commonly found in the construction trench backfill. The wall is pointed on both sides above the usual trench-built foundation.

A deposit of great importance, if it survives, is the weathering product from the front of the bank. If this is intruded by the wall, then it is unlikely that bank and wall are part of the same original plan.

Pits

A pit can be dug in the ground for a number of reasons, and these will control its shape and size.

The largest type of pit is the quarry pit. This is intended for the extraction of some material such as gravel or chalk. These features are dug in the fashion that most rapidly yields the desired product for the minimum amount of effort. They are rarely deliberately backfilled unless later used to shoot rubbish in. The sparsity of artefact content along with no sign of lining is usually a good indication of the purpose of a pit and the local geology will suggest the material sought.

The mine is a specialised variant of the quarry pit, and the flint mines at Grimes Graves, Norfolk, are a primary example. Here interest will centre on the nature of the sides, for marks that will indicate the technology employed, and on any associated artefacts or structures near the shafts.

Pits were much used in antiquity for the burying of rubbish and are a common feature of archaeological sites. If a pit was in use only for a short time and received the rubbish of a few days, then its excavation is important in yielding strictly contemporary groups of artefacts and food refuse. Some care is necessary in interpreting pit stratification. To seal off a rancid pit earth scraped up from nearby might be used, and if the site was long-occupied this might contain much earlier material. A reverse stratigraphy will have been created in effect. It can usually be ascertained whether a pit had a relatively long life or not by checking for evidence of erosion of the sides and for stages in the shooting of rubbish separated by sealing layers. Continuous pit digging is a feature of long-occupied or intensively occupied sites. The number of pits per habitation unit is a useful figure to use in guessing populations. Pits should be studied as assemblages and examined for specialisation of content, grouping with other pits or houses and their general location in the settlement. To do this effectively it is necessary to be able to know as near as possible the total number of pits present. Pits were often recut, so that only a trace of the fill of the earlier pit remains. Recuts must be carefully sought. The overlying layers can sink into the top of pits. At Wroxeter the tops of the pits and trenches of the final legionary phase are

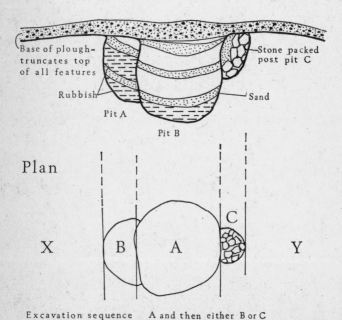

Section

Base of plough-
truncates top
of all features

Stone packed
post pit C

Rubbish

Sand

Pit A

Pit B

Plan

X

B

A

C

Y

Excavation sequence   A and then either B or C

Fig. 8 Pits

filled with the material formed from the spreading of demolition rubble over the abandoned site by the Roman army. Where the tops of the pits have been truncated it is not always obvious that the top fills are such sunk deposits and care must be taken, otherwise non-contemporary material might be ascribed to the period of the pit. Continual pit-digging can lead to the raising of the ground surface generally, as has been demonstrated for parts of medieval Cambridge (Addyman and Biddle, 1965).

It is not uncommon for a pit that served as a rubbish pit to have started life as a storage pit of some sort. At Little Woodbury Iron Age farmstead, G. Bersu in a classic excavation demonstrated the use of pits there as grain storage pits with subsequent reuse as rubbish pits (Bersu, 1940). In the Roman Rhineland, pits have been found to be so stereotyped in form as to warrant classification in morphological terms (*Bonner Jahrbücher*, 152 (1952)). The excavator should be on the lookout for signs of lining such as basketry, wood, stone and clay. The material in the latter case is used for water retention.

Large pits are dug in quadrants, but normally it is only necessary to section along one axis.

The special case of the well can be appended here. Because of the possibility of preservation in waterlogging conditions, their excavation can prove fruitful. Many wells have yielded timber, cloth, plant remains, insect remains and leather where the surrounding subsoil has proved unfavourable to preservation. Information about water levels is also available. Excavation presents practical problems of spoil removal, access, safety and working space. It is worth contemplating these difficulties before engaging in the task.

Timber buildings

Before considering the specific case of the post sunk into the ground, it is worth just considering the general excavation approach to a site suspected of being composed largely of ephemeral timber buildings. Whilst a number of distinguished excavators have contributed significantly to this approach (notably Brian Hope-Taylor and Philip Rahtz), the current exemplar of the achievements of the method is the meticulous work being carried out by Philip Barker at Wroxeter. The implications of some of the structural possibilities thrown up by the discoveries are truly revolutionary for our understanding of late Roman and early post-Roman Britain. Careful cleaning of rubble surfaces over virtually all the area of the Baths basilica and in areas immediately adjacent have revealed the platforms for a whole complex of timber buildings, one of which was 40 m long by 16 m wide. Very few of these structures had posts or beams that penetrated the ground. It is clear that the nature and, presumably, function of the centre of this Roman cantonal capital radically altered within the later part of the Roman occupation. What is also abundantly clear is that, if the site had been dug in any other fashion than in massive open strips, none of this information would have been forthcoming. Trenches had been dug across the area in the past and the upper layers of rubble noticed without any understanding of their meaning.

The methods being used at Wroxeter were developed in Britain on post-Roman sites. Philip Barker's other major excavation was the motte-and-bailey castle of Hen Domen, where he established his working method. Here he began his digging by simply lifting the turf and topsoil off an area and scrutinising the surface immediately below. A study of the distribution pattern of the stone showed circles of stone around shallow depressions containing 25 mm of stone-free soil. These were interpreted as being the emplacements for posts that had been set on, rather than in, the ground. Having made this interpretive step it was possible to see alignments of stone circles and associated stones, representing a fence, a rectangular building and other structures.

The next step in the dig was the following season to remove just the earth loosened during the winter and the dislodged stones onto the next definable layer. This revealed a new complex of stone alignments representing buildings—especially Building IX, tentatively interpreted as a twelfth-century chapel, a fully framed structure with horizontal timbers resting on the ground.

It is salutary to recall that this wealth of data was included in the first 15 cm of the site, and if the site had been ploughed just once it would have been obliterated. How much has been lost of this kind of building evidence will never be known. At least work like Barker's gives us an inkling of its presence and makes it imperative that no further potential sites are lost.

Therefore the only proper way to dig an extensive site with many timber buildings is to strip by hand large continuous areas, plotting the distribution of all artefacts and other patterned features immediately below the topsoil. The work can be monotonous and psychologically depressing because of its apparent lack of readily discernible results, but the archaeological rewards are great. It is not the sort of method that an amateur could be expected to deal with and, indeed, the lessons of the work should show up the increasing irrelevance of the small-scale excavation and its possible dangers.

A common method of erecting an upright timber is to set it in a pit. The timber can be set centrally in the hole or up against the side. It can be packed around with stones and earth or simply with the material dug out of the hole. Sometimes it is set on a foundation plate of wood or stone. It can even be wedged with small timbers. At the end of the life of the structure a number of things could happen. The building might be left to decay slowly with the posts rotting in the ground. There will be little disturbance to the pit and the outline of the timber upright should be clearly distinguishable in hardly altered form in sections from the packing. The term post hole should strictly be reserved for the void of the actual timber as distinct from the pit in which it is set. If the building is dismantled but the posts are only cut off at floor level, then again there will be little disturbance of the filling of the post pit. However, if the posts are withdrawn by moving backwards and forwards and yanking, then the packing and backfill will be disturbed and the profile of the post hole distorted.

A labour-saving and accurate way of laying out wooden

buildings was to dig a continuous trench rather than post pits. Attention should be paid by the excavator to the nature of the post hole, otherwise the feature is dug after the fashion of a ditch.

Shallow trenches are often found in which had sat horizontal timbers to which the uprights of the wall had been fixed. Sometimes the beams were laid on, rather than in, the ground and such arrangements are only detectable in the slightest discolorations and the distributions of artefacts.

Stone walls

The first questions to be asked of a stone wall are, of what material is it constructed and from where was it obtained? This is a task for a petrologist.

In excavating, the archaeologist will be able to define the method of construction. A wall can be set directly on the surface of the ground, but it is common for it to be set in the ground. A distinction can be drawn between trench-building and construction trench-building. A trench-built wall is set in a trench hardly wider than the wall itself and not allowing the mason any space to face the outer blocks or to point if the construction is with mortar. A construction trench is much wider than the wall being built, and working within it the mason can square the masonry and point from below the level that will constitute the final ground or floor surface. A construction trench is backfilled as the mason works upwards. It is common in Roman monumental building to find a combination of trench-building and construction trench working for different levels of the same wall. Another feature worth looking for associated with the building of a wall is the post holes of any scaffolding that might have been used.

Foundations can vary tremendously. Rubble on its own, rubble in clay, rubble in mortar are some of the possibilities, but coursed and pitched foundations are to be expected as well as materials very different from the body of the wall, such as pure compacted clay or timber piling. It is necessary for the

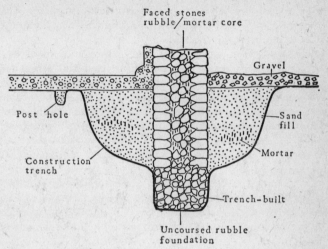

Fig. 9 Wall construction

excavator to familiarise himself with the building practices of the people or cultures which he is studying.

The same is true of the main body of the wall. Drystone walling is found in most places at most periods, but at certain times specialised practices developed. The common general Roman form was to construct with a rigid rubble core set in mortar, faced with small ashlar. Often at vertical intervals, double or triple courses of tiles were incorporated in the structure ostensibly to add strength and save on stone, although in some instances, such as the Godmanchester baths, it is likely that the wall structure was actually weakened by the bonding courses (Green, 1959, 224).

When a wall is part of a building it must be considered in terms of the general attempt to reconstruct the edifice. As Graham Webster and others have emphasised, there can be no intelligent reconstruction that does not clearly specify the nature of the roof. A scheme that cannot be sensibly roofed is nonsense. This, of course, applies to timber as well. This is a most difficult aspect as so little data actually survives. It is necessary to study comparative material in standing buildings and the ethnographic record.

In the study of any structure its constructional history will be of interest, especially to decide the plan and aspect (at various periods) which can undergo radical alteration. The obvious signs are building superimposition, where walls cross earlier walls or are set onto the footings of a demolished one. Study of floor sequences is revealing if later footings trenches are cut through pre-existing floors or later floors are run over robbed outwalls. This sort of relationship is best studied in cross-sections along the line of a wall. It is very important not to dig along a wall face until the precise stratigraphical relationship of every deposit to the wall has been defined. It is bad enough untangling the mess left by stone robbers without compounding it with the misguided efforts of archaeological bandits.

The manner in which adjacent walls meet often betrays different phases of work. Strictly contemporary walls are likely to be closely bonded together. A later wall can be bonded into an earlier, but the disjunction in coursing, if not in materials, allows this to be spotted. Often no attempt is made to bond at all and a straight joint is formed between the earlier and later structure.

Robber trenches

Ancient sites have always provided a ready source of stone and many have been so extensively robbed that the plans of the buildings are only recoverable in the outlines of the robber trenches.

The tracing of these trenches is clearly important to the understanding of a site, and the content of the fills, comprised as it is of waste from the rob, can yield details of the materials of the vanished structure, something of its dating if associated artefacts have been disturbed and possibly the dating of the robbing.

The robber operated on a least effort principle. Having

found a stretch of wall he would work down from the top of it extracting the useful stone. To save effort he would not dig much, if at all, beyond the line of the wall; and having created a working space in the trench he could work along the course of the wall. Good stone was tossed to the surface and carted away, whilst small chips, mortar and rubble were discarded in the trench dug. There would be no incentive for the robber to backfill and so the open trench would become subject to similar denudation processes to a ditch. The method of digging both features is very similar.

M. Biddle has made a special study of the habits of robbers and the information latent in their trenches on the site of the Old Minster, Winchester. He noted that, because the top of the trenches weathered, the base of the trenches was more important for defining the line of the robbed wall. Sometimes the impressions of blocks were preserved in the bottoms of trenches (Biddle and Kjølbye-Biddle, 1969).

Biddle carried the study further than simply outlining buildings. He was able to show periodisation in structures. If walls at different periods were of different depths or widths, this could be reflected in the dimensions of the robber trench. Small baulks of soil often occur at footing level where one wall is added to another, and this can survive robbing. These same signs can also occur if gang-working was employed in the construction of the building. The sequence of robbing should always be checked as parts of a building may have continued in use whilst other parts were completely dismantled. Different fills in different robbers can show different periods by changes in mortar or stone type. By the same token, similar fills will help to connect a complicated plan (Biddle and Kjølbye-Biddle, 1969).

Bibliography

Addyman, P. V., and Biddle, M., *Medieval Cambridge: Recent Finds and Excavations. Proceedings of the Cambridge Antiquarian Society*, LVIII, 1965, 74–137.

Ashbee, P., *The Bronze Age Round Barrow in Britain*. London: Dent, 1960.

Ashbee, P., *The Earthen Long Barrow in Britain*. London: Dent, 1970.

Barker, P., *Some aspects of the excavation of timber buildings*. *World Archaeology* I, 1969, 220–35.

Barker, P., *Excavations on the Site of the Baths Basilica at Wroxeter 1966–71*. Birmingham: University of Birmingham, 1971.

Barker, P., *Excavations on the Site of the Baths Basilica at Wroxeter 1972*. Birmingham: University of Birmingham, 1972.

Bersu, G., *Excavations at Little Woodbury, Wiltshire*. *Proceedings of Prehistoric Society*, 6, 1940, 30–111.

Biddle, M., and Kjølbye-Biddle, B., *Metres, areas, robbing*. *World Archaeology* I, 1969, 208–19.

Coles, J., *Field Archaeology in Britain*. London: Methuen, 1972.

Fox, C., in *Arch. Cambrensis*, 1926, 48ff.

Fryer, D. H., *Surveying for Archaeologists*. 2nd ed. Durham: University of Durham, 1961.

Green, H., *An Architectural Survey of the Roman Baths at Godmanchester. Part One: Walls, Floors, Doorways and Windows*. *Archaeological News Letter* 6, No. 10, 1969, 223–9.

Grimes, W. F., *Excavations on Defence Sites 1939–45; 1 Mainly Neolithic—Bronze Age*. London: HMSO, 1960.

Jewell, P. A., *An Experiment in Field Archaeology*. *Advancement of Science*, May 1961, 106–9.

Jewell, P. A., and Dimbleby, G. W. (eds), *Experimental Earthwork on Overton Down, Wiltshire, England: The First Four Years*. *Proceedings of Prehistoric Society*, XXXII, 1966, 313–42.

Lethbridge, T., *The Anglo-Saxon Cemetery, Burwell, Cambs*. *Proceedings of the Cambridge Antiquarian Society*, XXVII, 1926, 79.

Webster, G., *Practical Archaeology*. London: A. & C. Black, 1963; new edition, 1974.

Wheeler, R. E. M., *Archaeology from the Earth*. London: Oxford University Press, 1954 (Pelican edition 1956 for references).

Additional reading

Alexander, J., *The Directing of Archaeological Excavations*. London: John Baker, 1970.

Atkinson, R. J. C., *Field Archaeology*. 2nd ed. London: Methuen, 1953.

Cookson, M. B., *Photography for Archaeologists*. London: Parrish, 1954.

Cornwall, I. W., *Soils for the Archaeologist*. London: Dent, 1958.

Feininger, A., *Manual of Advanced Photography*. London: Thames & Hudson, 1970.

Heizer, R. F. (ed.), *The Archaeologist at Work*. New York: Harper & Row, 1959.

Heizer, R. F., *A Guide to Archaeological Field Methods*. 3rd ed., Palo Alto: California University Press, 1966.

Heizer, R. F., and Graham, J. A., *A Guide to Field Methods in Archaeology*. Palo Alto: California University Press, 1967.

Kenyon, K. M., *Beginning in Archaeology*. London: Dent, 1964.

Matthews, S., *Photography in Archaeology and Art*. London: John Baker, 1968.

Pyddoke, E., *Stratification for the Archaeologist*. London: Dent, 1961.

Simmons, H., *Archaeological Photography*. London: London University, 1969.

Wendorf, F., *A Guide For Salvage Archaeology*. Sante Fe: Museum of New Mexico Press, 1962.

Williams, J. C., *Simple Photogrammetry*. London: Academic Press, 1970.

Woolley, L., *Digging up the Past*. 2nd ed. London: Penguin Books, 1954; repr. 1963.

4   Conservation

Few of the objects excavated by the archaeologist will not require some treatment, having been removed from the ground in order to guarantee their preservation in storage or on display. Fortunately pottery, which, in the historic periods at least, comprises the bulk of the finds, is usually one of these exceptions. Nevertheless, the sheer quantity of perishable items dug up annually is staggering and at present beyond existing resources to deal with. There is an urgent need for public recognition of the vital role of the conservator and the provision of finance for adequate laboratory facilities and appropriate staffing.

The problem is accentuated by the fact that conservation is not a do-it-yourself operation but a job for specialists, of whom there are far too few. Wherever possible, *no first aid or attempt to use preservatives should be made except by an expert in the laboratory or under an expert's explicit guidance.* It is only when this is impracticable that the excavator will attempt such work himself. Indeed, it should be asked whether it is justified to dig without adequate provision for preservation. There is no place for amateur conservation work, which can do irreparable harm by extracting material from its original preserving environment.

This chapter describes some of the techniques in use in

conservation laboratories and some of the elementary procedures that the archaeologist can observe in getting his
material to a laboratory. The chapter draws heavily on the
excellent *Conservation in Field Archaeology* by Elizabeth A. Dowman which, along with the other works mentioned in the
notes, should be consulted for further details.

Consolidation

Objects commonly need strengthening before they can be
removed from the earth. Various resins and waxes are used for
this purpose, depending on the material. A preliminary to consolidation is cleaning, if this is feasible. If any scientific investigation is intended for the object, it should be left untreated.

Five methods of consolidation are available. Gentle spraying
is rapid and effective and has the advantage over the commonly
used brushing of minimising the mechanical disturbance of an
object. If the material has been freed from the ground it can be
put on a polythene sieve and lowered into a consolidant. This
immersion procedure is continued at short intervals until
satisfactory penetration is achieved. A variant of this is to im-
merse the material only partly, so that penetration is by up-
ward evaporation. The best method of impregnation is to
utilise a vacuum chamber, in which the consolidating agent is
forced into the material under pressure. This method is rarely
used in the field because of the difficulty of setting up the
equipment satisfactorily.

The synthetic resins and waxes that are used as consolidants
and adhesives are chosen for their possession of certain necessary properties. It must be possible to break down the substance utilised in case it proves to be unsatisfactory. Some
shrinkage of resins is inevitable and only low-shrinkage ones
are used. The nature of an object determines the amount of
impregnation to occur and the strength of the resin to be
applied. The resin should not be quite as strong as the fabric
of the object to be treated. Both the resin and the solvent for
it must do no damage to the object.

Of the resin consolidants in use, the most frequently employed is polyvinyl acetate. It is purchased as crystals and made up into a solution using either acetone or toluene, although methyl ethyl ketone, industrial methylated spirit, xylene or ethyl acetate are also used. A solution of 10% to 15% in industrial methylated spirit is a standard concentration. Application can be by brush, spray, dipping or vacuum impregnation. The solution can be applied to dry subjects, excluding metal ones and organic material. PVA emulsion which has been diluted in water is applied to wet materials (exclusive of metals and also of wood and leather). Polyvinyl alcohol in solution with water is equally applicable to wet and dry objects, especially bone, but is not for use on timber, leather or metal. Polyvinyl butyral has greater strength than PVA and is suitable for dry materials other than metal.

Polyethylene glycol waxes come in a variety of forms of different molecular weights and extend the range of materials it is possible to consolidate. Carbowax 1500 is especially utilised on leather and does not destroy the pliability of the object. PEG 4000 can consolidate timber and can be employed as a temporary measure when raising fragile metal artefacts. PEG 6000 is used as a consolidant for pottery.

A large number of adhesives are commercially available and, provided that they can be broken down and have the requisite strength without doing violence to the object, most can be used for some archaeological purpose. Well-known multipurpose brands include UHU grade R and Evostick, although the latter is somewhat difficult to break down.

The solvents that are required in conservation work vary according to the particular case. Most entail some degree of danger in their handling, being either toxic or inflammable, or both. Commonly used solvents include industrial methylated spirit (for PVA, PEG and shellac), toluene, xylene (for resins, PVA, rubber), acetone and methyl ethyl ketone (for oil, PVA, shellac), ethylene dichloride (for oils and waxes) and amyl acetate (for PVA).

Pure water is essential for many operations, particularly for treating metals and soaking away salts. Distilled or deionised water is used. In Britain it is possible to get distilled water from the local chemist or garage for a small charge, or to distill it personally in a laborious process of condensing water vapour or steam. Buying a deionising column is the alternative and this requires drinking-standard water.

Raising

Fortunately, the average site does not yield many objects that require special measures for their lifting from the ground. In any case, the pressure of time would rule out such measures for all but the most precious of pieces.

If a small artefact is very fragile, consolidant is first applied, then further solutions in conjunction with bandages are added before lifting. Bigger pieces need to be supported by a stiff frame. This can be achieved by the use of strips of scrim dipped in plaster of paris and wood or metal splints. A typical procedure described by Dowman and based on the practice of the British Museum (Natural History) Palaeontology Laboratory involves successively isolating the object in the ground, applying a consolidant if necessary, using damp paper or polythene to cover the surfaces and then laying on strips of scrim dipped in plaster. Splints are incorporated whilst applying the scrim, and eventually the whole object is wrapped in scrim. When the plaster has dried, the specimen is removed from the ground. Other methods include lifting materials in blocks of earth by putting a box frame in around the block and encasing it with plaster and scrim. Damage can be caused if too much plaster is used.

Another method, only recommended when plaster is not practicable, is to use fibre-glass matting or, for small specimens, a powerful resin like polyvinyl butyral.

Polyurethane foam is suitable for specimens of a wide range of size. A small ditch is cut around the object and aluminium foil is laid over both. Cardboard is used to wall in the object and the foam is then poured in to cover the top of it. Usually this is sufficient to allow for lifting, but if not extra foam can be poured into hollows created by selective undermining.

Plaster of paris is easily obtained as fine industrial plaster. It is made up in water and, depending on local conditions, is relatively quick-setting. The setting time can be speeded up by adding either ammonium hydroxide (tablespoon to a gallon) or zinc sulphate (two teaspoons to a gallon). Conversely, it will set more slowly if citric acid crystals are added to the water used for mixing. The advantage of the material is its low cost and easy manageability, but if it is used carelessly it can be damaging as it is not chemically reversible. It must never be brought directly in contact with the specimen but should be separated with something like dampened paper or polythene.

Scrim is a coarse jute bandage. Plaster bandage serves the same function as scrim dipped in plaster. This is the hospital bandage and when dampened is fairly easy to apply in strips.

Fibre-glass is light and malleable but does tend to adhere to surfaces, causing them to come away without adequate prior consolidation.

Rubber latex is limited in usage to raising mosaics or soil profiles.

Polyurethane foam has considerable strength without being very heavy. It is very quick-setting. Its main disadvantages are that it cannot be applied directly to an object but must have aluminium intervening; it is poisonous; and it is costly.

Moulds and casts

If it is necessary to make a copy of a sculptured surface or the like, rubber latex can be used to make a mould. The surface of the object is prepared either by sprinkling talcum powder or french chalk or by spraying with a silicon polish. Three layers of latex are then brushed on. On to these are applied bandages, with more coats of latex. The mould is ready to be detached as soon as the latex is dry. Use of a plaster backing can keep the mould flat.

It is a slightly more complicated and time-consuming operation to make a two-piece mould, but better reproductions are
obtained. The object is placed on a flat surface. Either plasticine or clay, the surface of which is flattened and which makes
sharp joins with the object's surface, is put around it. Standing
above the plasticine surface is the part of the object that is the
subject of the first piece of the mould. Both the object and the
plasticine are dusted or polished and then rubber latex and
bandage is applied as described above. To give strength to the
mould a backing of plaster of paris and scrim is added. Before
the latex is brushed on, small holes are made in the surface of
the plasticine to give keying points between the parts of the
mould. After the plaster has set, the block is lifted from the flat
surface and inverted. The plasticine is removed. The other
part of the mould is constructed over the unmodelled part of
the object by exactly the same method as before, using the first
part rather than plasticine as a base. The object is freed from
the mould by removing the plaster encasement and then roll-
ing off the rubber.

Casting techniques are highly sophisticated nowadays, using
epoxy or polyester resins to produce commercially saleable
items, and this belongs to the museum rather than the archaeological sphere. Dental plaster is adequate for archaeological
purposes on site and can, with due care to its filling all crevices,
be easily poured into the relevant mould. The product can be
waterproofed with shellac in solution with industrial methylated spirit.

Rubber latex has the major disadvantage that it suffers from
shrinkage and therefore requires reinforcement when used in
reproduction work. It must not be applied directly to an
object, unless that object has first been dusted with ordinary
talcum powder or sprayed with furniture polish. Ammonia
and copper react together, and if the latex is used on bronze it
must first be mixed with thiourea solution. Thiourea is available from suppliers of chemicals and is used to prevent the
reaction of ammonia and copper.

Equipment

An important part of an excavator's and a conservator's equipment will be suitable containers for the portage and storage of finds in a way not detrimental to their long-term preservation.

Polythene bags are widely used, but some caution is needed. It is dangerous to store dry metal objects in polythene unless a desiccating agent such as silica gel is included in the bag. Silica gel comes in two forms. The first is clear crystals and their absorption of water is registered by indicating paper. The other is blue crystals which turn pink as they take up moisture. They are reusable if the water is driven out of them in an oven.

Polythene bags come in a variety of sizes and grades of heaviness of polythene. It is advisable to carry a selection of these for different purposes. If organic material is being stored, then it is necessary to seal the bag. Normally it will be kept within three sealed bags. Various methods of sealing are used, heat-sealing with an electric heat-sealer being the most effective. Other cruder methods include folding the top of the bag several times, stapling or clipping it and tying it with string or wire. Sealing is also required in storing other materials.

Plastic-foam sheeting and polythene sheeting are commonly needed to wrap around objects such as large wet timbers in order to retain moisture.

Standard sizes of cardboard box are indispensable as a bulk storage alternative to polythene. It is advisable to obtain sizes that will telescope conveniently one into another. A good stout grade of cardboard such as 50 LKC or 60 LKC is required. Typical, useful sizes that can be packed within a box $17 \times 9 \times 7$ inches are: $2 \times 3 \times 1$ in, $4\frac{1}{2} \times 2\frac{1}{2} \times 1\frac{1}{2}$ in, $5\frac{1}{2} \times 4 \times 1\frac{1}{2}$ in, $8 \times 5\frac{1}{2} \times 3$ in and $16\frac{1}{2} \times 4\frac{1}{2} \times 3$ in.

Hinged-lidded polystyrene boxes come in a number of sizes, such as $2\frac{1}{4} \times 1\frac{3}{4} \times \frac{3}{4}$ in and $3 \times 2\frac{1}{8} \times 1\frac{1}{8}$ in. They are strong, transparent and excellent for smaller artefacts.

Wood or metal crates might be required for distance transport. If objects are to be moved about, it is obviously necessary to take precautions in packing in proportion to the strength of the objects being moved and the degree of movement likely to be encountered. Common packing materials are plastic foam, screwed-up paper and tissue paper. The latter must be of the non-acid type, such as Kleenex. The Victoria and Albert Museum uses wads of brown paper wrapped in tissue paper. Cotton wool can also be utilised, provided that it is not touching the specimen directly. In packing the best results are obtained if the same classes of objects are packed together and if within one case there is a grading of heavy objects from bottom to top, laid in layers each of which is securely lined and wedged.

It is usually possible to mark directly much of the material excavated, especially pottery. The preferred method is to write in indelible indian ink on a prepared lacquered patch on the object. The writing itself is then lacquered over to ensure permanency. However, marking is unsuitable for many kinds of finds and labels must be attached either to the object or to its container. A very suitable multi-purpose plastic label in different colours is available. This should be marked in indelible ink.

It is not possible to describe here all the possible tools and containers that might be found in a well-equipped laboratory, and comment is restricted to a few of immediate use in treating objects in the field lab. The conservator needs a whole range of fine probes, such as are available to a dentist or chiropodist. In addition, knives of various sizes and strengths—from the scalpel to the carving knife—are essential. For cleaning and applying fluids, paint brushes, toothbrushes and nailbrushes are used. Mechanical cleaning of metal objects, especially iron, can be accomplished using a vibrating drill with a special fine attachment. If it is used excessively without protective clothing, the dust from this power-driven implement constitutes a health hazard.

For applying consolidant, a spray and soft paint brushes are required. Other useful implements and equipment include wooden sticks, pin vices, tweezers, spatulas, plaster tools, rubber gloves, magnifying glass and sticking tape, in addition to those things already mentioned in the previous sections on procedures.

The following sections describe the sort of treatment that particular materials might need to undergo.

Organic material

Bone

Bone can normally be washed with little danger to it and then be allowed to dry out thoroughly before being stored. A 15% solution of glacial acetic acid can help to clear away calcium accretions. The consolidants that are relevant are PVA and polyvinyl alcohol, the latter requiring removal within two years otherwise it will turn insoluble. In very acid soil, bone can be very badly rotted and, if its recovery is of importance, necessitates careful, *in situ*, mechanical cleaning and consolidation before lifting. Bone deposits in Palaeolithic caves are treated with particular care because of their rarity and fragility. Mechanical cleaning only is recommended for bone objects.

Ivory

Ivory is cleaned by taking dirt away with wooden tools. Dry ivory is never washed and soft tools are used to save scratching the delicate surface. PVA emulsion can be used to consolidate wet ivory, though this is not universally recommended. Alternatives are to allow the piece to dry *in situ* or to lift it and keep it damp in sealed polythene bags accompanied by fungicide.

Leather, textiles and basketry

As with most conservation techniques, the requirement for leather preservation is *the accurate recreation or maintenance of the favourable conditions that have allowed for survival to the present.* Thus wet leather is kept in water in a polythene bag along with some fungicide. Two fungicides commonly used are Topane WS and Dowicide A. They are used in very diluted form. If the leather is dry, it is transferred to a dry environment. A consolidant used for both conditions is molten Carbo-wax 1500 and treatment is by immersion.

Textile fragments and basketry are similarly kept damp if wet and dry if dry. The Rescue booklet suggests that wet textile should be kept wet in its own earth but not accompanied by fungicide. A wax consolidant can be used for wet pieces if really necessary.

Wood

Wet wood must be kept wet at all costs or it will begin to break down and warp. Small wooden objects can be put into sealed polythene bags with water and fungicide solution. Large pieces present many practical problems. They can be kept damp on exposure by spraying or covering with a wet bandaging. It is desirable that they are transferred as soon as possible to a tank in which they can be totally immersed. The bulk storage problem that the provision of adequate tanks imposes is immense; and the necessity of preserving large quantities of substantial timber must be seriously questioned. The surface of wet wood is spongy to the touch and can easily be damaged; if it is to be lifted, this should be effected by bandaging the timber in foam rubber, polythene sheeting or some similar material and supporting it with a wood splint. If it is necessary to cut the wood up, then substantial timbers will need to be cut with a power saw as the ordinary hand saw is quickly blunted. Wet timber weighs considerably more than the dry article and anything up to a 20-ton telescopic crane may be required to do the lifting.

If the wood is very weak, then the polyethylene glycol wax 4000 can be applied undiluted as a temporary measure. Long-term preservation is effected with diluted PEG 4000, which is introduced by immersion to replace the water over a period of several months.

If the timber is to be used for analysis, it should not be subjected to any treatment at all. Instead, a sample should be swiftly taken and dispatched to the relevant specialist, say for C14 dating.

Plaster casts are recommended as suitable ways of recording the structure of a composite timber artefact for the purposes of reconstruction.

Dry wood is maintained in a dry state. PEG 4000 undiluted may be used as a temporary consolidant if really necessary, but long-term preservation is achieved by using epoxy or polyester resins. Finds of dry wood are unlikely in Britain.

It is worth stressing the importance of the closest possible study of preserved wood, especially if it can't be saved. A substantial part of man's early technology was in this material and still too little is known of the history of carpentry.

Samples for plant and pollen analysis are kept damp in a polythene bag along with some fungicide. If the samples have been extracted they can be preserved in a solution of 90% water/ethyl alcohol, 10% glycerol and a small part of formalin.

Soil samples are taken either as a monolith using an aluminium column driven into the section face or simply by digging out with a trowel. The sample must be allowed to dry before being bagged otherwise mould will develop.

Metals

Iron

All conservators will give the same advice to the field archaeologist when it comes to dealing with metals and that is simply *don't touch them*. The processes of true conservation require controlled conditions because of the many variables involved in alloys.

Iron is not washed but simply carefully cleaned mechanically when encountered in the field. The corrosion products on an object may preserve valuable evidence, such as the impression of textiles, so they should not be removed unexamined.

Dry iron is kept dry by placing it in a plastic or cardboard box wedged in with tissue along with some silica gel. Under no circumstances should a polythene bag be used for dry iron without the provision of silica gel.

It has been recommended that wet iron be immersed in a 5% solution of sodium sesquicarbonate to stop rusting, but this is frowned upon by laboratories, who prefer the iron not to be treated at all. It is advisable to get any iron finds rapidly to a conservator for specialist treatment.

An essential procedure which is the standard preliminary to conservation of iron is to take an X-ray photograph of the object. This has two advantages. First, it indicates the state of the object beneath the corrosion and allows the appropriate treatment to be undertaken and, secondly, it gives a permanent record of the shape of the specimen, which may be invaluable should no cleaning be undertaken or a disaster occur during that process.

Bronze

Bronze is likely to be fragile when found and, as with iron, should not be washed but should be carefully relieved of excess dirt. The corrosion product can reveal impressions, for example, of cloth on brooches.

Dry bronze is stored dry in a container with silica gel. Wet bronze is gradually dried out.

Mechanical cleaning is preferred to use of chemicals as it can be better controlled, but this is time-consuming and impractical for a large site's output. There are three chemical methods. To clean coins rapidly a 30% solution of formic acid continually renewed can be employed. Cupric salts on bronze can be dispelled using alkaline glycerol or alkaline rochelle salt, and hydrogen peroxide in combination with either of these removes cuprous salts. Tin reacts with alkalis and therefore this treatment is unsuitable for a bronze with a high tin content. Chemicals should not be used in uncontrolled conditions—which usually obtain in the field.

Electrochemical reduction is designed to remove the chlorides responsible for corrosion. The specimen is encased in aluminium foil and immersed in a 10% to 20% sodium hydroxide solution, which is heated. The main products of the reaction are hydrochloric acid and copper. The object is dried thoroughly after treatment. Care has to be taken to avoid the redeposition of copper on the object being treated.

Two methods have been successful in arresting further corrosion or bronze disease. In the first, the object is thoroughly impregnated with 3% benzotriazole in industrial methylated spirit in a vacuum chamber. The object is subsequently dried completely. Much of the bronze work in even well-known museums is in a deplorable state simply because no attempt to counteract the possibility of growing corrosion has been made and storage is not in a controlled atmosphere. The second method is only suitable for localised small-scale corrosion. The corrosion product is removed manually and silver oxide applied to stabilise the metal. If the atmosphere of the store is kept dry along with the metal, then no further problems will arise. Silver oxide is not applicable to far-gone cases.

Silver

This can appear as a dark purple or black colour in the ground. Silver objects can be extremely fragile and, because of their rarity, are to be treated with absolute care. They are cleaned gently by hand, not washed. The corrosion product silver chloride can be dispersed with ammonia. Alkali cleaners are to be avoided if the silver is alloyed with lead. It is to be remembered that silver was extracted from lead mines as a major source in, for example, the Roman period.

Gold

It is not normally necessary to take any special precautions for substantial gold objects. They can be cleaned by washing in water. They should not be roughly treated, however, otherwise damage will result. If the object in question is only gilded, then great care must be taken with the underlying material so as not to destroy the surface. A particularly difficult example found is gilded leather, where shrinkage of the leather must be avoided.

Lead, tin and pewter

All these metals can be found in badly deteriorated state and should not be treated in the field. The main effort will be to lift them safely. They should not be placed in cardboard or wooden boxes as they are liable to hastened destruction through contact with the vapours of organic acids. Polythene bags are suitable receptacles. Lead is vulnerable to surface damage. Tin can be treated in a similar fashion to bronze and iron.

Stone

It is rare to have to undertake any conservation on stone arte-facts beyond simple washing. If soluble accretions are present, they can be soaked away in ordinary water. If the material adhering is insoluble, then it is taken off by hand-tools, possibly aided by the discreet use of hydrochloric acid. It is probably inadvisable to consolidate stone unless it is to be stored in controlled conditions. Recommended consolidants are PVA in toluene and acetone and Bedacryl 122x.

Shale

Shale is kept according to the conditions it is found under. Wet, it is kept in water in polythene. Dry, it can be kept dry—providing the conditions are fully controlled. Impregnation with PEG 4000 is one long-term method of preservation.

Amber

This is kept wet if found wet and dry if found dry. As it is common to analyse amber chemically to define its source, no consolidant or other chemical preparation should be allowed to come into contact with it.

Building materials

Plaster

Painted wall plaster is commonly encountered on Roman sites and is not always accorded the care it deserves. Whilst small individual pieces do not require special arrangements for lifting, when large deposits are encountered standard techniques are available. These are described by Dowman. The basis of the technique is to provide a strong but not too heavy backing of scrim and plaster of paris to the piece. Provided that a separating agent is used, the plaster of paris can be applied to a painted face as well as to the back of the specimen. Slight wetting of the piece avoids damage that might be caused by chemical reactions set up. Isolated fragments can be lifted using PVA emulsion and bandaging.

Procedures for the removal of wall-paintings intact are not the province of the archaeologist but entirely of the art-conservator. An archaeologist would seek advice and help immediately should he come across wall-paintings that must be removed. Ideally, paintings should be left as found with relevant controls on the atmosphere. In one removal technique, layers of glue, gauze and canvas are affixed to the surface of the painting and when the glue is dry the painted surface is literally rolled off. Other methods involve the removal of rigid blocks of painted surface and plaster or paint, plaster and wall, again using glue and canvas (Dowman, 1970, 126–31).

Mosaics

There are three common ways in which mosaics are treated. Some are preserved at the site of finding under coverings. The standard of covering and care does vary. Good examples of on-site display are provided at Fishbourne. Other mosaics are kept buried *in situ* and possibly periodically exposed to the public, as at Woodchester. Many mosaics have been lifted and taken to museums. The earlier method was to lift the mosaic as a rigid block. Canvas was securely glued on to the surface of the floor and provided with a timber backing. Sandwiched between timber, planks having been inserted beneath the bedding, the mosaic was lifted onto a prepared platform and carried away to be prepared for exhibition.

A current method is to dry out the floor completely and to clean out the interstices between the tesserae. A layer of synthetic resin, a layer of thin cotton and another layer of resin are applied to the surface of the floor. The mosaic is released from its bedding and then rolled up on a drum. It is transported flat, face-downwards. A variant on this method uses rubber latex and is designed for lifting small segments flat.

Glass

Wet glass is stored damp, unless it can be shown by experiment that gradual drying will not damage it. Dry glass is packed dry. If sheets or sherds of glass are to be stored together in the same box, then they are separated and wrapped in acid-free tissue paper. This procedure for wet glass includes enclosing the tissue-covered pieces in damp cotton wool. The water used to dampen the cotton wool should have had some fungicide added to it.

If the surface of glass is peeling, dilute, soluble nylon can be applied. PVA is a suitable consolidant and UHU a general-purpose adhesive.

Pottery

Generally most pottery found does not require any special treatment. It is washed in ordinary water using softish nailbrushes or toothbrushes. Brushes should not be used if the surface will be marked by them. The pottery is then left to dry out thoroughly before being put into store. Certain circumstances make it undesirable to wash sherds. Poorly fired prehistoric pottery is apt to disintegrate in water and should be cleaned mechanically. Some paints on pots can be washed away if treated carelessly. It is often worthwhile keeping unwashed a sample of the pottery from a site, so that it can be examined for any traces of food remains, and for subsequent thermoluminescence tests.

Soluble salts are washed out of pottery by repeated soaking in reasonably pure water such as is obtained from household taps. Insoluble salts are best removed by hand, but if really necessary then careful use of hydrochloric acid achieves an acceptable effect, although if the sherd has any form of calcitic temper this should be avoided. Hydrochloric acid deals with carbonates, whilst nitric acid can be used to dissolve sulphates and carbonates.

Dilute soluble nylon is used in thin coats to fix a flaking surface. If consolidation is needed, PVA, Butvar or Elvacite can be employed. A long-term method used by the British Museum for fragile pieces is impregnation with PEG 6000.

To obtain accurate profiles it is necessary to rebuild broken pots, if enough joining sherds remain. A tray filled with sand is required in which sherds glued together can rest supported. UHU or similar adhesive does an adequate job. The best results are obtained if the work is done slowly, fixing only one piece to another at a time and working from the base upwards. Restoration of missing sherds is done in plaster of paris, the surface of which can be painted to resemble the colour of the original.

Notes

It is worth stressing again that conservation is a job for experts and that there is no place in archaeology for amateur work in this sphere. The books listed here should be seen as explanatory of the techniques involved, not as working manuals. Under no circumstances should the few notes given in this chapter serve as the basis for attempted conservation. Major source book for this chapter:

Dowman, E. A., *Conservation in Field Archaeology*, London: Methuen, 1970.

Further reading:

Biek, L., *Archaeology and the Microscope*. London: Lutterworth Press, 1963.

Hodges, H., *Artifacts*. London: John Baker, 1964.

Leigh, D. *et al.*, *First Aid for Finds*. Southampton, 1972. (This is the Rescue Publication No. 1.)

Plenderleith, H. J., and Werner, A. E., *The Conservation of Antiquities and Works of Art*. London: Oxford University Press, 1972.

Thomson, G. (ed.), *Recent Advances in Conservation*. London: Butterworth, 1963.

UNESCO, *The Conservation of Cultural Property*. Paris: UNESCO, 1968.

These books contain detailed bibliographies which lead the reader to the specialist literature on the subject. The Rescue pamphlet contains a useful list of conservators in Britain who are prepared to give advice on conservation problems. The same publication gives the names and addresses of suppliers of various basic materials.

5 Analysis of Organic Remains

Objects made from living things have formed part of man's cultural equipment from earliest times. It has been claimed that Australopithecines at the site of Makapansgat, South Africa, were using animal long-bones as clubs, digging tools and perforators. The various species of *Australopithecus* occupied Southern Africa one to two million years ago and were antecedents and relatives of the earliest true man. The culture at Makapansgat has been termed the Osteodontokeratic (Dart, 1957). The degree to which Palaeolithic man used weapons and tools of wood and bone can only be guessed at as so little has survived. We must remember that, although archaeologists must of necessity be concerned with stone tools, many of these were probably part of composite implements or concerned in the manufacture of primary tools of organic origin.

Analysis of organic material is not solely concerned with the source, the method of production and the function of tools. It is much more involved in environmental reconstruction. Human cultural systems are in a continuing interchange relationship with their natural surroundings, which provide their economic basis. Through time, man has increasingly mastered his environment and it is the chronicling of this process that is one of archaeology's major contributions to knowledge. In order to do this the researcher makes use of as much evidence as he can from non-human sources. The particular contributions of these are discussed below. It should be stressed that the archaeologist's interest is in man, and he pursues environmental studies only as a means of gaining explanations for observed patterning in material culture, which remains his primary data. If he is to interest others in his work, however, he must be prepared to give aid to allied scientists, particularly as he might be dependent on their skills for analysis.

Animal remains: Bone—human
(Source: Brothwell, 1965.)

The study of the physical remains of man is the domain of the physical anthropologist. The student of material culture cannot ignore the morphology of the populations to which that culture belonged. Culture does not exist independently of man and its configuration is affected by demographic changes, some of which are ascertainable through the study of human remains. Many distinctions in culture and society are directly related to age and sex.

The field archaeologist needs to be able to identify human remains, record them correctly and have an appreciation of how they might aid him in his job of reconstruction. As he is dealing with somebody else's data he must be informed enough to treat it with due respect.

Identification of individual bones is not a difficult matter and can be learnt with the help of an anatomy atlas. Useful books are given at the end of this chapter. Wherever possible, actual bones should be handled. The articulation of the skeleton must be learnt as at least a guide to excavating an inhumation burial.

Measurement plays a large part in the study of skeletal morphology. Intelligent metrical analysis is the basis of comparative studies of population by statistical means. Use of figures can give greater definition to descriptions. Standard points from which readings are taken are given in books such as Brothwell's. The anthropologist uses for measurement spreading callipers, sliding callipers, tape and osteometric board.

Indices have been much used in the past by physical anthropologists. One, constantly found in the literature, is the cephalic index, which assesses the degree of long-headedness in a specimen. This is obtained by multiplying the maximum skull width by 100 and then dividing by the maximum skull length. A person classed as dolichocephalic or long-headed has an index of less than 75.0. A mesocephalic person has an index of 75.0 to 79.9. The round-headed or brachycephalic individual's index is 80.0 to 84.9. Ancient populations show marked variations in their mean cephalic index, but the distribution of individual values within a single population is very broad and there is little point to the measurement unless it is part of a considerable series; even then, modern multivariate statistical techniques are rendering simple indices such as these obsolete. Other indices calculated for the femur and tibia proximal ends are designed to bring out the differences in shape found between populations.

In all metrical comparative work, care must be taken that what is being compared is truly comparable and that variations are not a function of differences in either age or sex.

Analysis of measurements is not the only method of studying morphological variation between populations. Many traits are observable that are not susceptible to meaningful measurement and it is their presence, absence, frequency or precise form that is of interest. A set of such traits is discussed by Brothwell (1965, 94–100). These enabled him to differentiate fourteen widely dispersed populations as effectively as if he had used cranial measurements. Ethnic differences included such things as the relative frequency or deficiency in the presence of the third molar.

Three identifications are of traditional importance in skeletal studies: sexing, ageing and ascertaining stature. Sexing can only be tentative with a fragmentary specimen as it is necessary to have some idea of the variability of the general population from which the skeleton is likely to have come. A combination of measurements is required and it is not satisfactory to determine sex on the basis of a single feature.

A greater robustness in certain skeletal features, along with some qualitative difference, usually distinguishes male from female in a population. A detailed list of features is provided by Brothwell (1965, 51–7) and the most important areas are the pelvis, the skull and face, and articular surfaces, especially of the long-bones. In the pelvis, the female has a wide sciatic notch and marked pre-auricular sulcus, whereas in males the sciatic notch is deep and narrow and the pre-auricular sulcus usually absent. In the skull, the male has a greater cranial capacity with more marked supra-orbital ridges and mastoid processes. The ridge at the upper rim of the auditory meatus is well marked in the male.

Sexing is required to help establish the sex ratio of a group. It is also of relevance to such questions as the degree of sexual dimorphism to be found in earlier specific populations.

It is easier to age an immature or young adult individual than a mature one. The older method of using the skull sutures has been shown to be unreliable and has largely been abandoned. Where feasible, teeth are the primary evidence used, as it has been possible to calculate the average age at which various teeth erupt and at which the stages of transformation from milk to permanent dentition occur. These age estimates are averages and there is considerable variability within populations. X-rays help in the study of the immature jaw. The post-cranial skeleton provides less satisfactory clues. The cartilagenous areas at the ends of every long-bone, known as the epiphyses, are used. Ossification of the epiphyses at first proceeds separately from the main bone. Between 12 and 25 years the epiphyses fuse with their various long-bones into single bones. The approximate age ranges at which such union occurs has been calculated for different bones; for example, it is complete by the age of 19 for the femur, tibia and fibula.

To carry ageing beyond early adulthood, observations can be made of changes at the face of the pubic symphysis.

Dental wear is dependent on how much mastication has occurred and how frequently abrasives were present in the food. Study of wear can help in age determination, as well as sometimes aiding the anthropologist to sort out from a jumble of teeth those belonging to the same individual on the basis of similar attrition patterns. Brothwell has tentatively worked out the degree of attrition to be expected at different age groups on the molar teeth of pre-medieval British skulls (Brothwell, 1965, 69). Wear-rates can be calculated by comparing the relative wear on the molars of immature individuals, as molars erupt at different and closely definable ages. Data from the pubic symphyses can be used to check estimates made from teeth.

Ageing is important in establishing mortality rates in populations. There seems to be a definite relationship between cultural level and average life expectancy. In the Upper Palaeolithic, only 2% of the population survived beyond 50, whilst over two-thirds lived to between 21 and 40. Another aspect of ageing is the age distribution in a society, which can have important effects. For example, excess of young males in a hunting band might lead to social fission and be a mechanism of diffusion of material culture.

Stature increases with adulthood and decreases with senility. Within a population there is much variability, even though the overall distribution is normal. There is some distinction in the mean stature of populations, although the overlaps are considerable. Male average height is greater than female in all groups. Height is generally genetically linked, but environment can be a modifying influence.

There is no fully satisfactory method for estimating stature. The most reliable way is to measure a complete long-bone, particularly the femur, and then apply the appropriate regression equation which has been calculated by various anthropologists for different populations in order to estimate stature. The most commonly used equations are those of Trotter and Gleser (Brothwell, 1965, 103). The normal practice is to calculate the stature from a number of different long-bones and to use the mean.

It should be borne in mind that stature is to be considered in two divisions: the axial (i.e. the head and trunk) and the lower limb length. The proportion of one to the other varies within a population. The ratio of the femoral length to the tibio-fibula length also varies.

It is worth re-emphasising the difficulty of the isolated specimen. Single finds should certainly be recorded fully, but they cannot be used in syntheses except in conjunction with individuals of the same population. A particular abuse of the past is the claim of racial affinities based on one example. More serious because it is more difficult to avoid is the continuing terminological battle that rages over specimens of early hominids in relation to their evolutionary status. Whole specific differences could be erected here on the basis of nothing more than within-population morphological variability.

Certain rather unusual bone features can be used to suggest that groups of bodies found closely associated in, say, the same megalithic tomb belong to the same family group. Five of the Roman skeletons found at the Arbury Road, Cambridge, showed sacralisation of the fifth lumbar vertebra, which is strongly suggestive of some family link between them. The possession of a long lower jaw and a stunted upper one was a notable trait of the Hapsburg dynasty from the fourteenth to the eighteenth centuries.

Some idea of the diet of ancient man can be gained from the study of bones. Differences in the patterns of teeth wear and decay between two groups might indicate dietary differences. The presence of grist in milled corn contributes markedly to teeth attrition. The absence of vitamin D in a diet can lead to rickets in children.

Rickets leaves bones abnormally light and brittle in texture and there is distortion of the leg bones, seen as knock knees and bow leggedness. Examples of rickets have been found in ancient Nubian cemeteries. Osteomalacia, found in adults and similar to rickets, is attested in Peruvian cemeteries.

Bone-breaking accidents are detectable in skeletal material, but the majority of the injuries noted on ancient bones come from intentional violence. A study of the nature of the injury can suggest the type of weapon used and therefore imply the form of the attack. It is usually possible to decide whether the injury was serious enough to have directly or indirectly caused death. The way that the wound healed may suggest doctoring —for example, the use of splints.

If large boulders or clubs were used, extensive fracturing is to be expected, with a depression from which marked cracks radiate. The use of less powerful clubbing weapons produces correspondingly less marked fractures. Perforations are caused by missiles, arrows or spears, or by pointed thrusting weapons. A metal sword or axe which slashes and cuts leaves marked incisions, often very deep, in the bone.

Care must be taken so as not to confuse accidental damage by the excavator or post-mortem fracturing with pre-mortem injury.

It has been claimed that if a greater degree of iron-based staining occurs near an injury this is due to blood-staining prior to death.

Trepanning was very widely practised in the ancient world. The operation involves making incisions into the cranial bones and removing a plate of bone. The classic cases come from Peru, but there are about a dozen confirmed cases from Britain. The reason for the operation is not certain, but in Peru it seems to have been undertaken to relieve pressure on the brain caused by a fractured skull. In other areas, such as Africa, it seems that roundels of human skull bones were sought as religious amulets and a prehistoric example comes from Crichel Down, Dorset.

The usual method of trepanning was to scour an annular groove on the skull to detach a roundel. Peruvian practice was to cut out a rectangular patch by four deep cuts into the bone. More than 50% of known examples show healing.

Openings in the skull can occur for other reasons, including sword slashes, rodent activity, syphilis, disturbance by excavators or grave robbers.

Head deformation was most widely practised in the

Americas. The skull growth of a baby was deliberately constricted by attaching two flat boards to the top and back of the head. Pre-Inca Peruvian and Mayan skulls provide particularly good examples of this practice. There are some Neolithic deformed skulls from Europe.

Tooth evulsion, the deliberate knocking out of teeth, was practised by some peoples, such as the Mesolithic inhabitants of north-western Africa. The incisors were usually chosen.

Examples of post-mortem decoration of skulls come from Mexico and New Zealand.

Various diseases can be detected through malformation of bones. Osteitis, inflammation causing thickening of the bone, is frequently met with, but it is often not possible to attribute it to a specific cause. When it affects the outer bone only, it is termed periostitis and when it affects the inner tissue, osteomyelitis. Osteomyelitis is known from the Neolithic.

Tuberculosis causes the disintegration of bone, especially in the thoracic and lumbar sectors of the spine, leading to a markedly hump-backed stance. The best evidence has come from Egyptian mummies, but the illness is also recorded in French prehistoric material.

Syphilis leads to the erosion of the vault of the skull, severe decay in the nasal area and bowing of the tibia. There is no definite example from the European prehistoric, but there are pre-Columbian cases in the Americas, although it is not certain that it originated there.

Leprosy was a well-known disease in early historic times and is referred to in the Bible. The bone changes include the degeneration of the bones of the hand and foot. The detailed effects of leprosy have been studied on remains from the Naestved Leper Hospital, a medieval sanatorium in Denmark. Leprosy was probably introduced into Britain by the Romans.

Yaws causes bowing and deformation of the lower leg and lower arm bones. Thickening of bone occurs. Depressed scars are formed on the skull and the face is progressively destroyed.

Ivory osteomata is the most frequently occurring bone tumour. Growths of compact bone are found, usually on the

cranium. Osteosarcoma, a malignant disease, has been attested
on Egyptian bones of the fifth dynasty and at the Munsingen
Iron Age cemetery. Multiple myeloma affects the spine particularly but also the humerus and the femur. Many tumours are
formed and perforations of the bone occur, particularly in the
skull. Examples can be found in the French Neolithic and the
prehistoric Americas.

Arthritis has been present in hominid populations since
Neanderthal man at least. It is attested for Cromagnon man
and was common in the Neolithic. Among the ancient Egyp-
tians it was the main disease. There are two main kinds of
arthritis. The first is rheumatoid arthritis, which is noticeable
mainly at the joints of the hands and feet where there is a decrease in joint spacing, bony 'lipping' and sometimes fusion.
The second kind is osteo-arthritis, which affects the middle-
aged and old. Bony 'lipping' is always present and decrease in
joint spacing common. The major joints usually suffer, for
example the head of the femur is distorted. The spine is the
most commonly affected part. Vertebrae develop lipping and
occasionally fusion of some of them occurs.

Just as modern man, ancient peoples suffered from dental
diseases. The frequency of disease seems to have been definitely lower in the earlier periods than at present, and this
seems to be linked with dietary changes. A diet derived from
hunting, fishing and gathering causes less decay than one in-
corporating refined flours and sugars.

Dental caries are found as early as *Australopithecus*. The
general trend in Britain since the Neolithic is of a steady increase in the frequency of carious teeth. The increase is particularly noticeable in post-Saxon times.

Periodontal disease involves an infection of the alveolar
bone and the soft tissues of the mouth. The alveolar bone
recedes and the teeth become loosened and lost. It was very
common in early man and is, for example, noted on a Neander-
thaler from Krapina.

A chronic dental abscess often forms a hole inside the alveolar bone at the root tip of a tooth. Abscess formations are

known from the Mount Carmel Neanderthalers and from Rhodesian man. The frequency of their occurrence differs between populations. Over half the skulls of the Pueblo Zuni Indians of south-western USA exhibited abscesses, whereas the incidence among British material of all periods is slight.

Inadequate development of the teeth, termed hypoplasia, which commonly takes the form of defects in the enamel, arises from either dietary failures or childhood illness such as scarlet fever. Hypoplasia has been found in *Australopithecus robustus*.

Poliomyelitis is not well attested in ancient material, but examples of reduced limbs might be attributable to it. Dysplasia, distortion of the hip joint, is a congenital disorder known in skeletons from Peru, Egypt and Neolithic France.

Malfunctioning of the pituitary gland gives rise to growth disorders which are reflected in skeletal material. Gigantism occurs during youth, whilst acromegaly is gigantism resulting from renewed growth in the adult. Pituitary dwarfs suffer from hormone deficiency. Their limbs are correctly proportioned, the abnormality being one of scale.

Paget's disease develops in the elderly. The pelvis, femur, tibia, skull and lower spine are affected by thickening of the bone. The long-bones are prone to bowing. The only definite ancient example comes from Neolithic France.

A number of abnormal conditions arise for genetical reasons. The usual type of dwarf is termed achondroplastic. Typical features of this dwarf are short legs, bones that are thick in relation to their length, a large head relative to the size of the face and stubby hands. Hydrocephaly, or 'water-on-the-brain', develops in very young children resulting in an enlarged cranium. There is a Roman example from Norton in Yorkshire.

Acrocephaly results from distorted growth at the coronal suture such that the cranial vault is very tall and brachycephalic. Early Dynastic Egypt has yielded a number of specimens. Any tiny-headed person can be described as microcephalic, although the condition can arise from a number of causes. An example of an idiot microcephalic is known from among multiple interments of the tenth century AD at Donnybrook, near Dublin, Eire.

A few abnormalities of skull shape may be mentioned. With scaphocephaly, the skull is markedly dolichocephalic because of arrested development of the sagittal suture. In trigonocephaly, the frontal bone is very restricted over the orbits. Plagiocephaly is the asymmetric growth of the cranium. The above three conditions derive mainly from unusual suture development.

Brothwell (1965), from whom much of the preceding section has been derived, concludes his discussion of skeletal pathology with the important advice that the archaeologist must be careful not to jump to conclusions about apparent deformities in bones that he finds. A number of post-depositional factors can cause distortions, such as the falling out of articulation of long-bones, the warping of the vertebral column, pressure exerted on the skull and chemical corrosion of the bones (Brothwell, 1965, 170).

It is possible with suitable specimens preserved under favourable soil conditions to use bones to identify the blood group of the deceased. There are many difficulties in doing this, such as the possibility that the type could actually change within the buried bone. Often the activity level of the blood group is so low that its type cannot be determined. After only four years' burial at Overton Down Experimental Earthwork, the bone specimens exhibited markedly lessened activity (Garlick, 1969, 507–8). The ABO antigens are those usually recognised, and it is very rare to detect Rh or MN antigens. Similar reactions to tests for blood groups can be caused by chemical conditions in the burial environment and complicated procedures are required to separate these.

If it is intended to undertake blood-group analysis, the bone selected should not be treated with preservatives before testing.

Special problems are presented to the anthropologist by cremations. Many societies have burnt, and still do burn, their dead. Cremation in a pottery or glass vessel was the standard rite in Roman Britain during the first and second centuries AD. It changed to inhumation during the later second century, with Christian ideas reinforcing the practice in the fourth century.

The amount of information that can be obtained is dependent on the state in which the bones survive. If burning was highly efficient or pre-cremation crushing particularly thorough, then little might remain.

Nils-Gustaf Gejvall of the Osteological Research Laboratory, Ulriksdal, Solna, who has made a special study of the problems of cremations, sees experience, a study at a modern crematorium of the way in which burning proceeds and a comparative study of ancient and modern cremated bone, as the key to extracting the maximum data from these burials (Gejvall, 1969).

Where multiple burials are encountered, in order to gauge the number of individuals present it is necessary to look for bones that occur in the body singly or in pairs. In ageing, teeth are the most valuable evidence as they have a high rate of survival.

Sexing is a much more difficult job. Gejvall has developed a method to deal with the problem, but even with this he calculates that 20% of the adults will be unsexable because they are morphologically intermediate or the diagnostic bones are lost. Gejvall's method rests on the observation that the wall thickness of bone is consistently less in females. Measurements are taken on the skull vault, the centre of the femur shafts and at the head and centre of the humerus. For dealing with a prehistoric group, take the average thickness for various points obtained on those examples that can be grouped into male or female on purely morphological grounds and then compare unassigned individuals to these figures.

Animal remains: Bone—non-human

Since the Second World War, the importance of studying the faunal remains on archaeological sites has been universally

recognised. Detailed analysis is for the specialist, but the excavator must, as with human bones, be aware of the significance
of this material. The most obvious value of the study is the
light thrown on man's utilisation of animal food resources.
Animals were also sources of clothing, transport, shelter,
lighting and warmth—not to mention companionship. Animal
remains also provide evidence of man's floral and climatic
environment. Some of these aspects are discussed in more
detail below.

Books by Cornwall (1968), Ryder (1968) and others are
available to help the fieldworker to identify bones. If possible,
access to a collection of labelled bones should be obtained and
the material studied at first hand. Unstratified bones from a
site can form the basis of a private reference collection, which
could be supplemented from the butcher's or by hunting—
although this author is strongly opposed in principle to the
latter method.

On site all stratified bone should be retained, however small.
It should be accorded the same treatment in respect of recording as any other find. It is not normal to record bone positions
in any greater precision than the layer context. Occasionally,
drawing and recording *in situ* is required—for example, of a
sacrificial deposit of a joint of meat, a joint accompanying the
dead or a foundation deposit. Stratified bone should only be
discarded after expert advice has established it as totally useless
in analysis. To destroy evidence through ignorance is inexcus-
able if it is avoidable. Many analyses depend on quantification,
which can be upset by disposal.

The primary study procedure is identification. This usually
proceeds by a process of elimination which becomes less explicit the more expert the worker is. The first step is to identify
the part of the skeleton from which the bone comes. To help
in this a 'key' to decisive attributes has been published by
Cornwall (1968, 185–91). The second stage is to limit the
possibilities by taking account of the size of the bone. By use
of comparative morphology it should then be possible to assign the specimen to an order. The final step sees the bone

assigned to a species often on the basis of size differentials within families. The inexperienced worker will then be wise to compare his identification with material from a labelled collection including specimens not thought to belong to the species identified. Sometimes there is considerable uncertainty in assigning a bone below family level, for example in the case of a large dog and wolf or that of sheep and goats. In the latter case Boessneck has recently discussed the detailed skeletal differences between the two (Boessneck, 1969).

Within each species, for each separate period attempts will be made to calculate the number of individuals present and the sex and age at death of those animals. Counting individuals is done on the basis of identifying both bones that occur either singly or in pairs in the body.

I. A. Silver has published an important contribution on the ageing of domestic animals, and his tables should be consulted (Silver, 1969). Archaeological conditions are rarely such that all the requirements for precise ageing are met. To do this we need to know the ageing characteristics of the species being studied and its plane of nutrition, to possess nearly all its teeth and several critical bones, and to be sure that it died before being fully grown. However, certain standard methods do guarantee a workable level of accuracy. For bones, age can be assessed from the degree of epiphysial fusion that has taken place. The ages at which ossification has occurred at various centres in the different bones has been calculated for the domestic species. These are available in Silver's article (1969, 285–6). Similarly, the eruption dates for the teeth of various animals have also been computed. Heavy wear is usually a sign of old age. Other general indicators of age are the 'greenstick' fracture which is found only in young beasts and arthritis which characterises the middle-aged and old. Horn exhibits annual growth rings.

Sex determination is carried out on the basis of the size differences that exist between male and female. In order to be able to set confidence limits to any assignation, it is necessary to have a good sample of a single population so that the degree of overlap in size between the sexes is known. Higham and Message have worked out a method of sexing cattle which is discussed below (Higham and Message, 1969).

After this work has been completed, the zoologist will be able to prepare a set of tables which show for each period the relative frequency of occurrence of different species and their distribution by age and sex. This tabulation, in conjunction with metrical tables for individual bones by species, forms the basis for the real analyses.

There are many questions that can be asked of such evidence and only a few can be mentioned here. Some are restricted to particular time periods. In this category falls the specialised study of Pleistocene mammalian remains for the purpose of understanding the processes at work in the evolution of *Homo sapiens*.

An ongoing study of fundamental importance to our understanding of the development of civilisations is that of the processes involved in the development of economies in which domesticated animals played an important part (Herre, 1969). Bone studies provide the basic data. In early bone material it is very difficult to differentiate wild from domestic forms. Many economically significant changes wrought by domestication are not evident osteologically—for example, sheep's wool, the increased output of hens' eggs and the increased milk yield of the cow. The sort of transformations that do occur may be illustrated from the case of the dog. The animal undergoes a general decrease in size. Its jaw is shortened but retains its width so that the teeth become crowded. The teeth also become smaller, with changes to the cusp pattern. The presence of periodontal disease caused by a soft diet probably indicates that the specimen was domestic and not wild (Clutton-Brock, 1969).

It is clear that the transformations involved in domestication take place within a single breeding community (species) and it is human interference that is the moving force, not natural selection (Herre, 1969).

Archaeological manifestations of domestication differ. The

relative frequency of species at a site can vary between hunters and owners of herds. A few species only are likely to be represented in quantity in the domesticated situation, whilst most hunting communities take a greater range of game.

The surest clues come from skeletal morphology which has undergone changes with domestication. To assess these alterations it is necessary to have a full acquaintance with the wild species from which the domesticates derive. The modern domestic beasts show more variation in their skeletons than their wild ancestors. In assessing differences in the early periods a large sample of the two populations, wild and domestic, is required to compare variability.

A decrease in size which initiates form changes is a common concomitant of domestication. This can arise from other causes too, such as sex differences or dietary deficiencies. Przewalski's horse, the wild ancestor of the modern breed, is about 140 cm at the withers. Iron Age horses had reduced to between 120 and 130 cm. In the Middle Ages the process of size reduction was reversed for some breeds, such as the war horses which could attain 160 cm at the withers (Herre, 1969, 269).

Present evidence favours the view that domestication was a process that occurred over a long period of time at a large number of places throughout the Middle East and Southeast Europe and independently in Central and Southern America. The idea of diffusion from a single source must be discarded.

The following broad dates can be regarded as *termini ante quem* for the primary domestication of the animals mentioned: *c.* 9000 BC, sheep (goats soon after); 6500 BC, pigs; 5000–4000 BC, cattle; 4000–3000 BC, horses. The dog was the oldest domesticated animal in Central Europe, where cattle and pigs were probably domesticated later than in the Middle East (*ibid.* 265–6).

For all periods, bones are primary evidence of the subsistence economy of a site. A study of the frequency of occurrence of species will show whether the group drew its meat supply from domestic herds or from hunting. The preponderance of a species in either case will be evidence of specialisation. It should be stressed that bones give direct indications only of consumption habits, not necessarily (in a sedentary community) of the actual emphasis in agriculture. Detailed examination of bones, particularly a count of the parts most commonly found, will inform on butchery practices. Ageing studies might show a preference for killing young animals and thus indicate a practice of autumn slaughter. The presence of quantities of non-mammalian bones will show the use of other sources of protein.

Many groups practised seasonal movements from site to site, exploiting a variety of ecological niches. Bone and other animal remains can indicate seasonal occupation. Some examples are given later.

A good example of a study of ancient husbandry is provided by the work of Higham and Message (1969). By comparing statistically the metrical characteristics of the metacarpal and radius in breeds of modern cattle and in a collection of bones from the Danish prehistoric settlement of Troldebjerg (end of the third millennium) they have been able to distinguish between male and female bones at the site. Ageing by means of examining the degree of epiphysial fusion of certain bones allowed the comparison of the mortality patterns of males and females.

This revealed valuable information about the kind of bovine husbandry practised at the site. For example, it is clear that the inhabitants were expert at overwintering their stock by providing adequate fodder. Meat production was the main economic objective and steers were kept until they were 3 or 4 years old and had achieved almost maximum body weight. Cows seem to have been kept longer to supply milk and for breeding. A few bulls were also supported for breeding. This sketch should give some idea of the potential of further work of this sort.

Animal species are often closely related in their distributions to particular climatic and vegetational zones. Habitat ranges of ancient animals can be gauged from their modern representatives, although changes have occurred. The range of the lion, for example, is now restricted to sub-Saharan Africa but was much broader in the ancient world. Given this limitation it is nevertheless possible to indicate the general environment of a site from its faunal remains and in a region chart environmental change through transformations in local faunal assemblages. It should be remembered that man has had the most profound effect on animal populations, and changes in assemblages can arise entirely from human causes.

Where faunal assemblages have been correlated with particular Pleistocene stratigraphies and absolute dates have been assigned to those deposits, further finds of similar assemblages can be used to date a site in the absence of other means or in conjunction with them. Kurtén suggests that a fauna can be placed in its approximate chronological position according to the percentage of modern types present; the less present, the older the assemblage. This is based on the assumption of a constant rate for the emergence of a new species. The assumption of constancy needs demonstration. This is a weakness of all chronometric systems based on rate estimates (Kurtén, 1969, 255).

The excavator might encounter animal remains in two other situations. The first is the pet relationship, a symbiosis peculiar to man, and the second is that of pests such as mice or rats.

Tools and ornaments of bone are fairly common in ancient societies, and it is instructive if the source of the raw material can be defined and its degree and range of utilisation assessed.

Finally, it should be remembered that, as excavators, the archaeologists are digging up material that is of potential interest to other disciplines, particularly zoology. Maximum co-operation is best achieved on the basis of a joint programme.

Animals, no less than humans, suffer from disease; osteological evidence can help trace the history of particular afflictions. Also, occasionally, the presence of disease will indicate environmental conditions. Presumably some diseases were

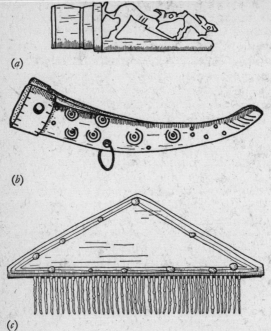

Fig. 10 Objects made from animal bone: (*a*) bone knife handle from Great Chesterford, Romano-British; (*b*) clasp-knife handle, Romano-British; (*c*) bone comb from Great Chesterford, Romano-British (partly reconstructed); *Cambridge MAE*

carried by other animals prior to the emergence of modern man and their origins may be discoverable. Particularly common disorders for which there is evidence among ancient animal remains include fractures, periostitis, osteomyelitis and arthritis. For example, the European cave-bear seems to have commonly suffered from osteo-arthritis (Brothwell, 1969a).

It is worth making the point that fossil bone and ancient bone are not the same thing. Most bone on sites is unmodified except for the effects of decay in the ground. Fossil bone has undergone certain definite alterations, including the decay of its organic structure and the substitution of minerals from the ground water for the organic elements.

Before looking at various analytical techniques that aid jointly the study of human and animal bone, this is a convenient place to examine the information that can be derived from the study of non-mammalian remains.

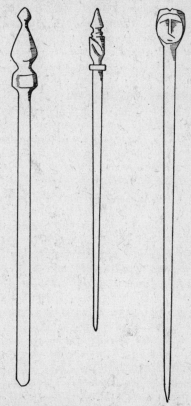

Fig. 11 Bone pins from Great Chesterford, Romano-British; *CMAE*

Birds
(Source: Dawson, 1969.)

The study of birds has been neglected in archaeology except in countries such as New Zealand, where the economic subsistence of the Maoris was at one period dominated by the hunting of the now extinct Moa. Bird remains comprise bones, feathers, mummies, shell and droppings.

Bird bones are treated in the same manner as other animal bones, i.e. by identification and tabulation of the relative frequencies of species present. It is not always easy to assign bones to species. The species table can be compared with the modern bird lists and the degree of and reasons for differences assessed. Present-day distributions and migrations of species can be a guide to whether the site was seasonally rather than permanently occupied. Distributions have been modified through time—for example, the Dalmatian pelican is known from Iron Age Glastonbury, but it has been possible with a high degree of probability to demonstrate seasonality. Occupation at the Upper Palaeolithic site of Meiendorf in north Germany was thought on the basis of the bones of hunted reindeer to be confined to the summer, and the avifauna of tundra species confirmed this. On the other hand, the bird bones from the Emeryville shellmound, San Francisco Bay, California, were used to show that the site was held all year round. As a corollary to using birds to indicate seasonal occupation, the same species can be taken to show climatic conditions.

Some birds were of ritual importance to various peoples. The vulture was held sacred by the Romans and a sacrificed bird is recorded from the Forum dating to the sixth or seventh century BC.

Bird bones were used for artefacts. Awls, needles and spearpoints were made by the Maori from Moa bones. Eggshells, particularly ostrich, have been used for ornaments such as beads among the Bushmen. Feathers were gathered for ornamentation and ceremonial dress, especially in the tropical forest areas, and exchanged over considerable distances with peoples outside that zone, for example in ancient Peru. Guano was an important fertiliser used in cultivation plots in the arid valleys of coastal Peru. Mummies of birds were made in ancient Egypt (Dawson, 1969).

Fish
(Source: Ryder, 1969a.)

Man has made use of the resources of the rivers and sea from earliest times. The Neanderthalers of Gibraltar consumed large numbers of limpets and mussels, and early hominids in Africa are known to have eaten catfish.

From the class of cartilaginous fishes (Chondrichthyes) such as sharks, skates and rays only the teeth and denticles are usually preserved. The bony fishes (Osteichthyes) are represented by their bones, but these are often so slight as to be easily missed, although sieving techniques can overcome this. Even then identification often cannot be carried as far as the species, especially if the bones are mainly vertebrae, because it is the skull that varies most between species.

The most familiar order containing all the common fish is the Teleostei. The scales of these fishes exhibit growth rings. During spring and summer with the fast rate of growth multiple rings are developed, but with the decline in the growth rate in winter less rings are formed and they crowd together in a zone marking the end of the annual growth. The age of a fish can be derived from these rings.

Otoliths (earstones) are small lumps of free calcium carbonate in the ear. These also have annual growth rings which are definitely the same age as the fish as they are not subject to differential growth in the way that scales can be. Some otoliths are peculiar to certain species. Otoliths may indicate fish in the absence of other evidence.

Some of the bones also have growth rings, often of microscopic proportions. For example, half-yearly rings occur on the horny plugs of the whale's ear.

Fish remains inform us in a number of ways. First, fish is a high protein source and has been important in the diet of various communities. The degree of importance of fish can be studied by comparing the relative food values represented by bones of fish and other animals at a site. The source of the fish, freshwater or marine, might indicate the technology and amount of organisation involved in procuring it, including exchange mechanisms. Study of the species present might show that only seasonal fishing was practised. There is a suggestion that Magdalenians (Upper Palaeolithic, Dordogne, France) migrated seasonally to catch salmon. Exploiting the salmon run was of great importance in the economy of several tribes of the north-west coast of America. Fishes can also give indications of local environments, particularly of changes. Finally, it is worth keeping in mind the many ingenious, and often very complex, specialised tool kits that have been developed in various societies, such as the Eskimo, in order to catch fish.

Besides fish and molluscs, which are dealt with below, man has also exploited other aquatic animals such as whales, seals, sea-lions, walruses, dolphins, dugongs, beavers, otters, turtles, frogs and newts (Ryder, 1969a).

Molluscs
(Sources: Meighan, 1969; Shackleton, 1969; Biggs, 1969.)

Shell middens are a special category of archaeological site found on the coasts of many countries throughout the world. They consist in varying degrees of the remains of marine molluscs which were consumed as food. The detailed examination of the shell refuse can yield considerable data on economy, environment and dating.

Meighan (1969) describes a standardised procedure for sampling from a midden. Such selection is made necessary by the sheer quantity of shells that can be present. Firstly, between fifteen and twenty samples weighing 2 or 3 kg each are taken from the section faces of a trench. If this is not possible, cores

Fieldwalking. Plotting a flint scatter prior to excavation.

Above: General view of modern area excavation with soil marks visible. *Below:* Area excavation in progress.

Above: Structure. Post holes and pit showing as soil marks prior to excavation. *Below:* Same structure after excavation.

Planning using a drawing frame.

Above: Quadrant excavation of pit. *Below:* Structure after excavation with wall and partition trenches for timber walls.

Post hole after excavation.

Horizontal timber trace, partially excavated.

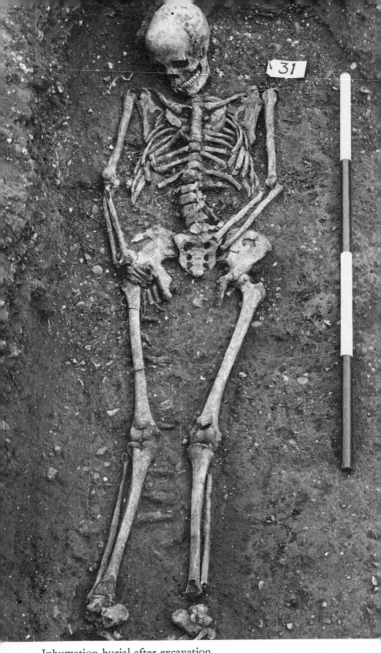

Inhumation burial after excavation.

are extracted with an auger. The sample is then screened and only material retained by a ¼-inch (6-mm) mesh is regarded for analysis. This is washed, and sorted according to its constituents. Meighan stresses the importance of analyses that recognise the importance of the other components of the mound as well as the shells. A simple weight preponderance of shell need not mean the same relative importance as a food supply. A hundred grams of clam shells have been estimated to have the same amount of edible meat as one gram of bird bone.

From an analysis of shells it should be possible to say what species were consumed, and in what absolute and relative quantities. The meat yield can be calculated for the average shell and if some idea of the rate of consumption can be gained, and provided that shellfish were the main food, then an informed guess at the population can be made.

Many of the middens were seasonally utilised places; or molluscs were only collected at certain times. Palaeotemperature analysis described below can help show this. Further, using modern distributions of species as a guide, the shells can indicate the sort of coastal environment existing at the time of capture.

Study of the size of the shells may reveal a preferred collecting size, and Shackleton (1969, 408) has made the interesting suggestion in connection with the site of Saliagos (Neolithic, Greece) that finds of groups of shells of smaller than average size may represent food shortages.

The shells should always be checked for signs of beach wear, which indicates that the molluscs were not taken alive.

Shells have been put to a variety of uses by man. Among the Hopewell Indians of prehistoric Illinois and Missouri, conch shells were made into vessels and mussels were utilised for hoes. Shells may have served as money among some groups and there is good evidence that shells figured in a widespread exchange network in the prehistoric south-west USA. An ancient and well-attested industry in the Near East was that of dye extraction from *Murex* shells. Axes and adzes of shell are found on the sites of Arawak Indians in the West Indies.

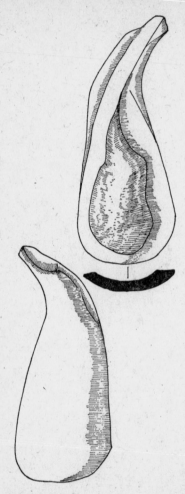

Fig. 12   Scoop; *CMAE*

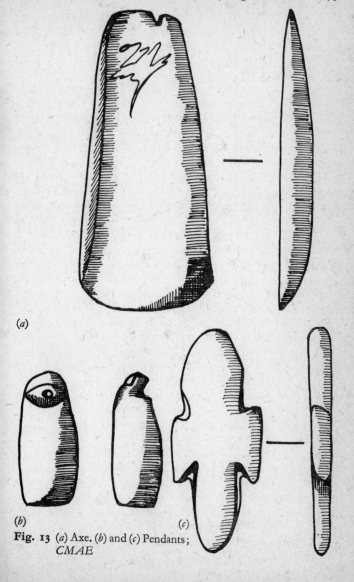

(a)

(b)   *(c)*

Fig. 13 *(a)* Axe. *(b)* and *(c)* Pendants;
CMAE

Trumpets, necklaces, pendants and bangles are among the many other artefacts made from this source (Biggs, 1969).

The temperature of ancient seawater can be obtained from the investigation of the isotopic composition of shells (Shackleton, 1969, 409–12). The value (δ-value) of the molecular ratio of the oxygen isotopes $^{18}O^{16}O/^{16}O_2$ for calcium carbonate which has been deposited from water by a mollusc is a function of the δ-value of the water and its temperature. If the δ-value of the carbonate, and of the water in which the carbonate was deposited, can be determined, then the water temperature is calculable by use of a standard formula. It had been assumed that the isotopic composition of the oceans was constant, but glaciation has been shown to have had the effect of making the seas appear colder than they actually were using the usual methods of estimating palaeotemperature. Because of this problem it is only strictly correct to use the estimate as showing relative, rather than actual, temperature values. Within this limitation stratified sequences of molluscs can be analysed and fluctuations in temperatures through time demonstrated. Air and sea temperatures seem to be closely correlated so that the information gained from marine molluscs can be validly applied to terrestrial conditions. The procedures have been used on material from the Haua Fteah cave (Cyrenaica); there the early Holocene rise in mean temperatures and the temperature maximum between 4500 and 2500 BC were both detectable (Shackleton, 1969, 410).

The variations of temperature according to season are preserved in the layers of the shell and it is thus possible to say at what season a mollusc died, and hence at what time of year it was collected.

A relative dating method for South African middens composed of *Mytilus perna* shells has been developed. The ratio of conchyolin to calcium carbonate in the shell decreases the older the shell is. Providing two mounds are on the same soils, it is possible to assign them chronological positions relative to each other (Ryder, 1969a, 393).

The radiocarbon method, which is described in detail elsewhere in this book, is applicable to shells. Carbon from the carbonate of the shell has been used for determinations, but this is subject to contamination with modern carbon. If possible, it is preferable to use the conchyolin or organic part of the shell because of its chemical stability. Normal carbon 14 analysis procedures are used once the calcium carbonate has been removed with acid.

Non-marine molluscs (source: Sparks, 1969) belong to another class of animal remains that can be used in dating and environmental reconstruction. The preservation of the shells depends on the chemical composition of the soil and the ground water conditions. The animals usually like lime-rich environments, such as the chalklands, where material for shell-building is available and are rarely found on non-calcareous soils. Molluscs are common and widespread, and less prone to human disturbance than other animals. This, combined with the probability that modern distributions in habitats for the various species do not seriously differ from the ancient, means that molluscs are useful for reconstruction.

The use of assemblages of molluscs as dating tools for the Pleistocene has been attempted but with very limited success. Occasionally it is possible to use certain species as giving a general indication of age; for example, in Britain, *Helix pomatia* and *Helix aspersa* in a deposit suggest a Roman or post-Roman date.

Molluscs are most use in indicating microenvironmental conditions. Sparks, a leading British expert, recognises four ecological groupings of freshwater snails: (1) slum species—those from inadequate water conditions; (2) catholic species—found in virtually all conditions; (3) ditch species—found in sluggish water with much vegetation; (4) moving-water species—from more open water. Land snails can be grouped into species of the marsh, woods and open lands (Sparks, 1969, 404–5). If the whole faunal assemblage of a deposit contains relatively more species characteristic of one of these groups than another, then it may be assumed that the local conditions approximated to those of the group. Such an

approach is of broader application than the alternative of looking for marker species, i.e. those species among a larger collection that are known to have only very restricted ranges.

This total approach to an assemblage is equally applicable to
the use of snails to indicate climate. A similar procedure to the
ecological with regard to the study of Pleistocene climatic
conditions and change is employed based on four distributional groups of species found in modern Scandinavia. These
groups are: (1) those found as far north as the Arctic circle;
(2) those found to *c.* 63°N; (3) those found to 60–1°N; (4)
those found only in south Scandinavia or in continental
Europe (Sparks, 1969, 403).

Archaeologists are in a position to help malacologists in
their studies of the history and ancient distributions of snails
by providing collections from relatively well-dated deposits,
and the feedback of increased knowledge is in turn of use to
archaeology.

Microscopy and X-rays

The microscope and X-rays are indispensable in the study of
ancient bones. More detailed discussion of the microscope is
reserved for the sections on artefacts. Microscopic analysis of
small bone fragments may allow assignation to species when
macroscopic analysis cannot. This should warn the archaeologist not to discard any material too quickly. It is worth men-
tioning here a development to which Brothwell has drawn
attention: the use of the scanning electron microscope (Brothwell, 1969b). Its use is not limited to bones alone. The microscope uses an electron probe to scan solid materials unsuitable
for investigation by the standard electron microscope. By this
means calcification processes can be studied, pathological
structures identified and bone picked out of unidentified
aggregates. Detailed examination of the structure of teeth and
features such as attrition can be made. The wear on artefacts,
the constituents of coprolites and the structure of hair are
other aspects that are studied. The scanning instrument ex-

tends the range of the standard work carried out by microscope on bone in the spheres outlined previously.

In the study of bones, X-rays make their main contribution in the field of ancient pathology. For example, healed fractures can be identified and there are radiographic differences in the structure of the bones of animals suffering from a deficient diet. Many of the diseases suffered by man and animal can be studied in more detail using X-rays. The teeth, as in modern dentistry, are examined by X-ray. This is important for study of eruption sequences and for taxonomic purposes in fossil hominids.

Fossilised material is often heavily mineralised and X-ray photography of it is difficult. Nevertheless, it is now the standard practice. The fossil is photographed from a number of different directions and at a set distance from the X-ray head to facilitate comparability. Stereoscopic radiography can be conducted on skulls. Age can be estimated from X-rays that show the amount of development of the frontal sinuses (Ascenzi, 1969).

Relative dating
(Source: Oakley, 1969.)

The fluorine test, the nitrogen test and the uranium test are all techniques that can be used on bone to establish that the specimen is contemporary with the layer from which it has come. The methods are for *relative dating*, not for assigning dates in years.

Bones and teeth buried in permeable deposits undergo a weightless change in their phosphatic composition and in most ground-water percolation conditions gradually accumulate fluorine ions, which become fixed in the bone. Fluorine accumulation is variable between different deposits, but bones of the same date and buried in the same deposit should contain roughly the same quantity of fluorine. Thus, if two bones supposedly contemporary with each other and with the deposit in which they were found are compared and found to differ markedly in their relative fluorine contents, there is good reason to suspect that the apparent association has arisen through intrusion, redeposition or fraud. By using this method it was shown that the Galley Hill skeleton found deep in gravels near Swanscombe and claimed as the remains of a Pleistocene hominid was, in fact, a much more recent burial.

The organic content of bone decays in the ground. The fats disappear quickly, but the structural protein, collagen, has been known to have been preserved in animals of Pleistocene age (for example, the woolly rhinoceros from Leadenhall Street, London). Bones deposited under similar conditions are known to lose their protein gradually but steadily. It is therefore possible to assess the relative ages of material from the same site on the basis of the amount of residual organic matter, particularly nitrogen, present. Whereas the amount of fluorine present in bone increases with age, the amount of nitrogen decreases. As over 90% of the nitrogen in bone is within the collagen, the nitrogen tests are really tests for residual protein, particularly as non-collagen nitrogen tends to disappear rapidly. There is some variation in the nitrogen content of bone during the lifetime of an animal, there being more nitrogen in young bones.

The Kjeldahl Method is the usual nitrogen test. In it, organic nitrogen is converted to ammonium sulphate and the quantity determined through the measurement of ammonia released by an alkali. The older method was the Dumas Method, which although more powerful was less rapid. By it, the nitrogen is converted to gas and direct measurement made (Garlick, 1969).

Nitrogen tests were run on the Galley Hill skeleton in an attempt to confirm the results for the fluorine test. This showed the expected relatively high quantity of nitrogen present when compared with fossil mammal bones from the Swanscombe gravels, consistent with the opinion that its position in the gravels was due to intrusive burial. Subsequent radiocarbon tests estimated an early Bronze Age date for the burial. As a more famous example, the combination of the fluorine and nitrogen tests helped expose the Piltdown forgery (Oakley, 1969; Weiner, Oakley, Le Gros Clark, 1953).

Bone in appropriate ground-water percolation conditions will also accumulate uranium in increasing quantities the longer it remains in the ground. There is a steady increase in the mean radioactivity of fossil bone with time despite the variability that exists between contemporaneous material from different locations. Bones and teeth of the same age at the same site should exhibit closely similar uranium contents. Thus the test can be used in a similar manner to the fluorine, with the advantage of not requiring the breaking up of the specimen. The uranium test suggests that *Gigantopithecus*, enormous fossil hominoid teeth from China, belong to a Middle Pleistocene horizon. The combined use of the three tests has led to the strongly based suggestion that the so-called sabre-toothed tiger survived in Britain into relatively late Pleistocene times (Oakley, 1969, 40 ff.).

Animal remains: Skin, etc.
(Sources: Sandison, 1969; Ryder, 1969b.)

The soft tissues of the body are rarely preserved in lands with temperate climates. The most frequent environments favourable to preservation are the waterlogged or the arid. Frozen conditions occasionally have the same effect as in the Iron Age barrows of the Altai Mountains. Many bodies have been preserved in the bogs of Denmark. Perhaps the most famous was that of the Iron Age Tollund Man who had been hanged to death. So beautifully preserved was the body that it was possible to examine the contents of his stomach and ascertain the nature of his last meal, a gruel (Glob, 1969).

Egyptian mummies (source: Sandison, 1969) have held a fascination for many years and been the unwitting source of much nonsense. They are very important scientific documents of the past and have been the subject of analysis by various techniques. Desiccated human skin can be rehydrated in various ways by using, for example, alcohols and formalin. In

examination normal staining methods can be used. Cell outlines and nuclei cannot normally be detected. Nerves, adipose
tissues, cartilage, tendon and bone are easily distinguished. It
is also possible to study blood vessels, hair follicles, sweat
glands and sebaceous glands. The bacteria present as the body
began to decay before mummification are regularly found and
have been mistaken for red blood cells.

Sandison (1969, 495 ff.) describes the procedure that is
followed in the investigation of a mummy. Before the object
is unwrapped X-rays are taken. This is capable of yielding
much information without unwrapping. First, it can verify
that there is indeed a body within the wrappings because some
examples obtained through dealers have been found to be
frauds. Both sex and age can be assessed and this checked to
see that it correlates with what the coffin inscriptions might
say. Lastly, small charms were often included in the bandages
and the positions of these can be identified.

Another important facet of X-raying is that it gives fore-
warning of the state of the body and so special unwrapping
techniques can be employed if necessary. As unravelling proceeds, much dust can be given off and protective clothing is
worn. The bottom layers are often stuck to the body surface
by resin and here care is required not to damage any skin preserved. At this stage a second set of X-rays might be taken to
increase detailed knowledge and the body is also photographed before further work. It is then possible to detach parts
for dissection which are first put in a rehydrating liquid. The
head often returns in a condition closer to real life. More photos
can be taken. The parts to undergo dissection are embedded in
paraffin blocks (having been decalcified if they contain bone).
Normal microtome methods are used for cutting.

The study of ancient disease has already been dealt with at
some length in the section on bones, but mummies are also
valuable in this study. Poliomyelitis, gout, leprosy, smallpox,
gallstones and anthracosis are among a number of complaints
diagnosed for mummies (Sandison, 1969, 497–8).

Microscopic study is essential for work on animal skin or on objects made from it. Specimens are softened, embedded in wax and then sectioned parallel to their surfaces. Details are brought out by staining. With samples mounted in this fashion it is possible to study the arrangement of hairs still in the skin. This method, described by Ryder (1969b), extends the possibilities of identifying the animal from which the skin came, a process which has previously been dependent on identifying the hairs that might survive above the surface. Leather has been assigned to species on the basis of its distinct surface patterns.

Sheep, as other mammals, have two types of hair follicle, termed primaries and secondaries. The secondaries are distinguished from the primaries by lacking sweat gland and erector muscle. The secondaries produce finer wool fibres, and the higher the ratio of secondary follicles to primaries, the finer the wool. There is an important distinction between the follicle disposition of domestic and wild sheep. The secondaries are usually between the primaries in the wild varieties, but since domestication they have come to lie on one side of the primaries, the primaries are smaller and the fibres produced are not as hairy. The study of the grouping of follicles combined with the examination of other characteristics of surviving hairs in skin remains can therefore help in the study of the progress of domestication of sheep and other animals, though the characteristics of these are less well known. It is also valuable in identifying the animal source of skin or parchment. For sheep, it is possible to find out what kind of wool was predominant on breeds at a particular period.

A very approximate method of dating parchment or leather is to extract collagen fibres from a specimen, heat them and observe at what temperature they start to shrink. The younger the sample, the higher the temperature will be within the range 25°C to 60°C. The temperature is then compared with those from specimens of known age (Ryder, 1969b, 543).

In staining procedures, vegetable tanned leather has been found to stain maroon, whilst untanned skin, such as parchment, stains blue-green like fresh skin.

Animal remains: Fibres
(Source: Ryder, 1969b.)

A detailed discussion of textiles is not possible in this book and this section only explains how fibres are studied. In temperate climates it is rare for textile or other fibre remains to survive unless they come from waterlogged deposits or have been in contact with the corrosion products of metals such as bronze. It is important to examine carefully objects such as brooches which may have tiny fragments of cloth attached.

Fibre specimens are often very small and delicate, requiring consolidation with substances such as polyvinyl acetate solution. Macroscopic features like the weave used can be studied by means of stereoscopic binoculars with low magnification. It is normal to make a whole mount of the fibre in liquid paraffin which enables the examination of differences in fibre thickness, the nature of the pigment present and the cuticular-scale patterns to be made. More detail can be obtained to aid identification by making a cross-section of the fibre with a hand micrometer. Cuticle thickness and medulla structure are better brought out.

The external margins of the cuticular scales are patterned in different ways in various animals and can therefore be used as a guide to identification. Casts are usually made of these scale patterns in polyvinyl acetate.

The microscope is essential in all identification procedures. With it, it is possible to differentiate between families and species but more difficult to distinguish subspecies. Using Ryder's methods mentioned above, it is possible to subdivide sheep on the basis of fibre types.

Radiocarbon dating
(Sources: Libby, 1955; Renfrew, C., 1973.)

The technique of radiocarbon dating can be applied to the whole range of organic remains. Dating by this method is now the basis of prehistoric chronology. As will be seen, it is less useful for historic periods, for which a higher degree of accuracy can be obtained by traditional archaeological methods. In the Americas, Africa, Australia and the Pacific, the technique is valuable for all periods up to European contact and even beyond.

Radiocarbon (C_{14}), a radioactive isotope of carbon, is produced by cosmic ray bombardment of the earth's atmosphere. It combines with oxygen to form carbon dioxide and is thus universally distributed through the air and sea. All living objects take in C_{14} in the same ratio to ordinary carbon C_{12} as it exists in the atmosphere. When a plant or animal dies it ceases to take in radiocarbon and radioactive decay sets in. The proportion of C_{14} to C_{12} in the dead organism declines exponentially with time. The time taken for half the original radiocarbon content of an object to disintegrate (half-life) has been calculated variously. This half-life is a constant, as in life all organisms take in C_{14} and C_{12} in carbon dioxide in a constant proportion. Thus if we know the proportion of radiocarbon to ordinary carbon remaining in a sample, we can calculate the age since death. As the decline is exponential it should be remembered that if, say, one-eighth of the original amount remains, then the time elapsed since death is three times the half-life.

The amount of decay that has occurred can be assessed by measuring the intensity of beta radiation given off by the sample. This is greater the more C_{14} there is present. Objects over 70 000 years old give off very weak radiation that cannot be accurately measured. Modern methods of determining age are highly sophisticated and require relatively small amounts of sample (5 g is enough). The liquid scintillation counter operates by changing the sample into liquid form (benzene or methyl alcohol). This is mixed with another liquid which gives off a light signal every time an electron is emitted. Photomultipliers pick up the signal and it is registered electronically.

Background cosmic radiation is a major problem. Radiation particles do contaminate the readings and limit their accuracy despite all precautions. Fluctuations in the background radiation in the laboratory occur daily and therefore a series of readings, over say six months, is taken and at each measurement the reading usually varies slightly from the previous one. Thus the mean of a series of readings is published with the variability to one standard deviation stated. The normal form in which the date is published will be, for example, 3000 ± 300 BP, which means that there is considered to be statistically a 66% probability that the sample is dated between 2700 and 3300 BP. It is important to be aware of this probability statement as too many archaeologists have carelessly pinned important arguments on the central date only.

The half-life, although a constant, has not yet been accurately determined. An internationally agreed estimate is used for the publication of dates. Libby calculated a value of 5568 ± 30 in 1949 and this has been used in most estimates since then (Libby, 1955). Dates are stated as being BP—'before present', which is conventionally AD 1950. The half-life value was reassessed subsequent to Libby's work and the present accepted figure is 5730 ± 30, showing that there is a longer time before half a sample's radiocarbon has decayed than was first thought. Adjustments of dates BP can be made by multiplying by 1·03 (BC × 1·03 and add 66 years). At present all dates continue to be quoted using the Libby half-life to maintain a standard system. It must be remembered that the necessary conversions must be made to obtain estimates in calendar years.

It is of great importance to be sure that the surviving C14 to C12 ratio has only come about through radioactive decay. Ancient samples can be potentially affected by coming into contact with older carbon samples such as coal or recent material like roots, leading to the recording of artificially old or young dates respectively. Contamination during collection is another danger and great care should always be taken to eliminate potential threats.

In interpretation, it should be remembered that C14 samples are subject to all the customary rules of association which govern other archaeological objects.

Libby originally assumed that there was a constant, uniform distribution of radiocarbon throughout the earth's atmosphere. There is, due to the effects of the earth's magnetic field, variation with latitude such that the southern hemisphere samples tend to appear to be forty years older than contemporary samples in the northern hemisphere.

Another assumption that Libby made was that all living organisms contained the same proportion of C_{14} to C_{12} as is found in the atmosphere. Freshwater molluscs, however, are known to contain a rather lower proportion of radiocarbon. Some plants during photosynthesis seem reluctant to take in C_{14} from the atmosphere, so that they contain relatively less C_{14} to C_{12} than the atmosphere. This effect is known as isotopic fractionation. The effects of fractionation can be checked and adjustments made in estimates by an analysis of any variation from the normal level of C_{13} present in the sample.

Libby also assumed that the proportion of C_{14} to C_{12} in the atmosphere had remained constant during the past. However, there are a number of events that have influenced the distribution of atmospheric carbon dioxide, particularly the vast quantities of water that were added to the oceans with the abating of the Pleistocene ice-caps and the massive consumption of fossil fuels since the early nineteenth century. Coal deposits are extremely ancient and their radiocarbon content is very low. The burning of them has diluted the C_{14} content of the atmosphere, so that the ratio of C_{14} to C_{12} in the atmosphere has dropped by 3% over the last two centuries. Adjustments have therefore had to be made in assessing the activity of modern control samples.

Atomic weapons' testing releases large quantities of C_{14} into the atmosphere, changing the balance of C_{14} to C_{12} by increasing the C_{14} content relative to C_{12}.

Important recent dendrochronological work has revealed that the C_{14} to C_{12} ratio in the atmosphere has oscillated significantly through time and some startling archaeological results have become apparent.

The technique of radiocarbon dating was invented by Willard F. Libby in New York in 1949. The so-called 'first radiocarbon revolution' (Renfrew, C., 1973) had the important consequence of revealing the unthought-of antiquity of many crucial events in prehistory, such as the beginnings of agriculture in the Old World, which was suddenly moved back from the fifth millennium to at least the eighth millennium. Agriculturalism was shown to be definitely earlier in Anatolia, the Zagros and the Levant than in Egypt. The Upper Palaeolithic sequence was firmly dated for the first time and the Abbé Breuil was shown to have been too generous in his estimate of the antiquity of the cave paintings of France and Spain. The beginnings of the Neolithic of Britain, put at 2000 BC by Professor Piggott in 1954, were seen to lie in the fourth millennium BC. In non-European prehistory it provided a reliable chronometric framework for the first time and allowed valid cross-cultural comparisons to be made.

The 'second radiocarbon revolution' has had even more drastic results, since it destroys the standard idea that the movement of culturo-technological inspiration from the Near East to Europe was a constant feature of European prehistory.

One of the main assumptions of the radiocarbon method was that the concentration of radiocarbon in the atmosphere has remained constant through time. Recent dendrochronological work has shown that the concentration has varied a great deal through time. The concentration around 4000 BC was higher than at present, and therefore samples have more radiocarbon in them than predicted and consequently give a date which can be hundreds of years too young.

Bristlecone pine lives in the White Mountains of California. The oldest tree is 4900 years old. It has been possible to build for this tree a dendrochronological sequence going back nearly 8200 years. This has provided an excellent check on radiocarbon and shown fairly conclusively that before 2000 BC radiocarbon estimates are consistently too young as a result of differential concentrations of radiocarbon in the atmosphere at different times. The changing concentration is thought to have arisen from fluctuations in the strength of the earth's magnetic field, which affects the intensity of cosmic radiation reaching the earth.

Intensive laboratory work, especially by Professor Suess in California, has allowed the production of a chart which can be used to calibrate radiocarbon years in calendar years. Examination of the Suess calibration chart shows, firstly, how consistently the expected radiocarbon date deviates from the actual, the deviation increasing the older the sample; secondly, the main trend curve shows a whole series of smaller kinks which represent shorter term fluctuations. Calibration is simple using this chart except where kinks are encountered, for they may allow alternative dates to be chosen of over 200 years apart. It must be stressed that radiocarbon dates are quoted with their associated standard error, and this must not be overlooked in calibration. The calibration curve also has its own set of associated standard errors. The general effect seems to be to widen the range of the estimated standard errors, giving a rather less precise value to the calibrated dates. This does not detract from the fact that radiocarbon dates are too young and need readjusting. One or two objections have been raised to the tree-ring evidence. The first is that it is possible that the radiocarbon composition of the wood has been contaminated by the recent sap of the tree. This does not seem to be a major factor judging from check experiments. The second objection has tried to question the assumption of the uniform distribution of the particular atmospheric concentration of C_{14} at any one time. There seems to be no good empirical evidence to deny the assumption. It has recently been suggested that lightning bombardment can lead to C_{14} enrichment.

Scientists do disagree in detail about the precise form of the calibration curve and revised ones are to be expected. Independent checks using thermoluminescence and historically dated material seem to support the calibration. It is hoped that work on varves will provide a check stretching back to the Pleistocene.

The most fundamental archaeological effect is the discrediting of the diffusion model for European prehistory. This saw all the major developments that occurred in western and northern Europe as having their inspiration, if not their physical origin, in the Near East or the Aegean Basin. Now such things as the megalithic burial chambers, the Maltese temples and Stonehenge are shown to be much earlier in date than their supposed oriental models. Prehistorians are now re-examining the evidence and considering seriously the likelihood of local economic and social developments accounting independently for all these phenomena.

Vegetable remains: Pollen
(Sources: Dimbleby, 1967; West, 1971; Dimbleby, 1969.)

The composition of the vegetation of any particular area depends on a number of factors, chief among which are soil and climate. Thus a change in vegetation pattern is likely to represent a change in climatic conditions, although this is not necessarily the case. Pollen is durable and can survive for a very long time, particularly in anaerobic conditions. A study of the pollens present, and the amounts in which they occur relative to each other within a deposit, will yield information on local ecology at the time of forming the deposit. Changes that are detected in the pollen composition in the vertical development of the deposit will represent changes occurring in the local vegetation. It is this ecological aspect of palynology that is the main concern of modern archaeologists.

Intensive work, particularly in Scandinavia and Britain since before the Second World War, has resulted in the identification for post-glacial Europe of a sequence of major pollen zones with distinctive pollen spectra. These zones form the basis of the series of climatic periods recognised for the late and post-glacial.

Palynologists recognise that there are limiting factors to the proper interpretation of pollen spectra. First, not all pollen survives well and some important species may be absent in a deposit though present in the actual flora. Some environments are more favourable to some pollens than others. Certain species are very productive of pollen, and their pollen can be present in a deposit in proportions greater than the actual ratio of trees in the forest. In this category fall *Corylus* (hazel), *Betula* (birch), *Alnus* (alder) and *Pinus* (pine). Conversely, some genera are small producers of pollen and can be present in unduly small proportion. Among these are *Salix* (willow), *Quercus* (oak), *Ulmus* (elm), *Tilia* (lime) and *Fagus* (beech). Genera that have pollens that do not survive well include *Populus* (poplar), *Fraxinus* (ash) and *Juniperus* (juniper). Very small percentages for some species may represent not local production but material derived from a considerable distance. Care is taken in examining the deposit that contains the pollen. It must be ascertained that the deposition has been uniform without lateral variation and that redeposited material has not been incorporated (Dimbleby, 1969, 172–3).

The best samples for analysis are obtained from peat or similar waterlogged deposits. However, there is a limit to the degree to which such information can be used in reconstruction of the ecology of the majority of settlements that were sited away from watery expanses. Except where directly associated with a lakeside settlement, like at Mesolithic Star Carr, pollen profiles from bogs must be regarded as generalisations for a region and not reflecting the specifics of inland situations (Star Carr: Clark, 1954).

Pollen analysis is feasible on ordinary soils provided that there has only been limited microbiological activity; Professor G. Dimbleby has been one of the main authorities responsible for developments in this field. Acid soils or very cold or arid soil environments tend to preserve pollens well. They are not normally well preserved on calcareous soils. In an undisturbed soil a rough superimposition of pollens in a time sequence can build up slowly as the pollen moves gradually downwards. Nevertheless, the largest percentage of pollen occurs at the top of the profile.

Burrowing animals, especially earthworms, destroy any stratification of pollen that might have built up in a soil.

As worms do not like acid soils they are not frequently a problem.

The importance of soil pollen is that it is derived from the immediate surroundings of an area and relates directly to a site's flora. Therefore every care must be taken on an archaeological site to identify buried soils and subject them to analysis. Earthworks and barrows are traditionally fruitful sources. If turf has been stripped off before the building of an earthwork, the pollen profile in the buried soil will be truncated. Such truncation will be detectable, as normally the majority of pollen is found in the top humus layer. If the stripped turves were incorporated in the structure and can still be isolated, then they can be used for analysis. Pollen analysis of the deposits of a mound may elucidate its construction. For example, a slight pollen content indicates the use of subsoil, and a high content the use of topsoil.

The standard idea that changes in marker species for the pollen zones reflect climatic changes has been increasingly challenged in recent years. It has been shown that changes in the frequencies of species such as elm, lime, ivy, mistletoe and birch can come about as a result of human activity, especially forest clearance and agriculture. Such alternative explanations weaken the use of the zone and subzone system as a universal time indicator. (For criticisms of standard interpretations see, for example, Raikes, 1967.)

The fact that man's impact on a landscape can be detected in the pollen profile has long been recognised and used. A greater percentage of grass pollens to tree pollens is an indication of forest clearance. Deforestation can be advanced through cutting, burning or grazing. Removal of the tree cover was particularly associated in Europe with the advent of agricultural man. Associated with the decline in tree pollen is a corresponding rise in the pollens of cultigens and the weeds of cultivation. By detailed linking of deposits across Europe, combined with radiocarbon dating, a very full picture of the timing and mechanism of the establishment of agricultural communities can be built up.

Plant remains: Palaeoethnobotany
(Sources: Helbaek, 1969; Renfrew, J. A., 1973.)

Plant remains, except where they have been found in unusually preserved states, have been sadly neglected by archaeologists despite the important light they throw on local environment and human diet. It is theoretically possible to subject the plant remains of a site to the same sort of analyses as bones. However, because of the very heavy expenditure of effort that would be required for wholesale recovery, it is necessary to take fairly limited samples and extrapolate statistically. It is important for the archaeologist to be aware that, if the soil conditions are suitable, then many seeds and other plant remains will be preserved on a site, although they will require sieving and the use of flotation machines to be recovered *en masse*.

Hans Helbaek has been pre-eminent in European and Near Eastern archaeology in advancing the study of palaeoethnobotany. His works mentioned in the notes and those of others in the field should be consulted for a detailed survey.

Not all the categories of plant remains mentioned by Helbaek are found in Britain. For example, mummy wheat, which is found in Egypt, is peculiar to that country, the grain having been preserved in perfect condition in storage pits dating back to Neolithic times by the extreme aridity of the climate. Similarly, siliceous skeletons that preserve the cell structure of grasses as a cast and allow identification are found in ash deposits in arid countries. The casts are of silica built up in the epidermis during growth.

The three other forms of remains can be found in western Europe. The anaerobic environment and humic acids of peat bogs favour preservation. As finds of the remains of food plants tend to indicate only the consumption of these in the general vicinity, directly preserved remains in a peat profile are of limited information value, but they are sometimes found associated with ancient marsh-side settlements such as in Switzerland or Somerset. The preserved, undigested remains of the person's last meal have been found in the stomachs of wonderfully intact Iron Age bodies; microscopic analysis of such remains has given important insights into the variety of vegetable diet in the Iron Age of the region. Fifty-nine of the identified species incorporated in the meal eaten by Grauballe Man were not cultivated. An experimental reconstruction of this meal by Sir Mortimer Wheeler and Glyn Daniel proved unappetising. Presumably most of the plants consumed had been obtained by close gleaning of fields, a common practice in peasant communities hardly above the basic subsistence line. It should be remembered, however, that as many of these bodies found their way into the bog as a result of sacrifice, the last meal may have been part of the ritual and possibly contained plants of religious significance, not normally eaten.

Carbonisation of organic matter will ensure its preservation in most conditions. Carbonisation can only come about if the matter comes into contact with heat. Grain drying was employed from early times for a variety of reasons. For example, it was necessary in order to allow the crushing of the spikelet of Einkorn, Emmer and Spelt. For storing in damp climates drying is used to guard against fungus growth, whilst in hot and damp climates it is used to prevent premature sprouting.

As there was often no close control over the temperature for drying, mistakes occurred and the grain was burnt and therefore discarded. Considerable distortion of the original can result from burning and the tar formed can be a hindrance to identification. Nevertheless, some structural elements usually survive, and these combined with microscopic examination allow the recognition of species.

It was very common in the past in different parts of the world to build with clay or mud and to incorporate in this, as a filler, straw and other waste from threshing. When fragments of the walls are examined today they are found to contain hundreds of impressions of the grain used. Similarly, prehistoric pottery for domestic use was often made by the women at the same spot as meals, and waste grains were accidentally incorporated into the clay of the pot as it was being worked. The seed or grain itself burnt out during firing but frequently left a very detailed impression of itself on the body of the pot. Helbaek and others have been able to make very detailed morphological studies from such imprints (Helbaek, 1969).

Coprolites

The remains yielded by coprolites are both animal and vegetable. The majority of the research work has been done by American scholars, who are mentioned in the bibliography. The main examples are also from the Americas, such as Huaca Prieta, Peru (2500–1250 BC), the Tehuacán Valley project, Mexico and Lovelock Cave, Nevada.

Coprolites are human faecal matter preserved under arid conditions or waterlogging, or fossilised. They can contain seeds, nuts, bones, hair, feathers, insect remains, shells, fish scales, pollen and the remains of parasites and their eggs.

Dry analysis, which entails crushing the coprolite, is satisfactory for recovering seeds, bones and fibres, but for more substantial recovery wet analysis is more suitable. The team from the University of California under the direction of Robert F. Heizer working at Lovelock Cave, Nevada, use a variant of the method developed by E. O. Callen (Heizer, 1969). One part of the coprolite is reserved for chemical and pollen analysis. Pollen analysis can inform about the local vegetation and can possibly suggest the season of excretion.

The sample is immersed in a 0·5% aqueous solution of trisodium phosphate. In this the coprolite slowly disintegrates and the materials contained rehydrate. Wet sieving follows and the residues are collected. The coarse elements are sorted under low magnification, dried and weighed. The fine elements are sorted under higher magnification and the percentages of the common elements and their weights calculated. Wet analysis, whilst being a more laborious process, has the major advantage of allowing more accurate recognition of the constituents of a coprolite.

Taking the example of Lovelock Cave, it is possible to see the sort of information that can be gleaned from such studies. First, the remains showed that meals of seeds and fish were prominent and that birds were also eaten. The varieties identified could all be obtained locally from the Humboldt Lake and its environs. Finds from the coprolites suggested that occupation of the interior of the cave took place in winter, whilst that at the entrance was during the autumn. The specimens could be directly dated using radiocarbon dating, and one from the entrance was estimated at 145 ± 80 BP. One from inside came to 1210 ± 60 BP. Despite the difference in dating, the dietary data is very similar, indicating a relatively constant pattern of exploitation for many centuries. There is no evidence of parasitic infestation in the coprolites and this conforms to the general trait of hunter-gatherers in unforested lands. The presence of Charcot-Leyden crystals indicates some incidence of diarrhoea and dysentery. By implication the coprolites suggest that the stomachs of the Indians were working normally. It does seem that the occupants of the caves were content to live within close proximity to their own excrement (Heizer, 1969).

Wood

There are four main ways in which wood can survive. It is most commonly encountered in the form of charcoal. Nearly every archaeological site seems to produce at least a little carbonised wood. Waterlogged wood is less common but more valuable in that it retains the original form of the object more exactly. Most of the timberwork of the Roman waterfront of London is intact through its immersion in Thames water and many Roman finds of wood, including writing tablets, have come from waterlogged levels in the City deep below the modern pavements. Another example of such preservation is the Roman barge from Blackfriars. Not of relevance to Britain are the finds of timber in totally arid conditions, a most spectacular example being the wooden objects amongst the treasure of Tutankhamun. Similarly, wood preserved in permafrost conditions, as in some of the Iron Age tombs of the Russian steppes, is not met with.

It should be appreciated just how much man owes to trees. A very large part of human technology has been directly dependent on wood, right up to the last hundred years. Taking the example of Britain alone, most buildings up to the end of the seventeenth century at least were largely of wood—and, of course, a brief glance around modern furniture and fittings will show little fundamental change. Most forms of transport were dependent on wood until Victoria's reign. Many artefacts were composites of metal or stone and wood. Wood was a major source of fuel. The example of wood shows up the partiality and incompleteness of archaeological evidence. How different might be the preoccupations of the Palaeolithic specialist, for example, were only the wooden elements of early cominid tool kits to survive instead of just the stone and bone.

By identifying the woods being used at a site it is possible to infer features of the local forest and, indirectly, the climate. Local timber can be distinguished from imported. Detailed examination of artefacts will indicate the level of craftsmanship reached by a community and which sort of trees they favoured for which jobs. Wood is, of course, directly datable through the C14 method.

The important structural features of woods are shown in Fig. 14. By making one or more of the three main types of section across a specimen it is normally possible to distinguish trees into genera. Greater detail of these procedures is given by A. Cecilia Western (1969).

Charcoal can be preliminarily sorted with a low-magnification hand-lens and then looked at in detail in one of three ways. In the first, the specimen is broken so that three main planes are available for study. These are examined microscopically. This method has the advantage of rapidity, but if it proves inadequate, having broken the piece in the three planes, the charcoal is impregnated with a suitable consolidant and

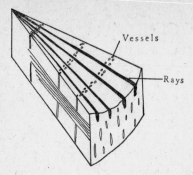

Vessels

Rays

Fig. 14 Main elements of wood shown in three section planes
(Based on Western, 1969)

ground down for mounting like petrological samples. The
alternative is to prepare for mounting by slicing on a microtome. Both the latter procedures are very time-consuming and
not practicable for large numbers of fragments. Microphoto-
graphs are taken as a permanent record, usually from thin
sections.

Dendrochronology

Many species of trees show in cross-section a series of rings,
each of which represents one year's growth of xylem. At the
beginning of the growing season sets of large, thin-walled
cells are added to the old growth. As the season advances, the
cells become smaller and more thickly walled until at the end
of the growing season no more cells are produced. The process
is repeated next season and a marked line occurs between the
thick-walled cells of the former season and the thin ones of the
new.

If there is no variability in a series of tree-rings, the sequence
is termed complacent and is not of much archaeological use.
However, if a sequence shows oscillation in the thickness of
the rings, this is termed sensitive.

Various factors are responsible for variation in thickness. The significant factor can be different in different regions. Temperature controls growth in Alaska and northern Europe, whilst soil moisture is critical in the American south-west. The mean size of rings lessens the older the tree is. Rings at the centre of the trunk are wider than those at the outer circumference. In the measurement and comparison of rings it is necessary to calculate an equation that converts each actual thickness to a common scale.

Climatic variation is a potent agent in affecting tree growth. In a very dry year or years, very thin rings are formed as growth is restricted. It is possible in studying a dated ring sequence also to follow variations in a region's climate. As climatic conditions will tend to be regional it follows that potentially all the trees within the same region will react in an approximately similar fashion and exhibit a similar trend in the variation of ring growth. It is found that microenvironmental factors can upset the theoretical position. In taking samples it is important to collect as much information as possible regarding geology, soil, aspect and drainage. Impeded drainage might produce the same growth pattern as drought even if the general rainfall is plentiful. Such individual variations can normally be set against the general trend.

The application of dendrochronology is limited by several factors. Many parts of the world are not favourable to the preservation of timber except under extraordinary conditions such as waterlogging. It has proved possible to arrive at a date for timbers from the Roman waterfront at London because of such preservation. Arid climates are far better and the most complete work has been done in the American south-west. It was here that A. E. Douglass, researching between 1901 and 1929, demonstrated the viability of the method.

Fundamental to all tree-ring dating is the principle of cross-dating. If the trees of a region do not cross-date, then no sequence can be established. Two trees are said to cross-date if they show the same sequence of variation in their ring series representing the same number of years. To establish an absolute date in calendar years it is necessary to start with modern trees, the dates of which are known. The sequence of these is overlapped with that of slightly older trees, and this process of overlapping the series of cross-dating specimens is carried successively back into the past as far as it will go. This is to several thousand years BC with the bristlecone pine.

Samples can be taken in a variety of ways. A complete section is preferred, but it is often necessary to restrict sampling to a core or V-shaped slice. Large waterlogged timbers are sectioned with a power-saw as they rapidly blunt the hand-tool. The specimen is consolidated with suitable preservatives. For analysis it is necessary to prepare the surface carefully so that all the rings can be observed, and various sanding machines are employed to produce a smooth finish.

The first part of the analysis depends on being able to count the number of rings present and to guarantee that each ring represents a single year's growth. Complicating features include double rings, which can arise through a temporary respite from and then renewed growth within the same year. Hardwoods are particularly prone to double-ring formation. Another feature found is the partial ring which does not complete the circumference of the tree. This presents clear dangers if only partial samples are being taken.

The reader should consult the specialist publications in the extensive bibliography at the end of Bannister (1969) for details of the many methods used to show ring variation and achieve reliable cross-dating. All methods are concerned to make sure that a single specimen is correctly correlated with the master sequence for a region, where such exists. The basic method is that of Douglass. The results of the ring count are recorded on strips of graph paper. Rings of ordinary thickness are not marked but only counted, whilst very narrow rings compared with their immediate neighbours are shown by a vertical line, the length of which is increased proportional to the greater narrowness of the ring. Wide rings are marked with a B or BB depending on the thickness. This has proved a very easy and rapid method for comparing two specimens.

Modern work studies variation and carries out comparison with the use of computers.

Besides the technical difficulties of the method itself, a number of standard archaeological problems of association should be borne in mind (Bannister, 1969, 199). In some buildings timber will be reused from another building or pieces will be used that died several years before being incorporated in the building. The timber will register a date earlier than the building in which it is found. This is the classic case for remembering the principle of *terminus post quem* in archaeological dating. The association between the timber in a house and the mobiliary content of that house is also problematic. It is perfectly possible for the timber to be several decades earlier than the latest objects found within the building. If repairs are made to a building, fresh wood may be used. If this is tested in isolation a falsely late date might be adduced for the construction. These pitfalls emphasise the need for multiple samples wherever possible.

Chronological studies are most advanced in south-western USA. The culture history of the Pueblo Indians is well documented in calendar years and it has been possible to progress to many more interesting anthropological studies on the basis of a secure time-scale. Bannister's bibliography should be consulted for details. Long chronologies are also established for Alaska and Germany. Other areas have sporadic coverage. Climatic studies are not as well advanced, but it has been possible to indicate periods of drought and consider the possible significance for settlement in south-west USA. Specific results, unfortunately limited in their ability to be reproduced, include the use of a relative chronology of beams at a site to show the development of a building complex. Bannister studied cutting dates at Chaco Canyon and suggested that timber stockpiling was practised. A study of dates might reveal earlier buildings of which all trace had gone. This will be indicated if a cluster of dates occurs that does not apparently relate to standing structures.

Bibliography

Ascenzi, A., *Microscopy and prehistoric bone*, in Brothwell and Higgs (eds), *Science in Archaeology*, 2nd ed. London: Thames & Hudson, 1969, 526–38.

Bannister, B., *Dendrochronology*, in Brothwell and Higgs (eds), 1969, 191–205.

Biggs, H. E. J., *Molluscs from Human Habitation Sites and the Problem of Ethnological Interpretation*, in Brothwell and Higgs (eds), 1969, 423–7.

Boessneck, J., *Osteological Differences between Sheep (Ovis aries Linné) and Goat (Capra hircus Linné)*, in Brothwell and Higgs (eds), 1969, 331–58.

Brothwell, D. R., *Digging up Bones*. London: British Museum, 1965.

Brothwell, D. R., *The Palaeopathology of Pleistocene and More Recent Mammals*, in Brothwell and Higgs (eds), 1969a, 310–14.

Brothwell, D. R., *The Study of Archaeological Materials by Means of the Scanning Electron Microscope: An Important New Field*, in Brothwell and Higgs (eds), 1969b, 564–6.

Clark, J. G. D., *Excavations at Star Carr*. Cambridge: Cambridge University Press, 1954.

Clutton-Brock, J., *The Origins of the Dog*, in Brothwell and Higgs (eds), 1969, 303–9.

Cornwall, I. W., *Bones for the Archaeologist*. London: Dent, 1968.

Dart, R. A., *The Osteodontokeratic Culture of Australopithecus Prometheus*. Pretoria: Transvaal Museum Memoir No. 10, 1957.

Dawson, E. W., *Bird Remains in Archaeology*, in Brothwell and Higgs (eds), 1969, 359–75.

Dimbleby, G. W., *Pollen Analysis*, in Brothwell and Higgs (eds), 1969, 167–77.

Garlick, J. D., *Buried Bone: The Experimental Approach in the Study of Nitrogen Content and Blood Group Activity*, in Brothwell and Higgs (eds), 1969, 503–12.

Gejvall, N.-G., *Cremations*, in Brothwell and Higgs (eds), 1969, 468–79.

Glob, P. V., *The Bog People*. London: Paladin, 1969.

Godwin, H., *The History of the British Flora*. Cambridge: Cambridge University Press, 1956.

Heizer, R. F., *The Anthropology of Prehistoric Great Basin Human Coprolites*, in Brothwell and Higgs (eds), 1969, 244–50.

Helbaek, H., *Palaeo-Ethnobotany*, in Brothwell and Higgs (eds), 1969, 206–14.

Herre, W., *The Science and History of Domestic Animals*, in Brothwell and Higgs (eds), 1969, 257–72.

Higham, C., and Message, M., *An Assessment of a Prehistoric Technique of Bovine Husbandry*, in Brothwell and Higgs (eds), 1969, 315–30.

Kurtén, B., *Pleistocene Mammals and the Origin of Species*, in Brothwell and Higgs (eds), 1969, 251–6.

Libby, W., *Radiocarbon Dating*. 2nd ed. Chicago: Chicago University Press, 1955.

Meighan, C. W., *Molluscs as Food Remains in Archaeological Sites*, in Brothwell and Higgs (eds), 1969, 415–22.

Oakley, K. P., *Analytical Methods of Dating Bones*, in Brothwell and Higgs (eds), 1969, 35–45.

Raikes, R., *Water, Weather and Prehistory*. London: John Baker, 1967.

Renfrew, C., *Before Civilisation*. London: Jonathan Cape, 1973.

Renfrew, J. A., *Palaeoethnobotany*. London: Methuen, 1973.

Ryder, M. L., *Animal Bones in Archaeology*. Oxford and Edinburgh: Blackwell Scientific Publications, 1968.

Ryder, M. L., *Remains of Fishes and other Aquatic Animals*, in Brothwell and Higgs (eds), 1969a, 376–94.

Ryder, M. L., *Remains derived from Skin*, in Brothwell and Higgs (eds), 1969, 539–54.

Sandison, A. T., *The Study of Mummified and Dried Human Tissues*, in Brothwell and Higgs (eds), 1969, 490–502.

Shackleton, N. J., *Marine Mollusca in Archaeology*, in Brothwell and Higgs (eds), 1969, 407–14.

Silver, I. A., *The Ageing of Domestic Animals*, in Brothwell and
Higgs (eds), 1969, 283–302.

Sparks, B. W., *Non-marine Mollusca and Archaeology*, in Brothwell and Higgs (eds), 1969, 395–406.

Weiner, J. S., Oakley, K. P., and Le Gros Clark, W. E., *The
Solution of the Piltdown Problem*. London: Bulletin of the
British Museum (Natural History) Geology Vol. 2, No. 3,
1953.

Western, A. C., *Wood and Charcoal in Archaeology*, in Brothwell
and Higgs (eds), 1969, 178–87.

Yarnell, R. A., *Palaeo-Ethnobotany in America*, in Brothwell and
Higgs (eds), 1969, 215–28.

Additional reading

Ager, D., *Principles of Palaeo-ecology*. New York: McGraw-Hill,
1963.

Agerter, S. R., and Glock, W. S., *An Annotated Bibliography of
Tree Growth and Growth Rings*, 1950–1962. Tucson: University of Arizona, 1965.

Appleyard, H. M., and Wildman, A. B., *Fibres of Archaeological Interest: Their Examination and Identification*, in Brothwell and Higgs (eds), 1969, 624–33.

Brothwell, D. R., and Sandison, A. T., *Diseases in Antiquity*.
Springfield: Charles C. Thomas, 1967.

Butzer, K. W., *Environment and Archaeology*. 2nd ed. London:
Methuen, 1971.

Callen, E. O., *Diet as revealed by Coprolites*, in Brothwell and
Higgs (eds), 1969, 235–43.

CBA, *Handbook of Scientific Aids and Evidence for Archaeologists*.
London: Cncl. Brit. Archaeol., 1970.

Dimbleby, G., *Environmental Studies and Archaeology*. London:
London University, 1963.

Dimbleby, G. W., *Plants and Archaeology*. London: John Baker,
1967.

Evans, J. G., *Land Snails in Archaeology*. London and New
York: Seminar Press, 1972.

Genovés, S., *Sex Determination in Earlier Man*, in Brothwell and Higgs (eds), 1969, 429–39.

Genovés, S., *Estimation of Age and Mortality*, in Brothwell and Higgs (eds), 1969, 440–52.

Higgs, E. S. (ed.), *Papers in Economic Prehistory*. Cambridge: Cambridge University Press, 1972.

Kurtén, B., *Pleistocene Mammals of Europe*. London: Weidenfeld & Nicholson, 1968.

Olsson, I. U., *Radiocarbon Variations and Absolute Chronology*. Nobel Symposium, 12, Uppsala: Interscience, 1970.

Schmid, E., *Atlas of Animal Bones*. London: Elsevier, 1972.

Tansley, A. G., *The British Islands and Their Vegetation*. Cambridge: Cambridge University Press, 1965.

Ucko, P. J., and Dimbleby, G. W. (eds), *The Domestication and Exploitation of Plants and Animals*. London: Duckworth, 1969.

Weiner, J. S., *The Piltdown Forgery*. London: Oxford University Press, 1955.

Wells, C., *Bones, Bodies and Disease*. London: Thames & Hudson, 1965.

Wells, L. H., *Stature in Earlier Races of Mankind*, in Brothwell and Higgs (eds), 1969, 453–67.

West, R. G., *Studying the Past by Pollen Analysis*. London: Oxford University Press, 1971.

Zeuner, F., *Dating the Past*. London: Methuen, 1952.

6 Analysis of Inorganic Remains

Stone: Chronological methods
(Sources: Gentner and Lippolt, 1969; Miller 1969; Fleischer, Price and Walker, 1969; Friedman, Smith and Clark, 1969.)

The *potassium-argon* dating method is a standard procedure for establishing the chronology of early geological ages, but it can also be applied, though there are difficulties, to Quaternary deposits and hence has importance for the study of early hominids. It has contributed towards a chronology of the European and American glaciations and given the date of $1 \cdot 75$ million years old to the crucial deposit at Olduvai Gorge, Tanzania, known as Bed 1, from which there is evidence of very early representatives of the modern genus of man.

The radioactive isotope of potassium, K40, decays partially to argon 40 at a known rate. Potassium is a very common constituent of minerals. The Ar40 concentration in a mineral is measured and it is possible to calculate how long it would have taken for such a concentration to have occurred through radioactive breakdown. The technical details of the method are discussed by W. Gentner and H. J. Lippolt, 1969.

A wide range of minerals can be used for dating, such as muscovite, biotite, sanidine, leucite, phlogopite, illite, glauconite and sylvite, the first three mentioned being most commonly employed. Archaeological samples tend to be whole rock ones which are not as suitable as unchanged minerals.

In dealing with geologically recent periods certain difficulties arise. Because of the low amount of argon present in the mineral, refined methods of mass spectrometry are needed, such as are provided by the omegatron-type mass spectro-

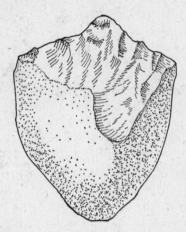

Fig. 15   Chipping tool from Olduvai

meter. Mineral samples must have a low content of atmospheric argon with a correspondingly high amount of potassium. It is possible that the age registered by the specimen will be too old because the rock has old minerals incorporated in it. The most careful mineralogical study is required of each deposit potentially to be dated to ensure that such a problem does not arise. A refinement of the customary technique of analysis termed the 40Ar/39Ar method has been described by Miller; it seems to improve the accuracy of the general method for younger ages (Miller, 1969).

Potassium-argon dating, besides bearing on questions of

direct relevance to archaeologists, has also made major contributions in two other spheres. First, it has provided a time-
scale to the study of changes in the earth's magnetic field. For
example, it is known that the poles were reversed between 2·5
million and 0·85 million years ago. Secondly, the glasslike
structures called tektites, probably of meteoric origin, have
been grouped according to their potassium-argon dating,
those of South-east Asia, Indonesia and Australia being 0·72
million years old and those of the Ivory Coast 1·3 million
(Gentner and Lippolt, 1969, 98–9).

Fission track dating is capable of dating glasses or crystalline
substances which range in age from a few years old to over a
thousand million years. In glasses or crystalline substances
very tiny damage trails are created by the fission of uranium 238
impurities. By counting the number of tracks, the date of
the material can be calculated. The number of tracks produced
is a function of both the age of the substance and the amount
of uranium initially present. The uranium present in each
sample is measured by artificially stimulating the fission of a
few of the uranium atoms of the specimen. The density of the
new damage trails is proportional to the amount of uranium
present, which can be measured by making another count of
the trails. The trails are so small as not to be detectable by
microscope directly. To be able to count them in order to
make an age estimate the specimen is placed in a chemical
which acts more quickly at the points of damage than elsewhere on the material. This chemical action creates etched
pits at the sites of the trails which can be viewed and counted.

It is important that the material used for dating is one capable of retaining its tracks relatively permanently and is not
affected by high temperatures. Such substances are muscovite,
tektite glass, silica glass, zircon and quartz. Poor materials in
this respect are autunite, aragonite and feldspar glass. Further,
the substance must contain enough uranium to create a track
density that does not take too long to count.

Further details of this method can be found in the publications of its developers Fleischer, Price and Walker (1969).

Some success has been achieved in various parts of the world with a technique for dating the volcanic glass, obsidian. A newly exposed surface of obsidian takes up water from its immediate environment, and a hydration layer that is visible microscopically develops at a constant, known rate through time (Friedman, Smith and Clark, 1969).

In order to measure the hydration layer, a thin slice is cut out of the object transverse to the plane of the surface being investigated. This slice is ground down on a microscope slide to a thickness of about 0·05 mm. The hydrated part is easily distinguished under a microscope as it has a higher refractive index. The thickness of the hydration layer is measured with a micrometer attached to the microscope. The expected standard error in the measurements is ±0·2 microns.

The rate at which hydration occurs has to be calculated from well-dated ancient specimens, which are unfortunately very rare, and therefore the present estimates of rate must be regarded as very tentative and subject to alteration with further research. One piece of important information that has emerged is that the rate of hydration of trachytic obsidian differs from that of the more common rhyolitic, being faster.

The temperature of an artefact's environment affects the rate of hydration, which increases in hotter climates. Workers calculate that rough estimates of ancient climatic situations at sites from which obsidian is used for dating should suffice to allow this important factor to be taken into account. Chemical variation between obsidians is also known to correlate with varying hydration rates.

If an obsidian artefact is exposed to mechanical weathering, its hydration layer can be damaged and it will then be essential to examine the object thoroughly to find a complete section of the layer. As a hydration layer grows, there is extra strain created at the surface which eventually leads to spalling and the initiation of a new hydration cycle. This is only likely to occur on tools of Palaeolithic age, and even these will probably retain remnants of the primary cycle. Fire is a serious damager of surfaces.

Useful results which seem to accord with general archaeological expectations have been obtained in various parts of the world. For example, in northern Japan rates of hydration have been determined back for about 20 000 years.

Finally, it is worth noting that a check for a hydration layer is a useful guard against forgery.

Stone: Source analysis

Petrological study of a stone artefact identifies the material from which it was manufactured and this enables a search for the source of the raw material to be made. Many types of object are amenable to this sort of study, such as querns, millstones, whetstones, roofing stones, building stone, axes, adzes and stone ornaments. Identification of the source of a stone then allows the construction of hypotheses about the nature of the distribution of objects made from it. These might have come about through trading, gift exchange, annual ritual journeys or some other mechanism.

A sample of the object is taken for study in the form of a slice. In the case of axes the slice is normally taken out of the edge at right angles to the long axis of the artefact. The slice is mounted on a glass slide with cement and then ground down to a thickness of 0·03 mm. The procedure is completed by cementing on a cover glass. It is now possible to examine the specimen under a petrological microscope, looking for the characteristic colour, sizes, shapes and textures of minerals that allow the identification of the rock.

A major example of such petrological work is that of the CBA committee on stone (non-flint) axes and hammers, which has succeeded in identifying for the Neolithic and Bronze Ages a series of groups, mapping their distributions and, in a number of cases, specifying the sources. No actual factory site has been found directly by the method, but it is possible to narrow down the possible source to fairly restricted geological areas. Major factories are known at the following places and their distribution has been intensively documented. The

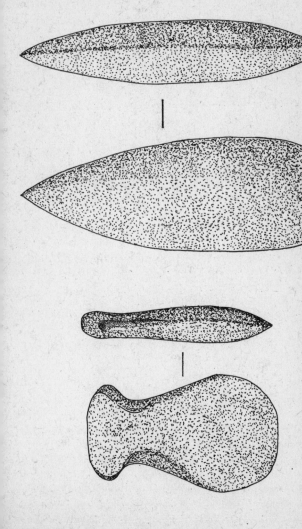

Fig. 16 Stone axes of the Arawak Indians of the West Indies

Roman numeral accompanying the name is the group number. VI Great Langdale, Westmorland: here the stone is ande-
sitic ash and a number of production centres are known on the

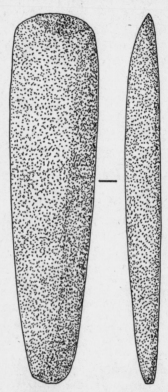

Fig. 17 Stone axe of the Arawak Indians of the West Indies

scree slope. VII Graig Lwyd, Penmaenmawr, Caernarvonshire: in this case the rock is an epidotised microgranodiorite
and again several sites were exploited. IX Tievebulliagh and
Rathlin Island, Antrim: these Irish factories used a special
stone, black and of volcanic origin. XXI Mynydd Rhiw,

Lleyn, Caernarvonshire: this factory exploited a volcanic ash. (Shotton, 1969, 573.)

Work on medieval hones from Yorkshire further shows the utility of the method. In this instance the researchers discovered that about half were of a rock, the source of which was Aberdeenshire (Morey and Dunham, 1953).

Thin sectioning is also being used with some success on pottery to characterise fabrics and their sources and on slags to specify the product and identify the type of ore.

It is not always necessary to resort to the petrological microscope in order to identify the kind of stone being used at a site. It is not difficult for an archaeologist to become familiar with the macroscopic characteristics of the local rocks in order to be able to identify these and also to spot intrusive pieces. Similarly, in some periods a few standard types of stone were used for particular artefacts, and these can be learnt and anomalies isolated. For example, in eastern England in the Roman period, a German lava, millstone grit and Hertfordshire conglomerate were commonly used materials for querns. It is only the less frequent sandstones and other rocks that are also found that require an expert to identify them. Nevertheless, if all the available information is to be extracted from a site, it is important to engage the co-operation of a geologist.

Petrological analysis does not help in the identification of the source of flint objects. This is unfortunate as so much of the stone tool kits of prehistoric man was composed of this stone. Of course, the vast majority of flint would be obtained in the immediate locale, and searching for its precise source would not be rewarding or informative work. However, it is more important to know the origin of the flint used for certain specialised objects which seem to have a wide distribution. The flint axes of Neolithic Britain are an example. They were made from flint mined from specific centres. This mining industry possessed a considerable degree of organisation judging from sites like Grimes Graves in Norfolk.

Recent work suggests that it is possible to distinguish between the products of different flint mines. Analysis using atomic absorption spectroscopy of samples from the mines of Easton Down, Grimes Graves, Black Patch, Peppard, Cissbury, Spiennes (France) and Grand Pressigny showed that there was a significant difference in the concentration of the trace elements aluminium, magnesium, potassium and iron (present in the flint) between these locations (Sieveking *et al.*, 1970).

Fig. 18   Hand-axe, middle Acheulean

Source analysis has also proved possible on obsidian. This stone was used in various parts of the world for such things as knife blades, arrowheads, spearheads, scrapers and ornaments.

There are three main kinds of obsidian: alkaline, calc-alkaline and peralkaline. These show differences physically; for

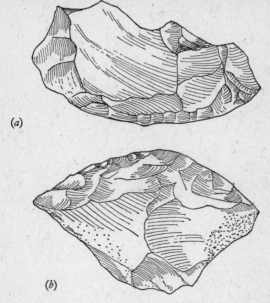

Fig. 19 Mousterian scraper: (*a*) convex side; (*b*) transversal

example, the alkaline and calc-alkaline varieties have a lower refractive index (less than 1·495) than the peralkaline (more than 1·505). The peralkaline shows up greeny in transmitted light, whilst the other two are either grey or colourless.

Chemical analysis, however, is utilised to characterise obsidian (particularly trace element analysis). It is known that there is considerable variability between obsidian from different sources, and this fact allows the ready assignation of a specimen to one of the three main types and to a definable subdivision within that type.

Cann, Dixon and Renfrew (1969) have reviewed the methods involved in a detailed analysis and some of the results of various attempts. Trace element analysis has been conducted in three ways. Optical spectroscopy has been used on

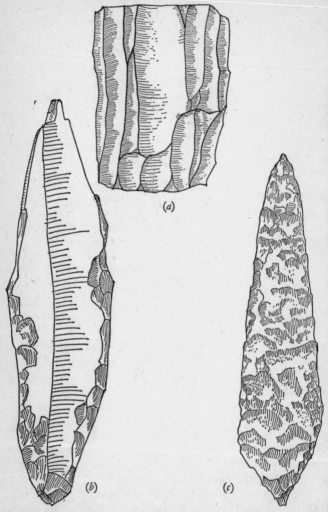

Fig. 20 (*a*) Blade core. (*b*) Burins on retouched blades. (*c*) Solutrean laurel leaf point

Mediterranean and Near Eastern samples and has produced satisfactory groupings. It requires 60 mg of an artefact and is therefore not seriously destructive, but the accuracy of the method is rather low. The X-ray fluorescence method is more accurate but does require larger samples of 2 g. It has been used on Central American obsidian. Neutron activation is the third method, used with success on Hopewellian obsidian in the USA.

Division into groups on the basis of these analyses is achieved by first dividing the specimens according to the quantities of zirconium and barium present. This results in placing all the artefacts from one place together, but it also lumps into the same group material from other sources. Sub-classification is effected by plotting other elements like iron and strontium. To secure the strict correlation of one group to one source is more difficult; it is being approached statistically and through the use of fission track dating that will distinguish obsidians according to age.

Obsidian has been shown to be one of the first raw materials to have been involved in extensive trade. In the seventh and sixth millennia BC intensive trading was taking place between sources like the Kayseri region in central Anatolia and the Levant. Sources near Lake Van in east Anatolia were also supplying Iraq. Melos was exporting to Thessaly, Macedonia and Crete in the sixth millennium.

Metals

In the study of metal artefacts, two questions of major interest are the exact nature of the metal and the source of the ore used in its manufacture. The technique of optical emission spectroscopy has been used for some time in the attempt to answer them.

The method is based on the fact that each individual element can emit light with a distinctive series of spectral lines. The intensity of these lines varies with the concentration of the element. Using only very small quantities for analysis, it is possible to identify over twenty constituents of an object, in concentrations as small as a thousandth. Simple identification can be achieved by comparing the spectral lines produced by a sample with the known lines of control samples. To measure the concentration of an element it is necessary to compare the intensity of the sample lines with the intensity of the same lines in a control of known concentration.

The structure of a large quartz spectograph is described by Britton and Richards (1969). A sample of the object is placed in the discharge between two electrodes and the atoms of the elements in the specimen collide with the discharge electrons, causing distinctive wavelengths of light to be given off according to the elements concerned. A photographic plate was used in the past to record the spectra of archaeological material, although this is now superseded by apparatus for direct reading. A microphotometer is used to calculate the intensity of the spectral line. All this work is subject to experimental error, which is usually quoted.

The analysis is the basis for the investigation of the method of manufacture. For example, if substantial amounts of arsenic or tin are found associated with copper, it is fairly certain that a deliberate alloy is involved.

The other lesser trace elements found as impurities in the metal arise because they were incorporated in the copper ore. This raises the possibility of being able to identify the ore source of particular objects. This would lead to a search for the ancient mines, and hence to an increased knowledge of prehistoric industrial archaeology and prehistoric trade and exchange mechanisms. Unfortunately, this easy hope is fraught with difficulties. A primary problem is, how is it possible to be sure that the proportions of impurities noted in the finished product are the same as those in the ore and have not been altered in the processing? Even if there were not this factor, it must still be noted that there is considerable variation in the impurity content of a lode, both vertically and horizontally. Also it is possible that in some processes old metal from different sources was resmelted. The answer to these problems seems to lie in mass analysis over many years and in the use of discriminating multivariate statistical techniques.

Successes in the application of the method have been scored in central Europe by a succession of workers, notably Witter, Otto, Pesta and Pittioni. For example, Pittioni in Austria has made an intensive examination of the actual ore sources. At Stuttgart the combined efforts of Junghans, Sangmeister, Scheufele, Klein and Schroder have led to the formulation of a generalised three-stage historical scheme for the development of metallurgy in Europe. In the first stage there was metal-working only in the south-east and south-west of Europe. In the second, it diffuses to central and western Europe. The Stuttgart researchers have identified thirteen groups of copper on the basis of different combinations of impurities. At this second stage (probably because new ore sources were being used) several of these emerge. Open moulds were the rule. The last stage is the period of the spread of bronze-working when more new lodes were extracted, particularly in Bavaria and the Austrian Alps. Closed-mould casting was very common.

Detailed studies of the structure of a metal artefact can be undertaken using a microscope with a special attachment known as a vertical illuminator which ensures that sufficient reflected light is directed to the surface of the metal under study. It is necessary to use reflected light as it is not practicable to produce translucent sections. The part of the specimen to be investigated is very highly polished and considerable care is exercised on the operation, first using successively finer types of emery paper and then finishing up with diamond powder. Certain structural features are looked for at this stage, but to bring out others the surface is etched using a suitable chemical reagent.

Such examination should reveal the nature of a non-ferrous alloy. This could be a solid-solution type, in which the alloying metals are in solution in each other in the molten and solid state; or it could be an eutectic, which is a mechanical combination of metals. A third possibility is that the alloying metals have become discrete chemical compounds. The main value of the microscopic study is not, however, in revealing precise details of composition, which it cannot, but in informing about the conditions in which the metal was manufactured. For example, if the so-called slip-bands (sets of parallel lines within crystals) are observed, this is evidence of cold working. Microscopic investigation has played an important part in the study of ancient iron-working (Thompson, 1969).

One of the ways in which it is possible to test ideas about how objects were made in the past, and what procedures were involved, is to try to reproduce the artefact experimentally. A whole range of experiments has been conducted on materials of various sorts, including metals, and this expanding and increasingly rigorous field of experimental archaeology has recently been systematically reviewed by John Coles (1973). Before considering some examples that concern metals, it is worthwhile repeating the guiding principles of experimental archaeology as listed by Coles.

It is important to realise that no experiment is conclusive. Even though a procedure may have proved effective, it is only proper to say that the experimenter has demonstrated the feasibility of the method he proposed, not that it was the method used in antiquity. He may only have shown one of a number of possible ways.

When undertaking the experiment the materials used should be as close to the ancient originals as possible. Similarly, the methods used must also be ancient. Some care is necessary in this respect, if measures of efficiency and output are being made, to ensure that the operator is fully conversant with the method before the experiment in order to avoid false, low estimates arising through modern incompetence. All modern aids must be rigorously omitted and care must be taken to regulate speed and scale in the work. Wherever possible, repeat experiments should be made.

The methods of casting in one-piece and two-piece moulds have been tried out successfully using the ancient moulds. Some experiments have been made to reproduce various procedures for casting particular objects by the ciré perdue method. Coles (1973, 137–8) describes the way in which a copper bell of the first millennium AD from Mexico was reproduced. First, a core of clay and charcoal with a pebble for the clanger was formed and over this a model in wax of the bell was made, with an extra stem to act as a reservoir for the molten metal. A slit was cut in the base of the wax model, this being plugged with the overlying clay and charcoal which helps hold the core in position after the melting of the wax. Straws were pushed into the upper part of the wax as outlets for gases. The wax model was plastered with layers of charcoal, clay and water, with a particularly thick outer coat for strength. A crucible containing pieces of copper was fixed to the stem on an incline so that molten metal could run down the stem. The crucible was sealed with clay and charcoal and the whole assembly placed in an oven raised to 1200°C. The wax melts and is displaced by molten metal, which takes on the form of the bell.

A series of studies have been made in Britain to investigate the production of iron in the Romano-British period. Attempts to produce iron in a bowl furnace modelled on one found at Great Casterton, Rutland, showed that such a furnace had a rather low efficiency of about 20% in terms of the ratio of produced iron to original ore weight. At Ashwicken, Norfolk, six shaft furnaces of the second century AD were found and one of these was reconstructed. It consisted of the shaft made by repeatedly firing a tree trunk coated with clay, removing the charred wood afterwards. In 8 hours 3·5 kg of iron was extracted (Coles, 1973, 140–2).

Pottery

The analysis of pottery is described in greater detail than the analysis of other classes of artefacts in order to illustrate its importance to the archaeologist and also to indicate through a particular example the sort of typological and functional analyses which are practised on artefacts in general, the background theory of which was dealt with in Chapter 1. It should be noted that it is very rare to find a study of a particular type of pottery that integrates all the lines of enquiry mentioned here. For example, most Romano-British excavators have until recently restricted their interest to the use of pottery for dating.

A pottery is normally sited where it will have ready access to three major resources, good clay, timber for kiln fuel and water for treating the raw clay. The Roman pottery industry in the Nene Valley, England, is a good example of such a siting. The potteries were strung out along the valley and exploited the local Jurassic clays. Small timber derived from bushes seems to have been mainly used in the kilns and this would have been obtained in the vicinity of the workings, although one imagines that the scale of consumption would have been such that more widely spaced sources in the local oak forest would have had to have been tapped. The Nene and its tributaries provided the water required in the processes and also the main means whereby the products were moved to their markets. It is presumed that batches were taken on the river to the Wash, from where they were coasted up to the northern military zone, which seems to have had a large supply contract with the Nene Valley potters. Another outlet was to the north and south by the artificial drain-come-canal known as the Car Dyke.

The clay from which a pot is made sets definite structural limitations on the form and size the pot can take. Therefore in any reasonably complex potting culture there would be a variety of forms of a clay or clays used, depending on the nature of the final product. Coarse, poorly levigated clays might suffice for large grain-storage jars; but thin-walled drinking cups, part of the better-use tableware, would require a finer, well-washed material. Another source of variation in clay type within a culture is geographical distribution. A demographically large culture spread over a considerable territory will have groups of people with differing degrees of access to different clay resources.

The ancient potter can be assumed to be selecting his clay in the light of experience of what is right for the job in hand. The archaeologist is not directly familiar with the clay source and has to analyse the finished product in order to define what qualities the maker was exploiting. Because of the mineralogical and chemical differences that exist between clays, various analyses can be undertaken which indicate the probable source of a clay or at least distinguish between two pieces that are superficially alike.

A simple method of examining the qualities of a clay is to make pots out of the clay thought to have been used for the ancient examples and to wash it in different ways, work it and fire it under different conditions, and compare the results with the actual. Roman samian pottery has been successfully reproduced in experiments making use of illite-rich clays, illite being considered to be the critical mineral in the slip producing the characteristic surface gloss.

Petrological study of sherds has proved successful in differentiating pottery and defining clay sources. A thin section is prepared from a sherd in a similar fashion as from a stone artefact and it is examined under a microscope in order to identify the minerals present. There are many examples of the successful application of mineralogical study to the problem of clay source. A recent one concerns the work of D. P. S. Peacock on the problem of the source of the Romano-British pottery called black-burnished 1. The mineral tourmaline is found to be present in an unusually high proportion in the fabric, and although such a high content is a feature of the Upper Greensand of the south-west it is known that the Greensand is not the temper because other features of the mineral content of the fabric differ from it. The Tertiary sands of the Wareham–Poole Harbour area, south Dorset, which are derived from the Greensand, have an identical mineral composition and are probably the source. This conclusion is supported by the finding of wasters at Corfe Mullen in the area and a kiln at Ower, Poole Harbour. Significantly, the native Durotrigian Iron Age pottery, which on typological grounds has been postulated as the precursor of the Roman age ware, has an identical tourmaline-rich fabric (Peacock, 1973).

Matson (1969, 597) has pointed out that thin-sectioning can also yield technological information by allowing microscopic study of grain sizes which will suggest whether the clay has been washed before being used. Similarly, the amount of oxidisation that has occurred in certain minerals can be observed and the information used to assess the degree of firing.

Spectrographic analysis can be used for distinguishing fabrics. The technique is essentially the same as that used for metal analyses and is concerned with the identification of trace elements. It is necessary to crush a sherd to produce a sample. It is essential that a representative sample is obtained and the most suitable type of pottery is fine-textured in which the minerals are well distributed.

Mrs E. E. Richards, working on the Romano-British pottery found in excavations at the fort of Mumrills, Scotland, used the method to draw an important distinction in the fabrics of the wares generally called black-burnished. She recognised two main fabrics, A and B. A corresponds to the typological category 1 which seems to have been manufactured in southern Dorset, whilst B is largely equivalent to category 2 and has its origins in eastern England, probably the Essex area. Both categories were supplied to the Army in the north, one being shipped up the west coast, the other up the east (Richards, 1963).

Sayre has been able to use the technique to indicate the sources of Greek amphorae working back from known examples and comparing the analyses with unlocated pieces (Sayre, 1959).

If the neutrons in a sample are activated by exposing it to radiation, it is known that the activity will decrease at a certain rate according to the chemical composition of the specimen. Thus by ascertaining this decay rate experimentally it is possible to define the chemical composition of an object. There is no need to break up a piece for nuclear bombardment analysis.

Important studies have already been made by nuclear activation on Roman Arretine, Gaulish samian and other classical wares. It has also helped confirm for Mesoamerican archaeologists that fine orange ware found at a number of ceremonial and habitation sites of the Maya originated from the site of Kixpec.

X-ray fluorescent spectrometry involves the exposure of the sample to X-rays and the identification of the constituent elements of a fabric by the distinctive fluorescence given off by each one. The technique is essentially concerned with those elements that group at the surface.

E. T. Hall has described a portable X-ray fluorescence machine. An example of the method at work is the identification of the ratio of manganese to cobalt in Chinese blue and white porcelain and the recognition that this can be used for dating purposes, as fifteenth- and sixteenth-century potters used an ore source with a low manganese content whilst eighteenth-century ones used a source that had distinctly more manganese.

A temper or filler is commonly incorporated into the clay of a pot to give added strength and to counteract any tendency to cracking on shrinkage through firing. A wide variety is found; chopped grass, straw, sand, crushed shell and crushed pottery are common. A number of important Romano-British wares can be characterised by their tempers; for example, the calcite-gritted wares made at a number of centres mainly in the later Roman period are easily recognised by the inclusions of calcite, shell and limestone particles. Calcitic material has a tendency to burn out during firing, leaving holes in the fabric and giving what is known as a vesicular effect.

As has been noted above, it is often the nature of the temper that reveals whether a pot was imported or not. Examples of studies of this aspect are noted in the bibliography.

Assuming the potter has selected a suitable clay and has washed and kneaded it in the required manner, the next stage is to form the pot. A fundamental distinction is drawn between wheel-made pottery and hand-formed. The time of the introduction of the use of the wheel in potting varies considerably throughout the world—for example, it is not known in the New World until post-Columbian times. In Britain it was introduced to the south-east on a limited scale in the last century before the Roman conquest but on a massive scale only with the provision of the new markets of Roman forts and towns. In order to be able to distinguish wheel-thrown pieces it is necessary to examine the inner surface of the sherd and look for the tell-tale wheel-marks, which are a spiral of lines or slight ridges formed by the maker's fingertips as he draws the vessel up on the turntable. These marks are not found on hand-thrown pots and should not be confused with the ridges often left on the inside when the pot has been formed by coiling. Small pots can be made by hand from a single block of clay, being formed by hollowing the middle of the lump out and shaping the walls by squeezing between the fingers. Unless great care is taken the result is usually crude. The more common method is to build the base of a single disc of clay and to form the walls by coiling. Often a pot will fracture along the junctions of the coils.

The pot should be examined for minor features of construction, such as the way lips or handles are attached to the main body and the manner in which the junction with the base was effected. One method of giving a smooth surface finish and strengthening the body was beating the exterior with a flattish paddle, holding an anvil against the corresponding inner surface. If the paddle was carved or wrapped in cloth, then impressions are left on the walls.

The third and least common technique of manufacture is moulding. The shape of the vessel is created in a clay mould. This was the method of mass production of Gaulish samian. The mould was reused several times. A pot is allowed to dry to the leather-hard state, shrinking a little, before it is extracted from the mould. Another example of the excellent results that can be obtained is the funerary pottery of the Mochica culture of the Classical period of the north coast of Peru. A great variety of subjects is found, including portrait heads, animals, mythological beasts and scenes from everyday life.

Many methods of finishing and decorating the surface of a pot were used in the past. Most were executed prior to firing. A smoothed surface can be obtained by polishing the exterior of the pot with a pebble or blunt stick, the effect being known as burnishing. This was a common practice on many Romano-British wares, and characteristic of the black-burnished types.

A slip is a mixture of clay and water in a liquid state into which a leather-hard vessel can be dipped to give it a fine finish. Gaulish sigillata was dipped in an illite-rich slip which gave the characteristic red colour if fired under oxidising conditions. A special case of slipping is the so-called colour-coated ware made in Roman Britain and chiefly characteristic of the third and fourth centuries. This was a major product of the Nene Valley. Vessels were immersed in an iron-enriched slip which fired to various colours, including black, chocolate brown, dark grey and red.

Not to be confused with a slip is the so-called self-slip, which is a darker zone at the surface of a vessel caused by the smoothing of the surface with wet hands or a wet rag which creates a skin of a very fine clay fraction. Thin-sectioning can be used to distinguish the two cases (Matson, 1969).

Paint applied pre-firing is also a form of slip, applied in the required patterns with a brush or stick.

The study of glazes is a specialised aspect of the ceramicist's work and involves the techniques of analysis mentioned above, such as spectrometry, X-ray fluorescence and nuclear bombardment, and is closely allied to studies of glass. Shepard's book should be consulted for further details (Shepard, 1965, 178–81). A glaze is a glassy deposit on the surface of a vessel. Various sorts are found, a very common one being the lead glaze, the main type used for British medieval pottery. Salt glazing was characteristic of stonewares. Glazed pottery found in Britain is almost certainly likely to be no earlier than Late Saxon in date, but a small amount of glazed pottery was imported from St Remy-en-Rollat, near Vichy, in the first century AD and some was manufactured at Littlechester, Derbyshire, during the reign of Trajan. Some experiments have been conducted that have reproduced the type of glaze found on ancient Egyptian pottery. A blue glaze was manufactured by heating potassium carbonate or natron with powdered malachite on silica-rich quartz pebbles (Coles, 1973, 153).

Post-firing painting is rarely found. It is a characteristic of certain types of funerary pottery from the Paracas peninsula, Peru—previously termed Paracas Cavernas—on which coloured areas of red, green, black and yellow are outlined with incised line motifs.

Negative painting is another feature of certain Peruvian ceramics, notably those of Gallinazo and Recuay. A design was painted on the vessel in a wax and then the rest of the pot either directly painted with a brush or immersed in a slip. On firing the wax melted away, leaving the unpainted area outlined as the main decorative motif. It is thought that the technique was copied from dyeing textiles.

The other decorative techniques can be divided into additive and non-additive. In the first category comes appliqué decoration. This involves the attachment of a figure or a device to the vessel. Examples are the face-urns that often accompany Romano-British burials and the lion-head spout found on the samian mortarium, form 45.

Barbotine decoration is executed by trailing a thick slip in a fashion not dissimilar to icing a cake over the exterior of a pot. In this manner very complicated motifs could be built up and, with careful finishing, could reach a considerable artistic standard. Examples of such fine work can be seen on the Romano-British hunt cups, which are drinking vessels adorned with scenes of hounds chasing hares and deer. Other types, such as the poppy-headed beakers of the second century, have designs of dots and circles. Drinking vessels imported to Britain from the Rhineland sometimes have drinking mottos written on them *en barbotine*.

A gilding effect can be produced by dusting the surface of a pot with fine mica grains. Products of the Romano-British Severn Valley are sometimes treated in this fashion.

The second group of techniques, the non-additive, includes

incised decoration. A knife or other sharp implement is used to cut a pattern or picture on the body of the vessel in the finer cases. In examples of coarse work, incision takes the form of crude slashes on various parts of the pot. The Forma-

Fig. 21 Colour-coated beaker with barbotine scrolls, Romano-British

tive period culture of Cupisnique in northern Peru produced some fine incised vessels with motifs, including the Chavinoid feline. It is not a common technique on classical wares.

Allied to incision is combing, by which patterns are created through dragging a comb across the surface leaving rows of parallel lines caused by the teeth. This is a common decorative method on local Romano-British coarse wares, such as the Horningsea industry of Cambridgeshire.

Minor modelling, which does not affect the general shape trend, is often found used for decorative effect. In this group could be included all the many non-functional variations in lip profile which often prove culturally and chronologically diagnostic. On the body, features such as cordons, raised lines

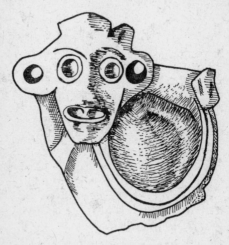

Fig. 22   Moulded head on pottery vessel—Arawak, West Indies

usually marking profile changes, corrugated surfaces, fluting and furrowing are devices encountered.

A number of methods of impressing designs on a surface were used. Two types of stamp are found, the single stamp and the roller stamp. The single stamp in the form of a figure or other device could be used in combination with others to produce a design. Stamps of this sort are found on the colour-coated products of Oxfordshire in Roman Britain and are an important feature in many of the pagan Saxon funerary products. With a roller stamp it is possible to repeat the same design several times on the same pot. A special case of the use of stamps is for decorated Gaulish samian (sigillata). The stamps of figures and standard classical motifs which were drawn from metal prototypes were not applied to the body of the vessels direct but were impressed in the mould. The same stamps were reused, often in differing compositions, for other vessels and the work of a single potter can be traced and the interrelationship between two potters studied if they shared some of their stamps. These stamps were of baked clay.

Rouletting is the form of decoration that can be created by holding a toothed wheel against a pot and revolving it slightly at regular intervals as the pot turns on the lathe, leaving characteristic horizontal bands of short vertical lines of teeth impression. It is common on Romano-British colour-coated vessels, such as the so-called Castor box where it was executed prior to dipping in the slip.

A variety of other media were utilised to give impressed designs. These included textiles wrapped around wooden paddles, carved wooden paddles, simple sticks, shells and bones—often bird bones such as the blackbird's used on British Neolithic pottery.

The final appearance of a pot, especially its coloration, depends on the way in which it is fired and this in turn is dependent on the type of structure used for this process. The essential requirements for a potter are that he can control the temperature and atmosphere of the kiln. The reader must consult the books mentioned in the bibliography for details of kiln structure, which are very variable. It is possible to produce very fine pottery with the minimum of structure, as is demonstrated by the fact that most of the black-burnished 1 types were fired in surface bonfires. The typical Romano-British kiln comprised the three elements usually found in such structures. First, there was a hollow for the stokehole in which the charcoal and wood for the fire were burnt. A short flue for draught connected the stokehole with the firing chamber, which was usually rounded in plan. Within, the firing chamber was normally split in two levels. Some form of pedestal supported a clay floor or fire bars on which the pots for firing were stacked. Experimental work at Barton-on-Humber has shown that it is likely that such kilns were first fired without pots in them or at least that the main purpose of the first firing was to produce a more airtight structure. It was no very difficult task to construct such a kiln, but it required skill to site the flue to best advantage. Loading was simple and the amount of fuel required low. Also it was shown that a permanent dome was unnecessary (Coles, 1973, 149–52).

Light-coloured pottery usually results if a free flow of oxygen is allowed in a kiln, i.e. if it is fired in an oxidising atmosphere. If the flow of oxygen is impeded and reducing conditions obtain, then dark ware is the usual outcome. Often it is found that pots were fired to differing states of total oxidisation. A study of the firing characteristics of the clays likely to have been used for a particular type of pot, particularly experimental firing under different conditions, will allow an assessment of the original firing process to be made. Texture, porosity and chemical make-up of a clay are closely related to the rate of oxidation.

A difficulty often met with in describing a vessel is finding an adequate terminology for the range of variation in colour that is encountered. Also, as many people vary in their assessment of colours, there is a need for standardisation. This is provided by use of colour charts, such as the Munsell chart for soils. Unfortunately, these are as yet not in common use. These comments can be extended beyond pottery to include wall plaster and other materials.

It is not possible in the restricted space available to examine at length all the possible directions that the secondary analysis of ceramics can take. The following comments are intended to indicate the general trends. It should be stressed that the principles behind such things as morphological analysis and distributional studies are common to other classes of artefact.

Form is a major aspect of a pot that can be used for archaeological purposes. The first problem for the analyst is to arrive at a standard description of form that is universal, not culturally or functionally restricted, and capable of expansion to assimilate new discoveries. The need for such a general reference system is not universally recognised. The student of Greek vases, for example, uses a terminology for the standardised shapes that he meets which, if it is not based securely on ancient usage, is at least hallowed by consistent scholarly repetition, whilst the student of Roman fine red wares uses a numerical system developed largely during the last and the beginning of this century. The data are not yet so arranged that questions of general form traditions and variations in Mediterranean ceramic history can be studied in detail.

Two attempts at achieving a standard description of form may be mentioned. One is to use standard templates of common geometric shapes to describe the profile. It is not possible to deal with minor variation in form by this method and its main use is to establish major classes of vessel. Even so, it is preferable to a poorly defined system based on functional descriptions such as jar, dish or bowl. The latter terms are interpretive and should be applied only after basic analysis.

The second means of describing form is that mentioned by Shepard (1965, 226). The profile of a pot is considered to be potentially composed of four types of critical points. The first are the end points, that is the terminations of the total profile. The second is the point of vertical tangency, which is that point at which a vertical line forms a tangent with the maximum lateral projection of the pot. The third is a corner point, the point at which any sharp change in profile trend occurs. The last is the inflection point, which is the point where the transition from one profile trend to another takes place, this change of profile being gradual.

Any pot's form can be described with reference to these four points. Qualitatively, it can be classed according to the particular combination of points and their positioning. Greater discrimination is achieved, and the nature of minor form variation studied, by using a numerical system to describe the position of the points. The author has used a simple system whereby all points on the profile are described by two figures, one expressing the distance below the upper end of the central

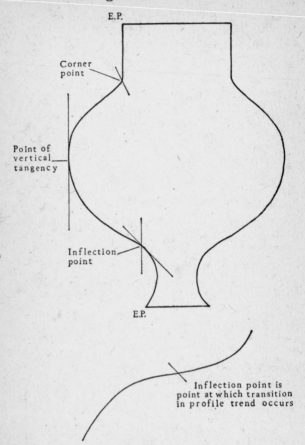

E.P.

Corner
point

Point of
vertical
tangency

Inflection
point

E.P.

Inflection point is
point at which transition
in profile trend occurs

Fig. 23 Profile points on a pot

vertical axis of the pot and the other giving its horizontal
distance from the same line.

It requires no great effort to devise other standardising
systems to the same end and a number have been published.
The advantages of ease of description and comparability are

substantial, and large numbers of vessels that it is not possible to draw can be registered precisely.

Decoration can be considered in three aspects: its technique of execution, and the content and style of the motifs. Only the third is diagnostic of a particular production centre or culture. Techniques have been discussed above and are shared by many centres of many periods. Similarly, the content of two decorative schemes can be very similar and yet the products be entirely distinctive because of the way in which the subject-matter is expressed. Style is partly arrangement of motif and this can be expressed numerically, but the actual configuration must usually be described with words and illustration.

Classification is the basis for most analysis. Archaeological categories have been discussed in Chapter 1. The application of such categories to pottery study has varied considerably in practice. The main stumbling block has been the very loose use of the term 'type'. Sometimes pots have been said to be of the same type if they have similar forms (e.g. beakers) or if they possess a common decoration characteristic such as colour-coating. In other cases pots have been excluded from being considered the same type because they did not possess features identical with one another.

The most profitable way in which to approach typing is to see types as being formed when two or more pots share a significant number of attributes of fabric, form and decoration such that the pots can be considered to have been made at the same production centre with the same function in mind. It is worth noting that an element of interpretation is essential even at this basic analytical stage and that pure objectivity cannot be employed.

It is also evident that it is not necessary for pots to be absolutely identical except in the key attributes (Clarke, 1968, 137). This conforms to real-life observations of the potter at work where he endeavours consistently to produce vessels according to a single idea but variation in form creeps in because of the limits of accuracy in reproduction in the method of manufacture and because non-essential variation in decoration is

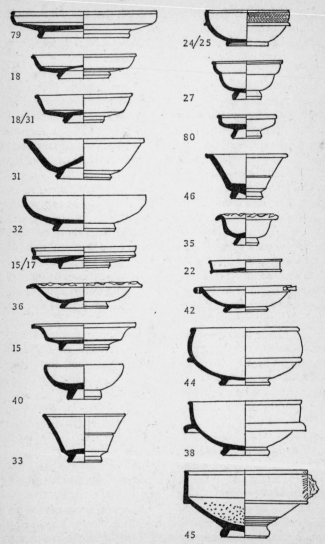

Fig. 24 A typology—Samian forms

allowed according to the predilections of the worker and his market.

Accepting this definition, we can therefore envisage at one point in time a given culture possessing a set number of production centres each producing a particular quantity of types of pots. A study in the changes that a pottery industry can undergo through time might observe one or more of the following trends. First, the number of centres of production can decrease, increase or stay constant. This can be accompanied by increase, decrease or no change in the number of types produced. Further, there could be quantitative change in the output absolutely and relative to individual vessels of a particular type. Detailed studies for whole cultures or even single industries are still rare in Europe, although recent work on beakers and Romano-British pottery is moving along these lines and the principles have long been the basis of pottery seriation analysis used by American archaeologists in their own hemisphere.

The variation that can arise in the production of one type is the starting-point for change. If a deviation from the normal practice proves advantageous it may be taken up as a modification to an existent type and the revised form might come to replace the original entirely. Thus it is possible through form and decoration analysis to follow the apparent growth one from another of a series of types. The arrangement of types into linked series with the implication of a sort of evolutionary relationship is termed typology. This is discussed at greater length in the first chapter. Besides its chronological purpose, the chief value of typology is the logical fashion in which it deals with the development of phenomena such as art-styles. Indeed, without the organising power of the typological concept, it is unlikely that the study of, for example, Greek pottery, sculpture and architecture would have made the progress it has. It has often been necessary to resort to the method because of the lack of adequate stratigraphic data to establish basic requirements such as sequences, as was for long the case with much of the funerary pottery of coastal Peru. The obvious problem with the method is that it is based on an assumption that populations of artefacts possess similar properties to biological populations, such as selection of useful variation, and the cycle of both quantitative and qualitative growth, middle age and death, or at least its analogy, development, fluorescence and decadence. It must be admitted that the idea is only a model when applied in individual cases, which must be tested rigorously using stratigraphic and other checks, but that also as a general model of the changes through time in an artefact population it has proved to be an accurate description.

The main use to which pottery has been put archaeologically has been to establish chronology, and this will remain a major function, especially where other evidence is lacking. The importance of pottery stems from its ubiquity. It is likely to be always present on sites of cultures that use it. Of course, it does not usually carry a date stamped on it. The excavator will compare the pottery he has found with types from other sites that have been assigned a date by various means. He will arrive at a dating on the basis of the degree of similarity that he considers exists between his material and that from dated groups.

Pottery is dated by its association with dated objects, such as coins or inscriptions, or through being found in a deposit which can be dated by one of the scientific methods already referred to. Another important means is the finding of a pot in a context that can be assigned to a particular historical event. Examples of these are the lava- and ash-covered buildings of Pompeii and Herculaneum dating to AD 79 and the burnt deposits at London, Verulamium and Colchester representing the destruction of these centres by Boudicca in AD 60.

A technique that is being rapidly developed for dating pottery directly is that of thermoluminescence dating. It is already a standard technique for testing authenticity and has been used to indicate the Hacilar forgeries and to detect modern reproductions of Etruscan sarcophagi. Its accuracy is not yet such that it can replace traditional methods for the historic periods in Europe, the present error being in the order of 10%—i.e. $\pm$100 years in a sample 1000 years old—but it has great potential beyond Europe and in the remoter prehistoric periods in conjunction with and as a check on radiocarbon dating.

A number of clay minerals absorb and store energy through exposure to nuclear radiation. Minute proportions of uranium and thorium are the chief source of radiation in pottery clay. The amount of energy stored increases with time. This energy can be released if the clay is heated, and light and heat are given off. The emission of light and heat is termed the thermoluminescence of a material and this is of greater intensity the more energy there has been stored. If fired to over 500°C a pot will have begun its 'life' with no thermoluminescence, and this will have accumulated during the years. Many factors, such as the constituent minerals and the degree of exposure to radiation, affect the absorption of energy.

The laboratory procedure establishes the thermoluminescence of a pot by comparing the quantity of light emitted during the rapid heating to a high temperature of a crushed sample with the output from extraneous sources isolated during another heating to 500°C of the same sample. The rate at which it accumulated is calculated by estimating the degree of radiation exposure required to produce the determined level of thermoluminescence. To do this the sample is exposed to a strong radiation source.

The principal development centre for this method is the Research Laboratory for Archaeology and History of Art, 6 Keble Road, Oxford. The laboratory can be consulted for details of its research programme.

The property of thermo-remanent magnetism discussed in connection with magnetic prospecting can be utilised for dating purposes. Fired clays generally have a stable remanent magnetism which records the direction and intensity of the earth's magnetic field at the time of firing (Cook, 1969).

If well-dated objects of fired clay are studied, then the changes in the direction and intensity of the earth's magnetic field can be plotted through time. The curves plotted can be used for assessing the date of an object the thermo-remanent magnetism of which, but not the age, is known. It is necessary to know the orientation at the time the object was fired in order to assess the direction of the magnetic field. This means that only *in situ* objects, especially kilns, are suitable. Pottery cannot be used as it is not usually possible to know its position during firing.

Specimens are extracted on site. About ten samples are taken from different parts of each kiln. These are detached as cubes, which are enclosed in a square box. The top of the box is filled with plaster, which is levelled off at its top. On this is marked the horizontal orientation, which is assessed by using a theodolite to sight between the sample and a known point. The remanent magnetism is measured with a magnetometer.

Interest in the method has waned in recent years owing to the difficulty in obtaining satisfactory specimens. However, the general history of the direction of the earth's field has been established for the Roman period in Britain such that it is possible to place a burnt structure in a date bracket of about fifty years. Longer curves are established for parts of the Continent. The method can also be used to indicate whether two burnt constructions were contemporaneously fired. Potsherds can be tested to check whether they are from the same vessel, as they should have the same orientations, and it is possible to assign the sherds to their relative positions on the pot.

Mobile objects as well as *in situ* structures can be tested to assess the intensity of the earth's magnetic field at the time of firing. It is not necessary to know the orientation of the specimen, but the place of firing must be ascertained because of the changes of intensity that occur with latitude and between areas. The remanent magnetism of an object is measured in the usual fashion. This is then obliterated by reheating and the object is remagnetised in a field of known intensity. The ratio of the newly acquired intensity to the old is theoretically equivalent to that between the present field and the original. For the process of remagnetisation it is essential that the sample is a clean, properly fired and fully oxidised example that is not likely to suffer from the conversion of the iron oxides present when heated. Intensity is registered in oersteds.

An intensity curve has been established for France, Czechoslovakia and Japan as well as other areas. This property does not allow for the same precision in dating as direction.

The study of ceramics can be of considerable importance for the study of the history of art. Chinese porcelains, Islamic glazed vessels and Mochica funerary pottery were small works of art in their own right and worthy of study as such. This is not the archaeologist's main task, but no study of social patterns can ignore the artistic products of a society. Vase painting was a highly developed minor art among the Greeks. Scholars have charted in detail the progressive development in Attic pottery from the early simple geometric motifs of the Proto-Geometric style, through the first tentative figure schemes of the late Geometric to the exquisite compositions of Black-Figure and Red-Figure (Cook, 1972). The chronology of vase painting has been established typologically by very detailed style analysis. The typological analysis has been combined with the evidence from a few well-dated deposits, such as that associated with the clearance after the sack of Athens in 480 BC. This same analysis in conjunction with signed works has allowed the detailed distinction of the works of individual potters and their workshops (Beazley, 1963). The study of Greek vases can be linked with that of sculpture as the style development in both media runs through similar parallel stages at approximately the same time. Particularly apparent is the progress towards representing three-dimensional space in two dimensions and portraying three-quarter views of the human body in the correct articulation.

Among Chinese and Greek potters the form of the vessel often ranked as important as any motifs that might appear on it.

A pot needs to be defined according to its function. A fundamental distinction is that between utilitarian and non-utilitarian. The difference that can occur between the funerary pottery and the household vessels of a culture can be demonstrated by comparing the moulded vessels of the Mochica culture, Peru, with the few, dull, strictly functional red and black wares usually found on their domestic sites. The differences can be so marked that on occasion the domestic pottery of one culture has been classified in a different culture from its burial pottery. Whatever the precise form that a funerary vessel might take, copying those of utilitarian vessels, its primary function was as a ceremonial accompaniment to the dead. It should be remembered, however, that vessels that have been used in the household were often interred as grave goods.

Utilitarian pottery can serve a broad range of functions, from a cheese press to a candelabrum. The specific function of some vessels, such as the amphora, is fully attested in literature and representational art, but the use of others must be deduced from less direct evidence. The term 'cooking pot' in Roman Britain is commonly used for any jar, but it should be strictly confined to those with accretions of carbonised matter which suggests the pot was in contact with a fire for cooking. Many jars must have acted as holders for liquid and have not been engaged in any cooking. Bowls and plates not only can be eaten from but also can be used simply for holding food such as fruit. Every attempt should be made on site to collect evidence that might suggest the function of vessels. This includes examining the earth adhering to a vessel for traces of food remains either as tangible fragments or as phosphatic traces. The difficulty of assigning a function to a piece with certainty means that classification by function is an unsatisfactory procedure.

Distribution studies are a major preoccupation of the archaeologist. Pottery was distributed in many different ways in the past according to its mode of manufacture and the system of marketing, or lack of it, that prevailed in various cultures. It was usually distributed for its own sake or as the container for a commodity. There was a variety of distribution patterns at work simultaneously in Roman Britain which demonstrates some of the features that can be found. The most restricted distribution was the purely local production by the women of vessels for direct household use in continuation of pre-Roman traditions. This practice undoubtedly continued throughout the Roman period, even though it is difficult to detect clearly. A broader distribution to several settlements within a geographically nodal region is the next stage in the market hierarchy. The kilns at Horningsea, Cambridgeshire, which supplied the southern Fens and south Cambridgeshire during the second century AD are a good example. The third stage is the distribution over large parts of the province from substantial factories. Prominent examples include the Nene Valley kilns, the Oxford area kilns and the black-burnished 1 industry. There was no type of pottery produced within the province that had a uniform distribution throughout it, but emanating from external sources in Gaul, samian pottery is found all over Britain in the first and second centuries AD on a wide variety of sites from cities to native subsistence farms.

Local and regional markets would be served by individual potters, or a small company of them who would establish kilns within an area which might not form a permanent factory. The products might be sold tinker-fashion from a travelling cart, but it is more likely that the wares were purchased at the periodic markets that were often held in conjunction with religious festivals. The larger factories might be owned by a wealthy individual or company. The workers were probably slaves, as was the case in many of the samian factories. As well as supplying periodic markets, they would also supply the regular markets of the towns and might have contracts with the Army to supply the frontier forts, as the Nene Valley potters seem to have had. Because of the practice of stamping the maker's or owner's name on samian vessels, the market distribution of individual factories can be studied in detail. It is possible to study through time the competitive relationships between rival potting centres vying for the same markets. A new type might flood the market initially and its incidence increase for a period but afterwards, as its popularity wanes and new varieties become available, its numbers and its range will diminish.

The distribution of amphorae fragments tells of the extent of the wine trade between Britain and Spain and Gaul. British chieftains in the south-east were importing wine from the Continent for many years before the Roman Conquest. Ointments, perfumes and oils were also transported in pottery containers. Grain was stored in large jars.

Various aspects of life and beliefs can be shown in the form of a pot or in its decoration. Mochica funerary pottery is famous for its stirrup-spouted vessels in the form of human

Fig. 25   Mochica portrait vase

heads so realistic as to be almost certainly portraits of the deceased. Many classical vases show contemporary dress, including military uniform, and this is valuable because so little of the actual items ever survive. Vessels in the form of houses or public buildings can inform on points concerning the superstructure of buildings only preserved at footings level. Certain Iron Age pots from central Italy are good examples of this. Greek and Mochica pottery both show a variety of daily activities such as hunting, food preparation and games.

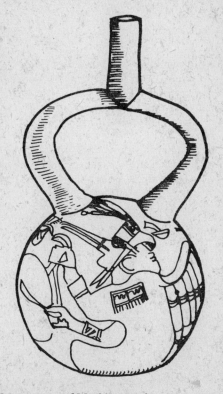

Fig. 26   Stirrup-spouted Mochica vessel

Mochica pottery often delights in showing the diseases and deformities suffered by the populace, and also the considerable variety of erotic practices that they indulged in.

Many of the scenes of Greek mythology are vividly portrayed on vases and the story of Odysseus, for example, can be detected as early as Geometric times. Often variants on the literary form of the myth are found in the painting. The gods of the Mochica pantheon can be detailed and their spheres of influence outlined because of their recurrent representation on pottery. Religious practices such as ritual head-hunting are shown.

A recent piece of research by Deetz on a site of the Arikara Indians, Missouri, has attempted to show that pottery decoration changes can be used to indicate social change. An analysis of the assemblages from the three main periods of the village of Medicine Crow showed that between 1690 and 1780 the cohesion of the Arikara pottery tradition broke down. Historical, ethnographic data showed that the Arikara had undergone a radical social change in terms of their inheritance and residential system, and Deetz suggested that this was reflected in the disintegration of the ceramic system. Whatever the criticisms of the details of the study, it does point the way to broader horizons in the study of pottery and its relationship to human society (Deetz, 1965).

Glass
(Source: Smith, 1969.)

The study of glass is directed to four main aims. The first is to achieve a more secure chronology for the glass of various cultures. The second is to study how the composition of glass varies regionally and temporally. Thirdly, much more knowledge is necessary for the understanding of the raw materials employed in glass-making and their source. Lastly, more investigation of the techniques of manufacture is required.

Three main methods of composition analysis are in use. Arc spectrography has been most extensively used, but it is not a favourite with museum curators as it is destructive. The method also fails to detect elements like phosphorus.

X-ray fluorescence analysis has the advantage of being non-destructive, but its results only apply to the surface of a specimen, which makes the study of decayed glass difficult. It is hoped that the use of the electron microbeam probe will lend further power to this form of analysis. The probe focuses on a point about 1 micron in diameter and so makes it possible to study very small pieces and parts of pieces. Flame photometry and colorimetry have also been employed for specialised work.

Neutron activation analysis is coming into more regular use after the initial experiments of Sayre.

Sayre has been able to identify five main compositional groups of Western glass. These are classified according to their relative concentrations of magnesium, potassium, manganese, antimony and lead (Smith, 1969, 616). The groups are as follows: second millennium BC group (high magnesium); antimony-rich group (sixth century BC to fourth century AD); Roman group (higher manganese content); early Islamic group (higher magnesium and potassium); and Islamic lead group. Russian and Chinese lead glasses are also known.

This chapter has by no means surveyed all the sorts of scientific analysis that are available to the archaeologist. It has sought to demonstrate that it is no longer possible for meaningful studies of culture to be made without recourse to such investigations. This means that the archaeologist must inevitably become better acquainted with the natural sciences. It also means that the role of the amateur requires careful redefinition. It is unlikely and increasingly undesirable that modern archaeology should be initiated by any one but fully trained professionals. The training of competent professionals is still a major headache, but the CBA and others are giving this urgent consideration and the likely result is the creation of some form of professional association.

The amateur will still be welcome to participate in the actual procedure of data recovery, but he will find himself under the very strict discipline of a scientific experiment. It is to be hoped that the majority of amateurs will accept this and, indeed, benefit from the process. Those who cannot reconcile their treasure-hunting instincts with science must per force face exclusion from our work.

Bibliography

Beazley, J. D., *Attic Red-figure Vase-painters*. 2nd ed. Oxford: Oxford University Press, 1963.

Britton, D., and Richards, E. E., *Optical Emission Spectroscopy and the Study of Metallurgy in the European Bronze Age*, in Brothwell and Higgs (eds), *Science in Archaeology*, 2nd edition London: Thames & Hudson, 1969, 603–13.

Cann, J. R., Dixon, J. E., and Renfrew, C., *Obsidian Analysis and the Obsidian Trade*, in Brothwell and Higgs (eds), 1969, 578–91.

Clarke, D. L., *Analytical Archaeology*. London: Methuen, 1968.

Coles, J., *Archaeology by Experiment*. London: Hutchinson, 1973.

Cook, R. M., *Greek Painted Pottery*. London: Methuen, 1972.

Deetz, J., *The dynamics of stylistic change in Arikara ceramics*. Illinois Studies in Anthropology, No. 4; Illinois: University of Illinois Press, 1965.

Fleischer, R. L., Price, P. B., and Walker, R. M., *Quaternary Dating by the Fission Track Technique*, in Brothwell and Higgs (eds), 1969, 58–61.

Friedman, I., Smith, R. L., and Clark, D., *Obsidian Dating*, in Brothwell and Higgs (eds), 1969, 62–75.

Gentner, W., and Lippolt, H. J., *The Potassium-Argon Dating of Upper Tertiary and Pleistocene Deposits*, in Brothwell and Higgs (eds), 1969, 88–100.

Matson, F. R., *Some Aspects of Ceramic Technology*, in Brothwell and Higgs (eds), 1969, 592–602.

Miller, J. A., *Dating by the Potassium-Argon Method—Some Advances in Technique*, in Brothwell and Higgs (eds), 1969, 101–5.

Morey, J. E., and Dunham, K. C., in *Proceedings Yorkshire Geological Society* 29, 1953, 141.

Peacock, D. P. S., *The Black-Burnished Pottery Industry in Dorset*, in CBA Research Report 10, 1973, 63–5.

Richards, E. E., *Report on Black-burnished Ware from Mumrills. Proc. Soc. Antiq. Scotland*, XCIV, 1963, 129–32.

Sayre, E. V., *Studies in Ancient Ceramic Objects by Means of Neutron Bombardment and Emission Spectroscopy*, in *Application of Science in the Examination of Works of Art*. Boston: Museum of Fine Arts, 1959, 153–80.

Shepard, A. O., *Ceramics for the Archaeologist*. Washington: Carnegie Institute of Washington Publications, 1965.

Shotton, F. W., *Petrological Examination*, in Brothwell and Higgs (eds), 1969, 571–7.

Sieveking, G. de G., Craddock, P. T., Hughes, M. J., Bush, P., and Ferguson, J., *Characterisation of Prehistoric Flint Mine Products. Nature* Vol. 228, No. 5268, 17 October 1970, 251–4.

Smith, R. W., *The Analytical Study of Glass in Archaeology*, in Brothwell and Higgs (eds), 1969, 614–23.

Thompson, F. C., *Microscopic Studies of Ancient Metals*, in Brothwell and Higgs (eds), 1969, 555–63.

Additional reading

Most of the above works contain useful bibliographies on this vast subject. Some other useful books include the following:

Aitken, M., *Physics and Archaeology*. 2nd ed. New York: Interscience Publications, 1974.

Biek, L., *Archaeology and the Microscope*. London: Lutterworth Press, 1963.

Bishop, W. W., and Miller, J. A. (eds), *Calibration of Hominoid Evolution*. Edinburgh: Edinburgh University Press, 1972.

Brill, R. H., *Science and Archaeology*. Cambridge, Mass.: Massachusetts Institute of Technology, 1971.

British Academy, *The Impact of the Natural Sciences on Archaeology*. London: British Academy, 1970.

Brodribb, C., *Drawing Archaeological Finds for Publication*. London: John Baker, 1970.

Centre National de la Recherche Scientifique, *Archéologie et Calculateurs*. Paris: Centre National de la Recherche Scientifique 1970.

Cook, R. M., *Archaeomagnetism*, in Brothwell and Higgs (eds), 1969, 76–87.

Forbes, R. J., *Metallurgy in Antiquity*. Leiden: Brill, 1950.

Forbes, R. J., *Studies in Ancient Technology* (I–VI). Leiden: Brill, 1955.

Hall, E. T., *Dating Pottery by Thermoluminescence*, in Brothwell and Higgs (eds), 1969, 106–8.

Heizer, R. F., and Cook, S. F. (eds), *The Application of Quantitative Methods in Archaeology*. Viking Fund Publications in Anthropology, 28, 1970.

Hodges, H., *Artifacts*. London: John Baker, 1964.

Hodson, F. R., Kendall, D. G., and Tăutu, P. (eds), *Mathematics in the Archaeological and Historical Sciences*. Edinburgh: Edinburgh University Press, 1970.

Levey, M. (ed.), *Archaeological Chemistry*. Philadelphia: Pennsylvania University Press, 1967.

Matson, F. R. (ed.), *Ceramics and Man*. Viking Fund Publications in Anthropology, 41, 1965.

Pyddoke, E. (ed.), *The Scientist and Archaeology*. London: Dent, 1963.

Rosenfeld, A., *The Inorganic Raw Materials of Antiquity*. London: Weidenfeld & Nicholson, 1965.

Schaeffer, O. A., and Zähringer, J., *Potassium-Argon Dating*. Berlin: Springer-Verlag, 1966.

Semenov, S. A., *Prehistoric Technology*. Bath: Adams & Dart, 1970.

Tite, M. S., *Methods of Physical Examination in Archaeology*. London: Seminar Press, 1972.

Tylecote, R. F., *Metallurgy in Archaeology*. London: Edward Arnold, 1962.

Appendix

Museums with Collections of Archaeological Importance

This appendix lists alphabetically by the town in which they are situated the main museums in Britain that contain archaeological collections. It is hoped that this will enable the reader to determine where he can most readily inspect antiquities. Anyone who is hoping to gain an understanding of our evidence for the past must regard diligent museum study as an essential part of his work.

Should the reader require more general information concerning the world of museums, he should write to the Museums Association, 87 Charlotte Street, London, W1P 2BX.

I would like to thank Max Hebditch, Director of the Guildhall Museum, London, and Deputy Director of the Museum of London, for his kindness in allowing me to use unpublished work of his in the compilation of this list.

Note that the counties mentioned in the addresses are those of the period prior to the reorganisation of local government that came into effect in 1974. It is not anticipated that this will cause any confusion. Revision can be effected by reference to the 1975 issue of the *Museums Calendar* issued annually by the Museums Association.

Aberdeen	Anthropological Museum, Marischal College, University of Aberdeen, AB9 1AS.
Abergavenny (Mon.)	Abergavenny and District Museum, Castle Grounds.
Abingdon (Berks.)	Borough Museum Collections, County Hall.
Aldborough (Yorks.)	Roman Town and Museum.
Alton (Hants.)	Curtis Museum, High Street.
Annan (Dumfries.)	Burgh Museum, Moat House.
Aylesbury (Bucks.)	Buckinghamshire County Museum, Church Street, HP20 2QP.
Ayr	Carnegie Library, Museum and Art Gallery, 12 Main Street, KA8 8ED.
Bangor (Caernarvon)	Museum of Welsh Antiquities, University College of North Wales.
Barnard Castle (Co. Durham)	The Bowes Museum.
Barnstaple (Devon)	North Devon Athenaeum, The Square.
Barrow-In-Furness (Lancs.)	Public Library and Museum, Ramsden Square.
Bath (Som.)	The Roman Baths and Museum, The Pump Room, BA1 1LZ.
Batley (Yorks.)	Bagshaw Museum, Wilton Park, WF17 0AS.
Bedford	Bedford Museum, The Embankment.
Berwick-Upon-Tweed (Northum.)	Museum and Art Gallery, Marygate, TD15 1BT.
Beverley (Yorks.)	Public Library, Art Gallery and Museum, Champney Road, HU17 9BQ.
Bexhill (Sussex)	Bexhill Museum, Egerton Park.

Bideford (Devon)	Public Library and Museum.
Birchover (Derbys.)	Heathcote Museum, Nr. Matlock, DE4 2BN.
Birmingham	City Museum and Art Gallery, Congreve Street, B3 3DH.
Bognor Regis (Sussex)	Museum Collection of Natural History, c/o The Town Hall.
Bolton (Lancs.)	Museum and Art Gallery, Civic Centre, BL1 1SE.
Bournemouth (Hants.)	Russell-Cotes Art Gallery and Museum, East Cliff.
Bradford (Yorks.)	City Art Gallery and Museum, Cartwright Hall, BD9 4NS.
Brechin (Angus)	Brechin Museum, Mechanics Institute.
Brecon	The Brecknock Museum, Glamorgan Street.
Bridgwater (Som.)	Admiral Blake Museum, Blake Street.
Bridlington (Yorks.)	Bridlington Art Gallery and Museum, Sewerby Hall.
Bridport (Dorset)	Museum and Art Gallery, South Street.
Brighton (Sussex)	Royal Pavilion, Art Gallery and Museums, North Gate House, Church Street, BN1 1UE.
Bristol	City Museum, Queen's Road, BS8 1RL.
Burton Upon Trent (Staffs.)	Museum and Art Gallery, Guild Street.
Bury St Edmunds (Suffolk)	Moyse's Hall Museum, Cornhill.
Buxton (Derbys.)	Buxton Museum, Terrace Road, SK17 6DU.
Caerleon (Mon.)	The Legionary Museum.
Caernarvon	Segontium Museum.

Cambridge	Fitzwilliam Museum, Trumpington Street, CB2 1RB.
	University Museum of Archaeology and Ethnology, Downing Street, CB2 3DZ.
	University Museum of Classical Archaeology, Little Saint, Mary's Lane, CB2 1RR.
Campbeltown (Argyll)	Public Library and Museum, Hall Street.
Canterbury (Kent)	The Royal Museum, High Street.
Cardiff	The National Museum of Wales, Cathays Park, CF1 3NP.
Carlisle (Cumb.)	Museum and Art Gallery, Tullie House, CA3 8TR.
Carmarthen	County Museum, Quay Street.
Cheddar (Som.)	Gough's Cave Museum, The Gorge, BS27 3QF.
Chelmsford (Essex)	Chelmsford and Essex Museum, Oaklands Park, Moulsham Street, CM2 9AQ.
Cheltenham (Glos.)	Art Gallery and Museum, Clarence Street, GL50 3JT.
Chertsey (Surrey)	The Museum (The Cedars), Windsor Street.
Chester	Grosvenor Museum, 27 Grosvenor Street, CH1 2DD.
Chesters (Northum.)	Roman Fort and Museum on Hadrian's Wall, Nr. Chollerford, Hexham.
Chichester (Sussex)	City Museum, 29 Little London.
	Roman Palace and Museum, Salthill Road, Fishbourne.
Cirencester (Glos.)	Corinium Roman Museum, Park Street.
Colchester (Essex)	Colchester and Essex Museum, The Castle, CO1 1TJ.

Corbridge (Northum.)	Corstopitum Roman Site and Museum.
Coventry (Warwicks.)	Herbert Art Gallery and Museum, Jordan Well, CV1 5QP.
Dartford (Kent)	Borough Museum, Central Park, DA1 1EU.
Deal (Kent)	The Museum, Town Hall, High Street.
Derby	Museums and Art Gallery, The Strand, DE1 1BS.
Devizes (Wilts.)	Museum of the Wiltshire Archaeological and Natural History Society, Long Street, SN10 1NS.
Doncaster (Yorks.)	Museum and Art Gallery, Chequer Road, DN1 2AE.
Dorchester (Dorset)	Dorset County Museum, High West Street.
Dover (Kent)	Corporation Museum, Ladywell.
Dumfries	Burgh Museum, The Observatory, Corberry Hill, DG2 7SW.
Dundee	City Museum and Art Gallery, Albert Square, DD1 1DA.
Durham	Gulbenkian Museum of Oriental Art and Archaeology, School of Oriental Studies, The University.
Edinburgh	National Museum of Antiquities of Scotland, Queen Street, EH2 1JD.
	Royal Scottish Museum, Chambers Street, EH1 1JF.
Eton (Bucks.)	The Myers Museum, Eton College, SL4 6DW.
Exeter (Devon)	City Museums and Art Gallery, Royal Albert Memorial Museum, Queen Street, EX4 3RX.
Faversham (Kent)	Maison Dieu Museum, Ospringe.

Glasgow	Art Gallery and Museum, Kelvingrove, G3 8AG.
	The Hunterian Museum, University of Glasgow, W.2.
Glastonbury (Som.)	Glastonbury Antiquarian Society Museum, The Tribunal, High Street.
Gloucester	City Museum and Art Gallery, Brunswick Road.
Godalming (Surrey)	Charterhouse Museum.
Grays (Essex)	Thurrock Local History Museum, Central Library, Orsett Road, RM17 50X.
Guildford (Surrey)	Guildford Museum, Castle Arch.
Halifax (Yorks.)	Bankfield Museum, Akroyd Park, HX3 6HG.
Harlyn Bay (Cornwall)	Harlyn Bay Museum of Prehistoric Discoveries and Ancient Burial Ground.
Harrogate (Yorks.)	Public Library and Art Gallery, Victoria Avenue, HG1 1EG.
Hartlebury (Worcs.)	Worcestershire County Museum, Hartlebury Castle, Nr. Kidderminster.
Hastings (Sussex)	Public Museum and Art Gallery, John's Place, Cambridge Road.
Haverfordwest (Pembroke.)	Pembrokeshire County Museum, The Castle.
Hawick (Roxburgh)	Hawick Museum.
Hereford	City Museum and Art Gallery, Broad Street.
Hertford	Hertford Museum, 18 Bull Plain.
Hitchin (Herts.)	Hitchin Museum and Art Gallery, Paynes Park, SG5 1EQ.
Horsham (Sussex)	Horsham Museum, Causeway House.

Housesteads (Northum.)	Housesteads Roman Fort and Museum, Haydon Bridge.
Huddersfield (Yorks.)	Tolson Memorial Museum, Ravensknowle Park.
Ilfracombe (Devon)	The Museum, Wilder Road.
Inverness	Public Museum, Castle Wynd.
Ipswich (Suffolk)	The Museum, High Street, IP1 3QH.
Keighley (Yorks.)	Art Gallery and Museum, Cliffe Castle, BD20 6LH.
Kilmarnock (Ayr.)	Public Library, Museum and Art Gallery, Dick Institute, Elmbank Avenue.
King's Lynn (Norfolk)	Museum and Art Gallery, Market Street.
Kingston-Upon-Hull (Yorks.)	Georgian Houses, 23–24 High Street, HU1 1NE.
Kingston Upon Thames (Surrey)	Central Library, Museum and Art Gallery, Fairfield Road.
Lancaster	Lancaster Museum, Old Town Hall, Market Square.
Leeds (Yorks.)	City Museum, Municipal Buildings, LS1 3AA.
Leicester	Museum and Art Gallery, New Walk, LE1 6TD.
Letchworth (Herts.)	Museum and Art Gallery, Broadway, SG6 3PD.
Lewes (Sussex)	The Barbican House Museum, The Sussex Archaeological Society, Barbican House, High Street.
Lincoln	City and County Museum, Broadgate.
Liverpool (Lancs.)	City of Liverpool Museums, William Brown Street, L3 8EN.
Llandrindod Wells (Radnor)	County Museum, Temple Street, LD1 5LD.

London	Barnet Museum, Wood Street, Barnet.
	Bexley Local Studies Service, Hall Place, Bourne Road, Bexley.
	British Museum, WC1B 3DG.
	Bromley Museum, The Priory, Church Hill, Orpington.
	The Cuming Museum, Walworth Road, Southwark, SE17 1RS.
	Epping Forest Museum at Queen Elizabeth's Hunting Lodge, Rangers Road, Chingford, E.4.
	Forty Hall, Forty Hill, Enfield, Middlesex, EN2 9HA.
	Guildhall Museum, Gillet House, 55 Basinghall Street, EC2V 5DT.
	Gunnersbury Park Museum, W.3.
	Hayes and Harlington Museum, Hayes Library, Golden Crescent, Hayes.
	The London Museum, Kensington Palace, W8 4PX.
	Museum of London (under construction).
	Passmore Edwards Museum, Romford Road, Stratford, E15 4LZ.
	Uxbridge Library and Local Museum, Council Buildings, High Street, Uxbridge, UB8 1HD.
	Walthamstow Museum of Local History, Old Vestry House, Vestry Road, E17 9NH.
Ludlow (Salop)	Ludlow Museum.
Lullingstone (Kent)	Roman Villa and Museum, Lullingstone Park.

Luton (Beds.)	Museum and Art Gallery, Wardown Park, LU2 7HA.
Macclesfield (Ches.)	West Park Museum and Art Gallery, Prestbury Road.
Maidstone (Kent)	Museum and Art Gallery, St Faith's Street.
Manchester (Lancs.)	The Manchester Museum, The University, M13 9PL.
Margate (Kent)	Public Library and Museum, Victoria Road.
Market Harborough (Leics.)	The Museum, Market Harborough Archaeological and Historical Society, The County Library.
Newark-On-Trent (Notts.)	Museum and Art Gallery, Appleton Gate.
Newbury (Berks.)	Borough Museum, Wharf Street.
Newcastle-Upon-Tyne	Laing Art Gallery and Museum, Higham Place, NE1 8AG.
	Museum of Antiquities, The Quadrangle, The University, NEI 7RU.
Newport (Isle of Wight)	Carisbrooke Castle Museum, PO30 1XY.
Newport (Mon.)	Museum and Art Gallery, John Frost Square, NPT 1PA.
Northampton	Central Museum and Art Gallery, Guildhall Road.
Norwich (Norfolk)	Castle Museum, NOR 65B.
Nottingham	City Art Gallery and Museum, NG1 6EL.
Nuneaton (Warwicks.)	Museum and Art Gallery, Riversley Park.
Oakham	Rutland County Museum, Catmos Street.
Oxford	Ashmolean Museum, Beaumont Street.

	Oxford City and County Museum, Fletcher's House, Woodstock, OX1 3AZ.
	Pitt Rivers Museum, Parks Road.
Penzance (Cornwall)	Natural History and Antiquarian Museum, Penlee House, Penlee Park.
Perth	Art Gallery and Museum, George Street.
Peterborough	City Museum and Art Gallery, Priestgate.
Plymouth (Devon)	City Museum and Art Gallery, Drake Circus, PL4 8AJ.
Poole (Dorset)	Poole Guildhall Museum, Market Street.
Portsmouth (Hants.)	City Museum and Art Gallery, Alexandra Road, PO1 2LJ.
Preston (Lancs.)	Harris Museum and Art Gallery, Market Square, PR1 2PP.
Reading (Berks.)	Museum and Art Gallery, Blagrave Street.
	Museum of Greek Archaeology, University of Reading, Whiteknights.
Ribchester (Lancs.)	Museum of Roman Antiquities.
Richborough (Kent)	Richborough Castle.
Rochester (Kent)	Eastgate House Museum.
Rotherham (Yorks.)	Municipal Museum and Art Gallery, Clifton Park, S65 2AA.
Rothesay (Bute)	The Bute Museum, Stuart Street.
Saffron Walden (Essex)	The Museum.
St Albans (Herts.)	Verulamium Museum and Hypocaust.
	City Museum, Hatfield Road.
St Andrews (Fife)	St Andrews Cathedral Museum.

St Mary's (Isles of Scilly)	Isles of Scilly Museum.
Salford (Lancs.)	Museum and Art Gallery, Peel Park, M5 4WU.
Salisbury (Wilts.)	Salisbury and South Wiltshire Museum, 42 St Ann Street.
Scarborough (Yorks.)	Museum of Archaeology, Vernon Road, YO11 2HB.
Scunthorpe (Lincs.)	Borough Museum and Art Gallery, Oswald Road.
Sheffield (Yorks.)	City Museum, Weston Park, Sheffield, S10 2TP.
Shrewsbury (Salop.)	Borough Museum and Art Gallery, Castle Gates.
	Rowley's House Museum, Barker Street.
Silchester (Hants.)	Calleva Museum, The Rectory, Silchester Common, Nr. Reading
Skipton (Yorks.)	Craven Museum, High Street, BD23 1JX.
South Shields (Durham)	Public Libraries and Museum, Ocean Road.
	Roman Fort and Museum, Baring Street.
Southampton (Hants.)	City Museums, Tower House, Town Quay, SO1 1LX.
Spalding (Lincs.)	Spalding Gentleman's Society Museum, Broad Street.
Stamford (Lincs.)	Public Library and Museum, High Street.
Stevenage (Herts.)	Stevenage Museum, Lytton Way, SG1 1XR.
Stirling	The Smith Art Gallery and Museum, Albert Place, FK8 2RQ.
Stoke-On-Trent (Staffs.)	City Museum and Art Gallery, Broad Street, Hanley, ST1 4HS.

Stroud (Glos.)	Stroud Museum, Lansdown, GL5 1BB.
Sunderland (Durham)	Public Museum and Art Gallery, Borough Road, SR1 1PP.
Swansea (Glam.)	Royal Institution of South Wales, Victoria Road.
Swindon (Wilts.)	Swindon Museum and Art Gallery, Bath Road.
Tamworth (Staffs.)	Castle Museum, Holloway.
Taunton (Som.)	Somerset County Museum, Taunton Castle.
Teesside	Dorman Museum, Linthorpe Road, Middlesbrough.
Tenby (Pembroke)	Tenby Museum, Castle Hill.
Tewkesbury (Glos.)	Tewkesbury Museum, Barton Street, GL20 5PX.
Thetford (Norfolk)	Ancient House Museum, White Hart Street.
Thurso (Caithness)	Thurso Museum, The Public Library.
Torbay (Devon)	Torquay Natural History Society Museum, 529 Babbacombe Road, TQ1 1HG.
Truro (Cornwall)	Royal Institution of Cornwall, County Museum and Art Gallery, 25 River Street.
Tunbridge Wells (Kent)	Municipal Museum, Civic Centre, Mount Pleasant.
Wall (Staffs.)	Letocetum Roman Site and Museum.
Warrington (Lancs.)	Municipal Museum and Art Gallery, Bold Street, WA1 1JG.
Warwick	County Museum, Market Place.
Wells (Som.)	Wells Museum, 8 Cathedral Green, BA5 2UE.
Weston-Super-Mare (Som.)	Public Library, Museum and Art Gallery, The Boulevard.

Weybridge (Surrey)	Weybridge Museum, Church Street, KT13 8DE.
Whitby (Yorks.)	Whitby Museum, Pannett Park, YO21 1RE.
Winchester (Hants.)	City Museum, The Square.
	Hampshire County Museum Service, Chilcomb House, Chilcomb Lane, Bar End.
Wisbech (Cambs.)	Wisbech and Fenland Museum, PE13 1ES.
Worcester	City Museum and Art Gallery, Foregate Street, WR1 1DT.
Worthing (Sussex)	Museum and Art Galley, Chapel Road, BN11 1HD.
Wroxeter (Salop.)	Viroconium Museum.
Yeovil (Som.)	Yeovil Borough Museum, Hendford Manor Hall.
York	The Yorkshire Museum, Museum Street, YO1 2DR.

General Bibliography

All abbreviations used are those of the CBA's *Archaeological Bibliography for Great Britain and Ireland*, 1975.

Addyman, P. V., and Biddle, M., *Medieval Cambridge: Recent Finds and Excavations. Proceedings of the Cambridge Antiquarian Society* LVIII, 1965, 74–137.

Ager, D., *Principles of Palaeo-ecology*. New York: McGraw-Hill, 1963.

Agerter, S. R., and Glock, W. S., *An Annotated Bibliography of Tree Growth and Growth Rings 1950–1962*. Tucson: University of Arizona, 1965.

Aitken, M., *Magnetic Location*, in Brothwell and Higgs (eds), *Science in Archaeology*. 2nd ed. London: Thames & Hudson, 1969. 681–94.

Aitken, M., *Physics and Archaeology*. 2nd ed. New York: Interscience Publications, 1974.

Alexander, J., *The Directing of Archaeological Excavations*. London: John Baker, 1970.

Appleyard, H. M., and Wildman, A. B., *Fibres of Archaeological Interest: Their Examination and Identification*, in Brothwell and Higgs (eds), 1969, 624–33.

Ascenzi, A., *Microscopy and Prehistoric Bone*, in Brothwell and Higgs (eds), 1969, 526–38.

Ashbee, P., *The Bronze Age Round Barrow in Britain*. London: Dent, 1960.

Ashbee, P., *The Earthen Long Barrow in Britain*. London: Dent, 1970.

Atkinson, R. J. C., *Field Archaeology*. 2nd ed. London: Methuen, 1953.

Bannister, B., *Dendrochronology*, in Brothwell and Higgs (eds), 1969, 191–205.

Barker, P., *Some aspects of the excavation of timber buildings. World Archaeology* I, 1969, 220–35.

Barker, P., *Excavations on the Site of the Baths Basilica at Wroxeter 1966–71*. Birmingham: University of Birmingham, 1971.

Barker, P., *Excavations on the Site of the Baths Basilica at Wroxeter 1972*. Birmingham: University of Birmingham, 1972.

Beazley, J. D., *Attic Red-figure Vase-painters*. 2nd ed. Oxford: Oxford University Press, 1963.

Beresford, M., *The Lost Villages of England*. London: Lutterworth Press, 1963.

Bersu, G., *Excavations at Little Woodbury, Wiltshire. Proceedings of Prehistoric Society*, 6, 1940, 30–111.

Biddle, M., and Kjølbye-Biddle, B., *Metres, areas, robbing. World Archaeology* I, 1969, 208–19.

Biek, L., *Archaeology and the Microscope*, London: Lutterworth Press, 1963.

Biek, L., *Soil Silhouettes*, in Brothwell and Higgs (eds), 1969, 118–23.

Biggs, H. E. J., *Molluscs from Human Habitation Sites and the Problem of Ethnological Interpretation*, in Brothwell and Higgs (eds), 1969, 423–7.

Binford, L. R., *An Archaeological Perspective*. New York: Seminar Press, 1972.

Binford, S. R., and Binford, L. R. (eds), *New Perspectives in Archaeology*. Chicago: Chicago University Press, 1968.

Bishop, W. W., and Miller, J. A. (eds), *Calibration of Hominoid Evolution*. Edinburgh: Edinburgh University Press, 1972.

Boessneck, J., *Osteological Differences between Sheep (Ovis aries*

Linné) and Goat (*Capra hircus Linné*), in Brothwell and Higgs (eds), 1969, 331–58.

Bradford, J., *Ancient Landscapes, Studies in Field Archaeology*. London: Bell, 1957.

Bray, W., and Trump, D., *A Dictionary of Archaeology*. London: Penguin Books, 1970.

Brill, R. H., *Science and Archaeology*. Cambridge, Mass.: Massachusetts Institute of Technology, 1971.

British Academy, *The Impact of the Natural Sciences on Archaeology*. London: British Academy, 1970.

Britton, D., and Richards, E. E., *Optical Emission Spectroscopy and the Study of Metallurgy in the European Bronze Age*, in Brothwell and Higgs (eds), 1969, 603–13.

Brodribb, C., *Drawing Archaeological Finds for Publication*. London: John Baker, 1970.

Brothwell, D. R., *Digging up Bones*. London: British Museum, 1965.

Brothwell, D. R., *The Palaeopathology of Pleistocene and More Recent Mammals*, in Brothwell and Higgs (eds), 1969a, 310–14.

Brothwell, D. R., *The Study of Archaeological Materials by Means of the Scanning Electron Microscope: An Important New Field*, in Brothwell and Higgs (eds), 1969b, 564–6.

Brothwell, D. R., and Higgs, E. S. (eds), *Science in Archaeology*, 2nd ed. London: Thames & Hudson, 1969.

Brothwell, D. R., and Sandison, A. T., *Diseases in Antiquity*. Springfield: Charles C. Thomas, 1967.

Butzer, K. W., *Environment and Archaeology*. 2nd ed. London: Methuen, 1971.

Callen, E. O., *Diet as revealed by Coprolites*, in Brothwell and Higgs (eds), 1969, 235–43.

Cann, J. R., Dixon, J. E., and Renfrew, C., *Obsidian Analysis and the Obsidian Trade*, in Brothwell and Higgs (eds), 1969, 578–91.

Centre National de la Recherche Scientifique, *Archéologie et Calculateurs*. Paris: Centre National de la Recherche Scientifique, 1970.

Ceram, C. W., *Archaeology*. London: Odyssey Press (NY), 1965.

Ceram, C. W., *The World of Archaeology*. London: Thames & Hudson, 1966.

Chang, K. C., *Rethinking Archaeology*. New York: Random House, 1967.

Chang, K. C. (ed.), *Settlement Archaeology*. Palo Alto, California: National Press Books, 1968.

Childe, V. G., *Man Makes Himself*. London: C. A. Watts, 1936.

Childe, V. G., *What Happened in History*. London: Penguin Books, 1942.

Childe, V. G., *A Short Introduction to Archaeology*. London: Muller, 1956.

Childe, V. G., *Piecing Together the Past*. London: Routledge & Kegan Paul, 1956.

Clark, A., *Resistivity Surveying*, in Brothwell and Higgs (eds), 1969, 695–707.

Clark, J. G. D., *Excavations at Star Carr*. Cambridge: Cambridge University Press, 1954.

Clark, J. G. D., *Archaeology and Society*. 3rd ed. London: Methuen, 1957.

Clark, J. G. D., *World Prehistory*. 2nd ed. Cambridge: Cambridge University Press, 1969.

Clark, J. G. D., and Piggott, S., *Prehistoric Societies*. London: Hutchinson, 1965.

Clarke, D. L., *Analytical Archaeology*. London: Methuen, 1968.

Clarke, D. L. (ed.), *Models in Archaeology*. London: Methuen, 1972.

Clutton-Brock, J., *The Origins of the Dog*, in Brothwell and Higgs (eds), 1969, 303–9.

Coles, J., *Field Archaeology in Britain*. London: Methuen, 1972.

Coles, J., *Archaeology by Experiment*. London: Hutchinson, 1973.

Cook, R. M., *Archaeomagnetism*, in Brothwell and Higgs (eds), 1969, 76–87.

Cook, R. M., *Greek Painted Pottery*. London: Methuen, 1972.

Cookson, M. B., *Photography for Archaeologists*. London: Parrish, 1954.

Cornwall, I. W., *Soils for the Archaeologist*. London: Dent, 1958.

Cornwall, I. W., *Bones for the Archaeologist*. London: Dent, 1968.

CBA (ed. G. Webster), *Romano-British Coarse Pottery: a student's guide*, Research Report 6. 2nd ed.: Cncl. Brit. Archaeol., 1969.

CBA, *Handbook of Scientific Aids and Evidence for Archaeologists*. London, 1970.

Crawford, O. G. S., *Archaeology in the Field*. London: Dent, 1953.

Daniel, G., *The Three Ages*, Cambridge University Press, 1943.

Daniel, G., *A Hundred Years of Archaeology*. London: Dent, 1950.

Daniel, G., *The Idea of Prehistory*. London: C. A. Watts, 1962, and Penguin Books.

Daniel, G., *The Origins and Growth of Archaeology*. London: Penguin Books, 1967.

Dart, R. A., *The Osteodontokeratic Culture of Australopithecus Prometheus*. Transvaal Museum Memoir No. 10, Pretoria, 1957.

Dawson, E. W., *Bird Remains in Archaeology*, in Brothwell and Higgs (eds), 1969, 359–75.

De Laet, S. J., *Archaeology and its Problems*. London: Dent, 1957.

Deetz, J., *The dynamics of stylistic change in Arikara ceramics*. Illinois Studies in Anthropology No. 4; Illinois: University of Illinois Press, 1965.

Deetz, J., *Invitation to Archaeology*. New York: American Museum of Natural History, 1967.

Dimbleby, G., *Environmental Studies and Archaeology*. London: University of London, 1963.

Dimbleby, G. W., *Plants and Archaeology*. London: John Baker, 1967.

Dimbleby, G. W., *Pollen Analysis*, in Brothwell and Higgs (eds), 1969, 167–77.

Dittert, A., and Wendorf, F. (eds), *Procedural Manual for Archaeological Field Research Projects*. Santa Fe: Museum of New Mexico Press, 1963.

Dowman, E. A., *Conservation in Field Archaeology*. London: Methuen, 1970.

Dymond, D. P., *Archaeology and History*. London: Thames & Hudson, 1974.

Ellesmere, Lord, *A Guide to Northern Antiquities*. London: Bain, 1848.

Evans, J. G., *Land Snails in Archaeology*. London and New York: Seminar Press, 1972.

Feininger, A., *Manual of Advanced Photography*. London: Thames & Hudson, 1970.

Fleischer, R. L., Price, P. B., and Walker, R. M., *Quaternary Dating by the Fission Track Technique*, in Brothwell and Higgs (eds), 1969, 58–61.

Forbes, R. J., *Metallurgy in Antiquity*. Leiden: Brill, 1950.

Forbes, R., *Studies in Ancient Technology* (I–VI). Leiden: Brill, 1955, 1956, 1957, 1958.

Forde, C. D., *Habitat, Economy and Society*. London: Methuen, 1964.

Foster, E., and Hackens, T., *Decco Metal Detector Survey on Delos*. Archaeometry 11, 1969, 165–72.

Fowler, E. (ed.), *Field Survey in British Archaeology*. London: CBA, 1972.

Fowler, P. (ed.), *Archaeology and the Landscape*. London: John Baker, 1972.

Fox, C., in *Arch. Cambrensis*, 1926, 48 ff.

Friedman, I., Smith, R. L., and Clark, D., *Obsidian Dating*, in Brothwell and Higgs (eds), 1969, 62–75.

Fryer, D. H., *Surveying for Archaeologists*. 2nd ed. Durham: University of Durham, 1961.

Garlick, J. D., *Buried Bone: The Experimental Approach in the Study of Nitrogen Content and Blood Group Activity*, in Brothwell and Higgs (eds), 1969, 503–12.

Gejvall, N.-G., *Cremations*, in Brothwell and Higgs (eds), 1969, 468–79.

Genovés, S., *Sex Determination in Earlier Man*, in Brothwell and Higgs (eds), 1969, 429–39.

Genovés, S., *Estimation of Age and Mortality*, in Brothwell and Higgs (eds), 1969, 440–52.

Gentner, W., and Lippolt, H. J., *The Potassium-Argon Dating of Upper Tertiary and Pleistocene Deposits*, in Brothwell and Higgs (eds), 1969, 88–100.

Glob, P. V., *The Bog People*. London: Paladin, 1969.

Godwin, H., *The History of the British Flora*. Cambridge: Cambridge University Press, 1956.

Goodyear, F. H., *Archaeological Site Science*. London: Heinemann Educational, 1971.

Green, H., *An Architectural Survey of the Roman Baths at Godmanchester. Part One: Walls, Floors, Doorways and Windows*. ANL 6, No. 10, 1969, 223–9.

Grimes, W. F., *Excavations on Defence Sites 1939–45; 1 Mainly Neolithic–Bronze Age*. London: HMSO, 1960.

Grinsell, L., Rahtz, P., and Warhurst, A., *The Preparation of Archaeological Reports*. London: John Baker, 1966.

Hall, E. T., *Dating Pottery by Thermoluminescence*, in Brothwell and Higgs (eds), 1969, 106–8.

Hawkes, J., *The World of the Past*, New York and London: Alfred A. Knopf and Thames & Hudson, 1963.

Heizer, R. F. (ed.), *The Archaeologist at Work*. New York: Harper & Row, 1959.

Heizer, R. F., *A Guide to Archaeological Field Methods*. 3rd ed. Palo Alto: California University Press, 1966.

Heizer, R. F., and Graham, J. A., *A Guide to Field Methods in Archaeology*. Palo Alto: California University Press, 1967.

Heizer, R. F., *The Anthropology of Prehistoric Great Basin Human Coprolites*, in Brothwell and Higgs (eds), 1969, 244–50.

Heizer, R. F., *Man's Discovery of his Past*. Palo Alto, California: Peek Publications, 1969b.

Heizer, R. F., and Cook, S. F. (eds), *The Application of*

Quantitative Methods in Archaeology. Viking Fund Publications in Anthropology, 28, 1960.

Helbaek, H., *Palaeo-Ethnobotany*, in Brothwell and Higgs (eds), 1969, 206–14.

Herre, W., *The Science and History of Domestic Animals*, in Brothwell and Higgs (eds), 1969, 257–72.

Higgs, E. S. (ed.), *Papers in Economic Prehistory*. Cambridge: Cambridge University Press, 1972.

Higham, C., and Message, M., *An Assessment of a Prehistoric Technique of Bovine Husbandry*, in Brothwell and Higgs (eds), 1969, 315–30.

Hodges, H., *Artifacts*. London: John Baker, 1964.

Hodson, F. R., Kendall, D. G., and Tăutu, P. (eds), *Mathematics in the Archaeological and Historical Sciences*. Edinburgh: Edinburgh University Press, 1970.

Hole, F., and Heizer, R. F., *An Introduction to Prehistoric Archaeology*. 3rd ed. New York: Holt, Rinehart & Winston, 1973.

Jewell, P. A., *An Experiment in Field Archaeology. Advancement of Science*, May 1961, 106–9.

Jewell, P. A., and Dimbleby, G. W. (eds), *Experimental Earthwork on Overton Down, Wiltshire, England: The First Four Years. PPS*, XXXII, 1966, 313–42.

Kenyon, K. M., *Beginning in Archaeology*. London: Dent, 1964.

Kurtén, B., *Pleistocene Mammals of Europe*. London: Weidenfeld & Nicholson, 1968.

Kurtén, B., *Pleistocene Mammals and the Origin of Species*, in Brothwell and Higgs (eds), 1969, 251–6.

Leigh, D. *et al.*, *First Aid for Finds*. Southampton: Rescue, 1972.

Leone, M. P. (ed.), *Contemporary Archaeology*. Carbondale and Edwardsville: Southern Illinois University Press, 1972.

Lethbridge, T., *The Anglo-Saxon Cemetery, Burwell, Cambs. Proceedings of the Cambridge Antiquarian Society*, XXVII, 1926, 79.

Levey, M. (ed.), *Archaeological Chemistry*. Philadelphia: University of Pennsylvania Press, 1967.

Libby, W., *Radiocarbon Dating*. 2nd ed. Chicago: Chicago University Press, 1955.

Lubbock, J., *Prehistoric Times*. 6th ed. London: Williams & Norgate, 1900.

Lyell, C., *Principles of Geology*. London: Murray, 1830–33.

Mason, J. A., *The Ancient Civilisations of Peru*. Harmondsworth Press, 1957.

Matson, F. R. (ed.), *Ceramics and Man*. Viking Fund Publications in Anthropology, 41, 1965.

Matson, F. R., *Some Aspects of Ceramic Technology*, in Brothwell and Higgs (eds), 1969, 592–602.

Matthews, S., *Photography in Archaeology and Art*. London: John Baker, 1968.

Meighan, C. W., *Molluscs as Food Remains in Archaeological Sites*, in Brothwell and Higgs (eds), 1969, 415–22.

Miller, J. A., *Dating by the Potassium-Argon Method—Some Advances in Technique*, in Brothwell and Higgs (eds), 1969, 101–5.

Morey, J. E., and Dunham, K. C., in *Proceedings Yorkshire Geological Society*, 29, 1953, 141.

Nilsson, S., *The Primitive Inhabitants of Scandinavia*. London: Longmans, Green & Co., 1868.

Oakley, K. P., *Analytical Methods of Dating Bones*, in Brothwell and Higgs (eds), 1969, 35–45.

Olsson, I. U. *Radiocarbon Variations and Absolute Chronology*. Nobel Symposium, 12, Uppsala: Interscience, 1970.

Ordnance Survey, *Field Archaeology in Great Britain*. New revised edition, Southampton: HMSO, 1974.

Peacock, D. P. S., *The Black-Burnished Pottery Industry in Dorset*, in CBA Research Report 10, 1973, 63–5.

Phillips, C. W. (ed.), *The Fenland in Roman Times*. London: Royal Geographical Society, 1970.

Piggott, S., *Approach to Archaeology*. London: A. & C. Black, 1959.

Plenderleith, H. J., and Werner, A. E., *The Conservation of Antiquities and Works of Art*. London: Oxford University Press, 1972.

Pyddoke, E., *Stratification for the Archaeologist*. London: Dent, 1961.

Pyddoke, E. (ed.), *The Scientist and Archaeology*. London: Dent, 1963.

Raikes, R., *Water, Weather and Prehistory*. London: John Baker, 1967.

Reaney, P. H., *The Place-names of Cambridgeshire and the Isle of Ely*. Cambridge: Cambridge University Press, 1943.

Renfrew, C., *Before Civilisation*. London: Jonathan Cape, 1973.

Renfrew, C. (ed.), *The Explanation of Cultural Change: Models in Prehistory*. London: Duckworth, 1973b.

Renfrew, J. A., *Palaeoethnobotany*. London: Methuen, 1973.

Richards, E. E., *Report on Black-burnished Ware from Mumrills*. Proc. Soc. Antiq. Scotland, XCIV, 1963, 129–32.

Rosenfeld, A., *The Inorganic Raw Materials of Antiquity*. London: Weidenfeld & Nicholson, 1965.

Rouse, I., *Introduction to Prehistory: a systematic approach*. New York: McGraw-Hill, 1972.

Rowley, T., and Davies, M., *Archaeology and the M40 Motorway*. Oxford University Press, 1973.

Ryder, M. L., *Animal Bones in Archaeology*. Oxford and Edinburgh: Blackwell Scientific Publications, 1968.

Ryder, M. L., *Remains of Fishes and other Aquatic Animals*, in Brothwell and Higgs (eds), 1969, 376–94.

Ryder, M. L., *Remains derived from Skin*, in Brothwell and Higgs (eds), 1969, 539–54.

Sandison, A. T., *The Study of Mummified and Dried Human Tissues*, in Brothwell and Higgs (eds), 1969, 490–502.

Sayre, E. V., *Studies in Ancient Ceramic Objects by Means of Neutron Bombardment and Emission Spectroscopy*, in *Application of Science in the Examination of Works of Art*. Boston: Museum of Fine Arts, 1959, 153–80.

Schaeffer, O. A., and Zähringer, J., *Potassium-Argon Dating*. Berlin: Springer-Verlag, 1966.

Schmid, E., *Atlas of Animal Bones*. London: Elsevier, 1972.

Scollar, I., in *Bonner Jahrbücher*, 159, 1959, 284.

Semenov, S. A., *Prehistoric Technology*. Bath: Adams & Dart, 1970.

Shackleton, N. J., *Marine Molluscs in Archaeology*, in Brothwell and Higgs (eds), 1969, 407–14.

Shepard, A. O., *Ceramics for the Archaeologist*. Washington: Carnegie Institute of Washington Publications, 1965.

Shotton, F. W., *Petrological Examination*, in Brothwell and Higgs (eds), 1969, 571–7.

Sieveking, G. de G., Craddock, P. T., Hughes, M. J., Bush, P., and Ferguson, J., *Characterisation of Prehistoric Flint Mine Products. Nature* Vol. 228, No. 5268, 17 October 1970, 251–4.

Silver, I. A., *The Ageing of Domestic Animals*, in Brothwell and Higgs (eds), 1969, 283–302.

Simmons, H., *Archaeological Photography*. London: London University, 1969.

Smith, R. W., *The Analytical Study of Glass in Archaeology*, in Brothwell and Higgs (eds), 1969, 614–23.

Sparks, B. W., *Non-marine Mollusca and Archaeology*, in Brothwell and Higgs (eds), 1969, 395–406.

St Joseph, J. K. S. (ed.), *The Uses of Air Photography*. London: John Baker, 1966.

Strong, D. E. (ed.), *Archaeological Theory and Practice*. London and New York: Seminar Press, 1973.

Tansley, A. G., *The British Islands and Their Vegetation*. Cambridge: Cambridge University Press, 1965.

Thompson, F. C., *Microscopic Studies of Ancient Metals*, in Brothwell and Higgs (eds), 1969, 555–63.

Thomson, G. (ed.), *Recent Advances in Conservation*. London: Butterworth, 1963.

Tite, M. S., and Mullins, C., *Electromagnetic Prospecting on archaeological sites using a soil conductivity meter. Archaeometry* 12, 1970, 97–104.

Tite, M. S., *Methods of Physical Examination in Archaeology*. London: Seminar Press, 1972.

Trigger, B. G., *Beyond History: The Methods of Prehistory*. New York: Holt, Rinehart and Winston, 1968.

Trorey, L., *Handbook of Aerial Mapping and Photogrammetry*. Cambridge: Cambridge University Press, 1950.

Tylecote, R. F., *Metallurgy in Archaeology*. London: Edward Arnold, 1962.

Ucko, P. J., and Dimbleby, G. W. (eds), *The Domestication and Exploitation of Plants and Animals*. London: Duckworth, 1969.

Ucko, P. J., Tringham, R., and Dimbleby, G. W., *Man, Settlement and Urbanism*. London: Duckworth, 1972.

UNESCO, *The Conservation of Cultural Property*. Paris: UNESCO, 1968.

Wainwright, F., *Archaeology, Place-names and History*. London: Oxford University Press, 1962.

Watson, P. J., Leblanc, S. A., and Redman, C. L., *Explanation in Archaeology*, New York and London: Columbia University Press, 1971.

Webster, G., *Practical Archaeology*. London: A. & C. Black, 1963 (new edition, 1974).

Webster, G., Hobley, B., Baker, A., and Pickering, J., *Aerial reconnaissance over the Warwickshire Avon*. *Archaeological Journal* 121 (for 1964), 1965, 1–22.

Weiner, J. S., *The Piltdown Forgery*. London: Oxford University Press, 1955.

Weiner, J. S., Oakley, K. P., and Le Gros Clark, W. E., *The Solution of the Piltdown Problem*. Bulletin of the British Museum (Natural History) Geology Vol. 2, No. 3, London, 1953.

Wells, C., *Bones, Bodies and Diseases*. London: Thames & Hudson, 1965.

Wells, L. H., *Stature in Earlier Races of Mankind*, in Brothwell and Higgs (eds), 1969, 453–67.

Wendorf, F., *A Guide For Salvage Archaeology*. Santa Fe: Museum of New Mexico Press, 1962.

West, R. G., *Studying the Past by Pollen Analysis*. London: Oxford University Press, 1971.

Western, A. C., *Wood and Charcoal in Archaeology*, in Brothwell and Higgs (eds), 1969, 178–87.

Wheeler, R. E. M., *Archaeology from the Earth*. London: Oxford University Press, 1954 (Pelican edition 1956 for references).

Willey, G. R., and Phillips, P., *Method and Theory in American Archaeology*. Chicago: Chicago University Press, 1958.

Williams, J. C., *Simple Photogrammetry*. London: Academic Press, 1970.

Woolley, L., *Digging up the Past*, Penguin Books 2nd ed., 1954; repr. 1963.

Yarnell, R. A., *Palaeo-Ethnobotany in America*, in Brothwell and Higgs (eds), 1969, 215–28.

Zeuner, F., *Dating the Past*. London: Methuen, 1952.

Index

This index comprises proper names and major subject references in the text.

Abbeville, 16
Aberdeenshire, 191
Acculturation, 14
Acetone, 112, 123
Acheulean cultures, 15, 192
Achondroplastic dwarf, 137
Acrocephaly, 137
Additive process, 4
Ageing
   animal bone, 141, 144
   human bone, 131, 132
Agriculture, 11, 12, 166
Air photography, 38–42
Aitken, M., 42, 43
Alaska, 177, 179
Alder, 169
Allen, Major G. W., 38
Altai Mountains (USSR), 159
Amber, conservation of, 123
Americas, general, 19, 62, 134, 135, 136, 163, 173
Ammonium hydroxide, 114
Amphorae, 222
Amyl acetate, 112
Anatolia, 166, 195
Ancient Monuments Act, 17
Ancient Monuments Laboratory, 72
Anthropology, 1, 2
Antiquity of man, 15, 16, 17
Arawak (WI), 151, 189, 190, 208
Arbury Road, Cambridge, 133
Arc spectrography, 224, 225
Arikara Indians (Missouri), 224
Artefacts, Chpt. 1

Arthritis, 136, 146
Articulation, 3, 9
Ash, 169
Ashbee, P., 86, 89
Ashwicken (Norfolk), 199
Assemblage, 9, 10, 11, 13, 14, 20, 21, 25
Assimilation, 14
Assistant site supervisor, 83, 84
Association, 3, 9, 21, 22, *et passim*
Athens, 219
Atkinson, R. J. C., 45, 46
Atomic absorption spectroscopy, 192
Attribute, 4, 5, Chpt. 1, *et passim*
Auger, 34
Australia, 186
Australian aborigine, 11
Australopithecus, 128, 136, 137
Austrian Alps, 197
Avon Valley, 39
Axe factories, 188–91
Azoic era, 15

Balkans, 24
Bank Holidays Act 1871, 17
Banks, 90, 91
Bannister, B., 178, 179
Barbarism, 18
Barbotine decoration, 206, 207
Barker, P., 95, 96, 102, 103
Barrows, 86–9
Barton-on-Humber, 210
Basketry, 118

Bavaria, 197
Bedacryl 122X, 123
Beech, 169
Benzotriazole, 122
Bersu, G., 101
Bible, 16, 135
Biddle, M., 65, 67, 68, 107
Birch, 169
Birds, 148, 149
Black-burnished pottery, 201, 202, 209, 221
Blackfriars, London, 174
Blood groups, 138
Boessneck, J., 141
Bog bodies, 159, 172
Bone
    animal, 139–47
    conservation of, 118
    human, 129–39
Boudiccan fire deposits, 25, 26, 216
Brachycephaly, 130
Breuil, Abbé, 166
Bristlecone pine, 166, 167
Britain
    Neolithic, 166, 191, 209
    Roman, 139, 155, 191, 199, 200, 218
British Academy, 12
British Association Committee on Archaeological Field Experiments, 90
Britton, D., 196
Bromwich, J., 36, 37
Bronze
    conservation of, 121
    sources of, 196, 197
Bronze Age, 17, 18, 19, 20, 86, 158, 188, 196, 197
Brothwell, D., 130, 131, 132, 138
Burial mounds, *see* barrows
Burial, *see* graves
Bushmen, 11, 148
Butvar, 126

Caenozoic era, 15
Calcite-gritted pottery, 203
California, 148, 166
Callen, E. O., 173
Cambridge, 101
Cambridge University Committee for Aerial Photography, 39
Cann, J. R., 193
Carbowax 1500, 112, 119
Cardboard box, 116
Car Dyke, 200
Casts, 114, 115, 198, 199
Cattle, 144
Cave-bear, 146

Celtic cultures, 14
Cephalic index, 130
Chaco Canyon (New Mexico), 179
Charcoal, 175, 176
Charcot–Leyden crystals, 174
Cheddar, 59
Chemical prospecting, 49, 50
Childe, V. G., 4, 9, 10, 18
China, 159
Chinese glass, 225
Ciré perdue, 199
Citric acid, 114
Clark, A., 45–8
Clarke, D., 6, 8, 13, 20, 21
Coin, Roman, 25
Coin hoard, 25, 26
Colchester, 25, 216
Coles, J., 65, 198, 199
Combing decoration, 207, 208
Complex, 6
Conservation, Chpt. 4
Consolidation, 111–13
Construction trench, 104
Copenhagen, National Museum, 17
Copper, 196, 197
Coprolites, 173, 174
Corfe Mullen (Dorset), 201
Cornwall, 32
Cornwall, I., 140
Cotswold megalithic tombs, 88
Crates, 116, 117
Crawford, O. G. S., 38, 39
Cremations, 9, 138, 139
Crete, 195
Crichel Down (Dorset), 134
Cromagnon Man, 136
Crop marks, 40f.
Cross-dating, 18, 20, 24, 25, 177, 178
Cultural development, 20, 21
Culture, 9, 10, 11, 14
    change, 13
    group, 14
    history, 10, 12, 13
Cupisnique (Peru), 207
Cyrenaica, 154
Czechoslovakia, 219

Dalmatian pelican, 148
Daniel, G., 19, 172
Dechelette, 18
Deetz, J., 4, 224
Delos, 49
de Mortillet, 18
Dendrochronology, 176–9
Denmark, 17, 159
Developmental stages, 19, 20
Diffusion, 13
Diluvialism, 16

Dimbleby, G. W., 90, 92, 169
Director of excavation, 81–3, 85–6
Distilled water, 113
Distribution map, 32
  studies, 220–2
Ditches, 90–7
Dixon, J. E., 193
Documentary evidence, 35–6
Dog, 142, 143
Dolichocephaly, 130
Domesday Book, 35
Domestication, 12, 142, 143
Donnybrook (Eire), 138
Dorchester (Oxon.), 45
Dordogne, 150
Double-dipole configuration, 48
Douglass, A. E., 177, 178
Dowman, E. A., 111, 113, 124, 126
Drawing (plans and sections), 66–71
  equipment, 68–9
Dumas method, 158
Durotriges, 201, 202
Dysplasia, 137

Easton Down (Dorset), 192
Egypt, 12, 24, 135, 136, 137, 149, 159, 166, 171, 206
Einkorn, 172
Electrochemical reduction, 121, 122
Electromagnetic survey, 48, 49
Electron microbeam probe, 225
Ellesmere, Lord, 17
Elm, 169, 170
Elvacite, 126
Emeryville shellmound, 148
Emmer, 172
Environment, 10, 11, 12, 128, 129, *et passim*
Eocene period, 15
Epiphyses, human, 131
Epoxy resin, 115, 120
Equipment
  conservation, 116–18
  excavation, 77–81
Eskimo, 150
Essex, 202
Ethyl acetate, 112
Ethyl alcohol, 120
Ethylene dichloride, 112
Etruscan, 216
Europe, prehistoric, 13, 14, 24, 143, 167, 168, 170, 197, 216, 217
Evans, Sir John, 16
Evostick, 112
Excavation, Chpt. 3 *et passim*
  equipment, 77–81
  personnel, 81–6

procedure, 61–5
recording, 65–75
Experimental archaeology, 198, 199

Fenland, 36, 37, 39
Fibre-glass, 113, 114
Fibres, 162
Field names, 35
Fieldwork, 32, 36
Finds assistant, 84
Fish, 149–50
Fishbourne, 124
Fission track dating, 186, 195
Flame photometry, 225
Fleischer, R. L., 186
Flint, 191–2
Fluorine test, 157–8
Form of pottery, 210–13
Formalin, 120, 159
Formic acid, 121
Forum (Rome), 148
Foster, E., 48, 49
Fowler, P., 36
Fox, C., 52, 86
France (prehistoric), 135, 136, 137, 150, 166, 219
Frere, J., 16
Fryer, D. H., 65
Fungicide, 118, 119

Galley Hill skeleton, 158
Gallinazo (Peru), 206
Gejvall, N-G., 139
Gentner, W., 184
Geology, 16, 21, 34, 41
Germany, 62, 179
Gibraltar, 149
Gigantopithecus, 159
Glacial acetic acid, 118
Glass
  conservation of, 125
  study of, 224–6
Glastonbury, 148
Glazes, 205, 206
Gleser, G. C., 132
Glycerol, 120, 121
Godmanchester (Hunts.), 105
Gold, conservation of, 122
Goodyear, F. H., 50
Gossen Geohm, 47
Gradiometer, proton, 44, 45
Graig Lwyd (Caernarvon.), 190
Grand Pressigny (France), 192
Grauballe Man, 172
Graves, 2, 3, 89–90
Great Casterton (Rutland), 199
Great Chesterford (Essex), 146, 147
Great Langdale (Westmorland), 190

Greece, 14, 24, 151, 202, 211, 215
Greek pottery, 202, 211, 215, 219, 223, 224
Gridding, 58, 59
Grimes, W. F., 88, 89
Grimes Graves (Norfolk), 99, 191, 192
Ground survey, 36, 37
Guano, 149

Hacilar (Turkey), 216
Hackens, T., 48, 49
Hadrian's Wall, 30, 39, 98
Hadstock (Essex), 35
Haematite, 42, 43
Hall, E. T., 203
Hallam, S., 36
Hand-axe cultures, 15, 16
Hapsburg dynasty, 133
Haua Fteah (Cyrenaica), 154
Hazel, 169
Head deformation, 134, 135
Hebditch, M., 229
Heizer, R. F., 173
Helbaek, H., 171, 173
Helix aspersa, 155
Helix pomatia, 155
Hen Domen (Montgomeryshire), 96, 102, 103
Herculaneum, 216
Higgs, E., 12
Higham, C., 142, 144
High House (Cumb.), 98
Holocene period, 15, 154
Hope-Taylor, B., 102
Hopewell Indians (USA), 151, 195
Horn, 141
Horningsea (Cambs.), 208, 221
Horse, 143
Housesteads, 39
Hoxne (Suffolk), 16
Huaca Prieta (Peru), 173
Humboldt Lake (Nevada), 174
Hunting and gathering, 11, 12
Hydrocephaly, 137
Hydrochloric acid, 123, 126
Hydrogen peroxide, 121
Hypoplasia, 137

Illinois (USA), 151
Incision decoration, 207
India, 12
Indian ink, 117
Indonesia, 186
Industrial methylated spirit, 112, 115, 122
Indus Valley Civilisation, 13
Institute of Geological Sciences, maps, services, 34, 35, 54, 55

Intrusion, 14
Iraq, 195
Iron
    ancient production, 199
    conservation of, 120, 121
Iron Age, 19, 159, 172, 175, 201, 222, 223
Iroquois, 18
Islamic glass, 225
Islamic pottery, 219
Italy, 223
Ivory, conservation of, 118
Ivory Coast, 186
Ivory osteomata, 135, 136
Ivy, 170

Japan, 188, 219
Jewell, P. A., 90, 92
Junghans, S., 197
Juniper, 169

Kayseri (Anatolia), 195
Kilns, 209, 210, 218
Kiva, 2, 3
Kixpec, 203
Kjeldahl method, 158
Krapina, 136
Kurten, B., 145

Labelling, 71, 72, 117
Lake Van (Anatolia), 195
Lead, conservation of, 123
Leadenhall Street, London, 158
Leather
    conservation of, 118
    study of, 161
Leprosy, 135, 160
Lethbridge, T., 89
Levant, 166, 195
Levelling, 65–8
Libby, W., 164, 165, 166
Lime, 169, 170
Lion, 145
Lippolt, H. J., 184
Liquid scintillation counter, 163
Littlechester (Derbyshire), 205
Little Woodbury (Wilts.), 101
London, 25
    Roman waterfront of, 174, 177, 216
Longthorpe (nr. Peterborough), 39
Lovelock Cave (Nevada), 173, 174
Lubbock, J., 17
Lyell, C., 16

Macedonia, 195
Magdalenians, 150
Magnetic prospecting, 42–5

Magnetite, 42, 43
Magnetometer
    differential fluxate, 45
    proton, 44
Makapansgat, 128
Malta, 168
Manuring, 38
Maoris, 148
Maps, 33, 34, 35
Martin-Clark Meter, 47, 48
Maya, 30, 135, 203
McCurdy, 18
Medicine Crow (Missouri), 224
Megaliths, 168
Megger Earth Tester, 46, 47
Meiendorf, Germany, 148
Meighan, C. W., 150, 151
Melos, 195
Mesocephaly, 130
Mesolithic, 18, 135, 169
Mesopotamia, 12, 13
Mesozoic era, 15
Message, M., 142, 144
Metals, study of, 195–9
Methyl ethyl ketone, 112
Mexico, 19, 135, 173, 199
Microcephaly, 137, 138
Microscopy, 156, 157, 160–2, 197,
    198
Microtome, 160, 161, 162, 176
Middens, 150, 151, 154
Midlands (England), 39
Middle Ages, 12
Miller, J. A., 185
Mine, 99
Miocene period, 15
Mistletoe, 170
Moa, 148
Mochica (Peru), 19, 204, 219, 220,
    222, 223, 224
Molluscs, 150–6
Monothetism, 5, 6
Montelius, O., 18
Morgan, L. H., 18
Mosaics, 124, 125
Motorways, 36
Moulds
    in casting metal, 198, 199
    in conservation, 114, 115
Mount Carmel, 137
Mousterian, 193
Mummies, 159, 160
Mummy wheat, 171
Mumrills (Scotland), 202
Munsell soil chart, 210
Munsingen cemetery, 136
Murex shells, 151
Museums Association, 229

Myeloma, 136
Mynydd Rhiw Lleyn (Caernarvon.)
    190, 191
Mytilus perna, 154

Naestved Leper Hospital, 135
National Grid, 34, 68
Neanderthalers, 136, 137, 149
Negative painting, 206
Nene Valley, 200, 205, 221
Neolithic, 17, 18, 86, 135, 151, 171,
    188
Neolithic Revolution, 18, 19
Neutron activation analysis, 195,
    202, 203, 225
Nevada, 173
New Zealand, 135, 148
Nilsson, S., 18
Nitric acid, 126
Nitrogen test, 158, 159
Northwest Coast Indians, 11, 12,
    150
Norton (Yorks.), 137
Notebooks, 72–5
Nubia, 133
Nylon, soluble, 125, 126

Oak, 169
Obsidian
    dating, 187, 188
    source analysis, 192–5
Odysseus, 224
Olduvai Gorge, 184, 185
Oligocene period, 15
Open stripping, 59–61, 102, 103
Optical spectroscopy, 193, 195,
    196, 202
Ordnance Survey services, 33, 34,
    35, 41, 51–4
Organic remains, Chpt. 5
Origin of Species, The, 17
Osteitis, 135
Osteodontokeratic culture, 128
Osteological Research Laboratory,
    Ulriksdal, Solna, 139
Osteomalacia, 133
Osteomyelitis, 135, 146
Osteosarcoma, 136
Otoliths, 149
Otto, H. 197
Overton Down, 90–7
Ower (Dorset), 201
Oxfordshire, pottery, 208, 221

Pacific, 16
Paget's disease, 137
Paiute Indians, 11
Palaeocene period, 15

Palaeoethnobotany, 171–3
Palaeolithic, 9, 15, 17, 21, 128, 132, 148, 150, 166, 175, 187
Palaeotemperature analysis, 154
Palaeozoic era, 15
Paracas (Peru), 206
Paraffin, liquid, 160, 162
Parish boundaries, 36
Peacock, D. P. S., 201
Peat bogs, 171, 172
Periostitis, 135, 146
Personnel, 81–6
Period, 20, 21
Periodontal disease, 136
Perthes, Boucher de, 16, 17
Peru, 14, 19, 133, 134, 135, 137, 149, 173, 204, 206, 215, 220
Petrological analysis, 188–95, 201, 202
Pewter, 123
Phase, 20, 21
Phosphate analysis, 49, 50
Photogrammetry, 41, 42, 77
Photography, 75–7
Physical anthropology, 129
Piggott, S., 166
Piltdown forgery, 159
Pine, 169
Pits, 99–101
Pituitary disorders, 137
Place names, 35, 36
Plagiocephaly, 138
Planning, 65–8
Plants, 171–3
Plaster, 124
Plaster of paris, 113, 114, 115, 124, 126
Pleistocene period, 15, 142, 145, 155, 156, 158, 159, 165, 167
Pliocene period, 15
Poliomyelitis, 137, 160
Pollen, 168–70
Polythetism, 6
Polyester resin, 115, 120
Polyethylene glycol waxes, 112, 119, 120, 123, 126
Polystyrene boxes, 116
Polythene bags, 116
Polyurethane foam, 113, 114
Polyvinyl acetate, 112, 118, 123, 124, 125, 126, 162
Polyvinyl alcohol, 112, 118
Polyvinyl butyral, 112, 113
Pompeii, 3, 25, 216
Poole Harbour (Dorset), 201
Poplar, 169
Porcelain, Chinese, 203, 219
Post holes, 103, 104

Potassium-argon dating, 184–6
Pottery
 conservation of, 125, 126
 Roman, 200–9, 211, 215, 220, 221
 study of, 199–224
Prestwich, J., 16
Price, P. B., 186
Proterozoic era, 15
Przewalski's horse, 143
Pueblo Indians, 2, 137, 151, 179
Pulsed induction meter, 48, 49
Punch-card, 72, 73

Quarry, 99
Quaternary, 15, 184
Querns, 191

Radiocarbon dating, 20, 24, 154, 155, 162–8
Rahtz, P., 59, 102
Raising objects, 113, 114
Raikes, R., 170
Ramparts, *see* banks
Rathlin Island (Antrim), 190
Recording excavation, 65–75
Record sheet, 37
Recuay (Peru), 206
Relative dating, 157–9
Renfrew, C., 193
Research Laboratory for Archaeology and History of Art, Oxford, 217
Resistivity survey, 45–8
Rhineland, 101, 206
Rhodesian Man, 137
Richards, E. E., 196, 202
Rickets, 133
Robber trenches, 31, 106, 107
Rochelle salt, 121
Roman glass, 225
Rouletting, 209
Royal Society, 17
Rubber latex, 114, 115, 125
Russian glass, 225
Ryder, M. L., 140, 161, 162

Sabre-toothed tiger, 159
Saint-Acheul, 16
Saliagos, 151
Salmon run, 11
Samian pottery, 201, 203, 204, 205, 206, 209, 214, 221
Sampling error, 32
Sampling in field, 38
Sandison, A. T., 160
San Francisco Bay, 148
Sangmeister, E., 197

Savagery, 18
Saxon
  cemeteries, 89
  pottery, 205, 208
Sayre, E. V., 202, 225
Scandinavia, 156, 168
Scanning electron microscope, 156, 157
Scaphocephaly, 138
Schroder, M., 197
Scollar, I., 46, 47
Scrim, 113, 114, 115, 124
Sections, 69–71
Severn Valley, 39, 206
Sexing
  animal bone, 130, 131, 139
  human bone, 141–2
Shackleton, N. J., 151
Shadow marks, 39, 40
Shale, 123
Sheep, 161
Shellac, 115
Shepard, A. O., 205, 211
Silica gel, 116, 120, 121
Silver, 122
Silver, I., 141
Silver oxide, 122
Site supervisor, 83
Skin, 159–61
Slips, 205
Small finds, 72
Snails, 155, 156
Society of Antiquaries, 17, 59
Sodium hydroxide, 121
Sodium sesquicarbonate, 121
Soil conductivity meter, 48
Soil marks, 39, 40
Soil Survey of England and Wales, 35, 55, 56
Soils, 35, 170
Solutrean point, 194
Somerset, 171
Somme Valley, 16
South Africa, 154
  ...h Cadbury, 48
  ...east Asia, 186
  ...ite, Stapleford (Wilts.), 36
  ...W., 155, 156
  ...ance.), 192
  ...ration, 208, 209
  ...S., 39
  ...t (France.) 205
  ...36

Stone
  conservation of, 123
  study of, 184–95
Stonehenge, 30, 168
Stratigraphy, 20–4, Chpt. 3 esp. 61–2
Stuttgart, 197
Subcultures, 10, 14
Subtractive process, 4
Suess, H. E., 167
Sumeria, 13
Sunken Church Field, Hadstock (Essex), 35
Sutton Hoo, 50
Surveying, 65–8
Swanscombe (Kent), 158
Switzerland, 171
Syphilis, 134, 135

Tanzania, 184
Technocomplex, 14, 15
Teeth, 131–3, 136, 137
Tehuacan Valley, 173
Tektites, 186
Tellohm, 47
Terminus ante quem, 26
Terminus post quem, 25, 179
Tertiary, 15
Textiles, 118
Thames, River, 174
Thermoluminescence, 216, 217
Thermo-remanent magnetism, 42, 45, 217–19
Thessaly, 195
Thiourea, 115
Thomsen, C. J., 17, 19
Three-Age system, 17
Tievebulliagh (Antrim), 190
Timber buildings, 101–4
Tin, 123
Tissue paper, 117
Tollund Man, 159
Toluene, 112, 123
Tools
  conservation of, 117, 118
  excavation of, 77–81
Tooth evulsion, 135
Tourmaline, 201, 202
Trace element analysis, 193, 195
Trench-built, 104
Trenching, 58
Trent Valley, 39
Trepanning, 134
Triassic period, 15
Trigonocephaly, 138
Trisodium phosphate, 173
Troldebjerg (Denmark), 144
Trotter, M., 132

Tuberculosis, 135
Tutankhamun, 175
Twin electrode configuration, 48
Type, 6, 7, 8, 9, 14, 213–16
  complex, 9
  group, 9
  series, 9
  survival, 24
Typology, 8, 18, 20, 214, 215, 216

UHU adhesive, 112, 125, 126
Uniformitarianism, 16
Upper Greensand, 201
Uranium test, 159
Urban Revolution, 18, 19
Ussher, Archbishop, 16

Vegetation, 35
Verulamium, 25, 31, 216
Volunteer diggers, 84, 85
Vulture, 148

Walls, 104–6
Walker, R. M., 186
Wareham, 92, 201
Webster, G., 98, 105
Wells, 101
Wenner configuration, 47, 48
Werateuuorde, 35

Wessex culture, 10
Western, A. C., 175, 176
West Indies, 151, 189, 190, 208
Westropp, H. M., 18
Wheeler, R. E. M., 58, 59, 61, 62, 88, 89, 172
White Mountains (Calif.), 166
Willow, 169
Wimpole parish (Cambs.), 35
Winchester, 107
Witter, W., 197
Wood
  conservation of, 119
  study of, 174–9
Woodland, place names, 35, 36
Woodchester, 124
Worsaae, J. J. A., 17
Wroxeter, 31, 59, 100–2

X-ray, 121, 131, 157, 160
X-ray fluorescence analysis, 195, 203, 225
Xylene, 112

Yaws, 135
Yorkshire medieval hones, 191

Zagros, 166
Zinc sulphate, 114

CENTRAL LIBRARY
THE BRITISH MUSEUM